CHOPIN

Caricature by Eugene Delacroix (1840). *(A. Meyer Collection in Paris.*
Photograph courtesy of the Chopin Society in Paris)

GEORGE R. MAREK

MARIA GORDON-SMITH

HARPER & ROW, PUBLISHERS

NEW YORK, HAGERSTOWN, SAN FRANCISCO, LONDON

To Antonia Fraser

Quotations of letters from *Selected Correspondence of Fryderyk Chopin*, translated by Arthur Hedley (London, 1963), courtesy William Heinemann Ltd.

FIRST EDITION

Designed by Sidney Feinberg

Library of Congress Cataloging in Publication Data

Marek, George Richard, 1902–
  Chopin.
  Bibliography: p.
  Includes index.
  1. Chopin, Fryderyk Franciszek, 1810–1849.
2. Composers—Biography. I. Gordon-Smith, Maria,
joint author.
ML410.C54M37   786.1'092'4 [B]   76–57880
ISBN 0–06–012843–7

---

78 79 80 81 82 10 9 8 7 6 5 4 3 2 1

CONTENTS

CONTENTS

Illustrations follow page 116.

ACKNOWLEDGMENTS

THE BOOK represents a collaboration.

The reason for the collaboration is this: Chopin's life was divided into two parts, the division being decisive and not geographical alone. He spent his first twenty years in or near Warsaw, absorbing the Slavic tradition of life, music, and literature. A few months after his twenty-first birthday he emigrated to Paris; there he became thoroughly French; there he remained for the eighteen years—few enough—that were granted him; there he died.

The books written about him by Polish authors are permeated by a fervent chauvinism. He is, of course, one of the national Polish heroes known in the West, and in his native country he is looked at through lowered eyelids. Conversely, to his French, British, and American biographers Poland seems an unexplored country, a *terra incognita*, and they often could not rightly estimate the heritage from which he drew. Some of his Western biographers did not know Chopin's native language at all, some had only a foreigner's acquaintance with it, and none had lived in Warsaw. My co-author, Maria Gordon-Smith, nee Maria Krystyna Broniewska, was born and educated in Warsaw, and taught at the university there. She was married to Dr. Arnold Szyfman, founder and director of Warsaw's famous repertory theater *(Teatr Polski),* and also responsible for the construction of the postwar Warsaw opera house *(Teatr Wielki).* She lived and studied in Paris; came to the United States at the invitation of the University of Michigan where she taught for two years; and is now a U.S. resident. She is as familiar as only actual experience can make one with the conditions under which Chopin grew up, be they the political climate or the school system or a Christmas festival.

It is, then, the *two* parts of Chopin's life which induced us to cooper-
ate, hoping to unite the elements that formed his personality, to give
a complete portrait of the man, to present, as it were, both Chopins.
Though all the final text of the book was written by myself, I could not
have done so without her.

We are most grateful for the help of Krystyna Kobylańska, the former
head of Warsaw's Chopin Museum, an internationally acknowledged
Chopin expert, author of *Chopin in His Native Land* (1956), *Chopin's
Correspondence with His Family* (1972), *Catalogue of Manuscripts of
Chopin's Works* (1977), and approximately two hundred articles on the
composer. She read the manuscript and spent many hours discussing it.
Adam Harasowski in England, who wrote *The Skein of Legends Around
Chopin,* turned over to us the fragments of the disputed Delfina letters.
Bernard Willerval and C. Bédarida in Paris examined the French news-
papers and periodicals published during the Chopin years and extracted
what was written about him; a great deal was written about him. Georges
Lubin, whose edition of the George Sand letters is a model of what fine
scholarship can achieve, took personal interest in our work, as did Henry
Pleasants, who is an authority on Schumann. Others who helped were J.
Rigbie Turner of the Pierpont Morgan Library; the staff of the Music
Division of the Library of Congress; Ludwik Erhardt, editor of the
Warsaw music periodical *Ruch Muzyczny;* Henri Musielak, musicologist
in Auberchicourt, France, who discovered several interesting posthu-
mous documents; Zdzislaw Sierpinski, director of the Polish Institute of
Arts and Sciences in America; Ordway Hilton, graphological expert in
New York; Michèle Maurois, daughter of André, who owns the sketch-
books of Maurice Sand; Professor Jan Kott, author of *Shakespeare Our
Contemporary,* and an authority on French and Polish literature of the
nineteenth century; Professor W. J. Wagner of the University of Detroit;
Wiktor Weinbaum, Director, the Chopin Society of Warsaw; Dr. Warren
O'Reilly, President, Chopin Foundation of the United States; Mrs. Lewis
S. Rosenstiel, President, American Institute of Polish Culture; Mrs. Alex-
ander Janta. Special thanks are due to Frances Lindley, the brilliant
editor who is almost a collaborator.

Chopin had no Alexander Wheelock Thayer, the biographer who
punctiliously interviewed the men and women who knew Beethoven
and who collected and sifted every scrap of paper about him. Too many
"if"s and "maybe"s beset the story, too many errors and hearsays, and
too many memorabilia have been dispersed. It is ironic that the plaque

affixed to No. 12 Place Vendôme, Paris, where Chopin died, gives the wrong birth date (February 22 instead of March 1, 1810). It is even more ironic that the apartment that is pointed out to visitors as his was *not* his, as Henri Musielak has established. What makes the biographical task especially difficult is the absence of some of his important correspondence. Letters are the bricks of a biography, but these bricks have been pulverized by a series of misfortunes:

c.1850—George Sand burns her letters to him. No trace of them remains.

1863—Russian invasion of Warsaw. Many letters are dumped and swept away by soldiers.

c.1870—Maurice Karasowski, one of his first biographers, extremely careless. Loses many letters, tampers with the text of others.

1939—Invasion by the Nazis. Letters Chopin wrote to a friend, Jan Bialoblocki, are destroyed, along with other documents.

1944—Warsaw insurrection. The valuable "Binental Collection" is burned.

c.1950—The great-granddaughter of his pupil and helper, Julian Fontana, living in New Orleans, cleans out the attic and throws away "useless papers."

A. Hedley's *Selected Correspondence* was used as a valuable source; however, many letters have been newly translated.

Though much documentation is missing, we were able to find quite a bit of fresh evidence which tends to change the conventional idea of the poor, frail, tubercular Chopin appearing like a wraith in the overheated salons of oversentimental countesses. Decidedly, he was not what James Huneker called him: "nature's most exquisite soundingboard."

A word about what the book is *not:* it is not a treatise on his music. Though some of his works are discussed briefly, no technical analysis is given. Our book tells the story of a man, one who was worldly yet an enigma, one who hugged success yet remained dissatisfied, and one whose work has given pleasure to the musically naïve, yet before whom the musically learned still stand in profound admiration.

GEORGE R. MAREK

New York, 1978

CHOPIN

I

GROWING UP IN WARSAW

WARSAW RACONTEURS, including Frederic Chopin's father, Nicolas, used to tell foreign visitors a story which ran something like this: Writers from several nations were commissioned to write books about the elephant. The Englishman wrote a book entitled "The Club Life of the Elephant"; the American, "Bigger and Better Elephants"; the Frenchman, a paperbound volume, *"L'Éléphant et ses amours";* while the German—after spending his entire life in the jungle—published a seven-volume work, "Introduction to a Study of the Elephant, As He Is, and As He *Ought* to Be." The Pole wrote, without ever having seen the animal, a slim treatise: "The Elephant and the Polish Question."

"The Polish Question" . . . The schoolteacher and the physician, the lawyer and the student, were aware of it, as were the butcher, the baker, and the postman. Poles breathed a politically polluted air. They could not call their country their own. Ruled by strangers, they had to watch every step they took, every word they uttered. The Question before them, for which they longed morning and evening to find the answer, was: "Can we ever regain our liberty?" A variant of the question was: "When?"—"When will we be able to breathe freely?"

Long before, Poland had been a free, strong, and liberal state. Then, weakened by the selfishness of the nobles, held back economically by serfdom, torn by civil strife, she had been unable to resist the attacks of her greedy neighbors, Prussia, Austria, and Russia. Three times the country had been partitioned, in 1772, 1793, and 1795, and by the early nineteenth century had almost disappeared from the map. Kosciuszko's heroic rebellion in 1794 had fizzled, and in 1810, the year of Chopin's birth, Poland was virtually a province of Russia, though Warsaw itself was controlled by Prussia. Both the Prussian and the Russian police operated there—and operated efficiently.

The police could not suppress Polish pride, the kind of pride that cometh *after* the fall, and that kept the big question open. It sounded in the refrain "Poland is not yet lost," when in practical fact Poland was lost.

Count Jozef Skarbek, an ancestor of the family that was to be decisive in Nicolas Chopin's life, rode out in service of King Boleslav III to meet the German Emperor Henry V, whose armies had invaded Poland from the Elbe to the Oder. Henry had ordered huge mounds of gold and jewels to be heaped up. "Here," he said to Skarbek, "are the arms which will enable me to conquer." Skarbek drew a precious ring from his finger, threw it on the pile, and answered, "Take a little more; you still won't succeed." It happened—if it did happen—early in the twelfth century, and the Poles had kept defiance alive through defeat after defeat. It was pride which perpetuated the legend of exquisite Queen Wanda, who drowned herself in the Vistula rather than marry a German king. The Poles treated her as a saint. It was pride as well as avarice which kept those who had—the magnates—from making any concession to those who had not, the peasants. It was pride which caused the Poles to suffer hardening of the political arteries. They could not change their outmoded ways, and they could not agree among themselves. They were thus an easy mark for those three neighbors who declared on January 3, 1796, in a manifesto which contained one particle of truth to a paragraph of opportunism: "Convinced by experience of the total incapacity of the Poles to enact a lawful Constitution and to live in peace and freedom under the law, Their Majesties have resolved in Their wisdom . . . to divide . . ."

Pride and prejudice go together, and of course there had to be a whipping boy. Centuries earlier the Poles had invited Jews to their country to take over banking and commerce. Some were successful, and most came to be regarded with the hatred with which the ignorant confront the strange. Anti-Semitism became a tradition. "Jew" became synonymous with "untrustworthy," "usurer," or, in milder form, "a merchant."

Paradoxically, educated Poles mixed their patriotism with an admiration for foreign customs, specifically all that was French. Though they wished to preserve their "unsullied Polishness," to which they ascribed a messianic role, most of them were sure that the French held the secret of the good life, most of them spoke French, the language was taught in the schools, many of the important public documents were written in French, the Radziwills or the Potockis had a French chef, whom they paid a lot more than the tutor of their children, and the seamstress studied the Paris periodicals to learn how to duplicate French chic in Polish hemp.

Another paradox: They were an emotional people, expressing their feelings amid showers of tears and the punctuation of kisses, the men hugging each other and walking arm in arm, the women forever caressing their children's cheeks. When a father or a son left for a journey of only a few days, everybody sobbed. Yet they waxed gaily ironic about their sentimentality; their newspapers, books, and poetry were filled with self-mockery. Every night in the cafés of Warsaw, self-deprecating jokes passed from table to table.

One needs to understand this politically tinted condition, this frustrated longing to shake themselves loose, this existence the watchword of which was "Be careful"—in short, "The Polish Question"—if one is to understand the influences which shaped the childhood of Frederic Chopin. He was the son of mixed parentage, a heritage which seems to favor talent. Nicolas, his father, was French; Justyna, his mother, was *echt* Polish. In time the Frenchman who became a Pole had a Polish son who became a Frenchman, but only "officially."

Warsaw's predilection for French culture was to help Nicolas Chopin. At the age of seventeen he left his native Lorraine for distant Warsaw. Why he emigrated nobody knows; he was anything but a man avid for adventure. A sizable Polish colony existed in Lorraine, and some member of this colony may have told young Nicolas to try his luck in a country which admired the French. He got a job as a bookkeeper in a small Warsaw snuff factory, owned by another Frenchman; the factory prospered because snuff was the form of tobacco favored by gentlemen (including Frederick the Great, Addison, Pope, and Napoleon), the use of which involved the graceful ritual of tapping the little box, opening the lid, offering the solace to your companion, and waving your handkerchief. Nicolas came carrying as his tangible goods a violin, a flute, and several volumes of Voltaire. As his intangible goods, he carried French thrift, French skepticism, French prudence, and the ability not to postulate too many hard-and-fast rules for the conduct of life. He worked long hours during the day and in the evenings explored the city or read his Voltaire, taking a pinch of snuff now and then. His mother and sisters* were illiterate, but books were honey cakes to him. He loved learning for the sake of learning. With zest and ability, he educated himself. A letter of his is preserved, dated 1790; it is written in crude French. Forty years later, his correspondence with his son is still written in French, but very literate French.

He soon began to like the Poles and their Warsaw, a city which was not quite a metropolis and not quite a small town, but a conglomerate of ostentatious palaces in the neoclassical style and miserable hovels in the ubiquitous style of poverty, with enough trees and shrubs and little gardens between to provide space to move in. It was a restless place; the carriages of the nobles, drawn by six horses and attended by four servants, cut their way through groups of men who never stopped talking and skirted the stalls where peasant women sold farm produce. Some peace and quiet could be found on the right bank of the river, a district called Praga and reached by a ferry; it was a sylvan site, good for picnics and lovers' walks, which afforded a view of Warsaw rendered romantic by distance and dominated by the Royal Palace and the Cathedral of St. John. (Bernardo Bellotto, who had come to Warsaw in 1767 on his way to Russia but decided to stay, painted the views with such architectural accuracy that his paintings served as guides in the reconstruction of the ancient part of the city after World War II.) Some citizens wore Western garb, others the *zupan,* a long robe pleated from the waist down and trimmed with fur, such men affecting fierce hanging mustaches, with only a single tuft of hair standing upright on their shaved heads.

An uprising in which Nicolas took part followed the Second Partition in 1793. He escaped death by sheer chance. Hard times came; the snuff factory closed its doors; he thought of returning to France, fell ill, and on his recovery decided to remain in Warsaw. Polish ardor, the struggle of its people, had by that time captured his imagination. Realist though he was, he felt that he should throw in his lot with this unrealistic nation.

He had a pretty shrewd idea of his assets: he was young, unattached, handsome, fluent in French, good enough in German, his handwriting was exemplary, and he knew something about music. It added up to his

*The sisters lived in France, but if Frederic Chopin knew of their existence, which is doubtful, he never got in touch with them during his years in Paris.

becoming a tutor. We are familiar with the figure of the household tutor from such plays as Turgenev's *A Month in the Country,* though Nicolas proved a better man than Belyayev. After six years as tutor to the two sons and two daughters of a Mme. Laczynska (one of the daughters became the famous Marie Walewska, who was Napoleon's mistress), Nicolas got a better position in the household of the Skarbeks, descendants of Henry V's antagonist.

Countess Louise Skarbek owned a small estate, known by the melodious name of Zelazowa Wola, some forty miles from Warsaw in a district called "the heart of Poland." The Skarbek manor house was a plain one-story structure, flanked on either side by an annex, the little complex representing, if not the heart of Poland, the heart of a woods in which chestnut trees, poplars, oaks, birches, and willows grew. A small river, the Utrata, meandered through the property and the reeds stood high on its banks. There one could hide to read or just lie and look at the sky. Nicolas guided the education of the five Skarbek children, of whom the eldest, Frederick, was then only ten years old. Soon he did more. Count Skarbek had drunk up, packed up, and gone abroad, leaving considerable debts behind, and the harassed countess was trying to save the family name and possessions. Nicolas, the only man in the house, soon became the steward of the estate.

Opposite him at the dinner table sat a young girl with blond hair, blue eyes, and an easy smile. She was Justyna Krzyzanowska, supposedly a distant relative of the Skarbeks (the matter is uncertain), who acted as housekeeper. At her waist, she carried the keys to the medicine chest, the symbol of her authority. She played the piano, and on many an evening, while the snow wrapped the house in isolation, she accompanied Nicolas's flute or violin.

It was certainly not love at first sight. It was rather a drawing together, favored by living under one roof as members of one family. It took Nicolas fully four years before he decided. They were married on June 2, 1806, when Nicolas was thirty-five, Justyna in her mid-twenties, and moved into one of the annexes, a modest four-room cottage.*

---

*It is preserved as a museum. On summer Sundays, concerts are given in the house or the garden.

The children came:

Louise, born April 6, 1807, in Warsaw, where the Skarbeks and the Chopins had gone to live temporarily, because troop movements made the country estate unsafe. (In July Napoleon concluded the Treaty of Tilsit, by which a reduced Poland became the "Grand Duchy of Warsaw," and the Skarbek household moved back to Zelazowa Wola.)

Frederic Franciszek, born March 1, 1810, at Zelazowa Wola.*

Isabella, born July 9, 1811, in Warsaw.

Emilia, born November 20, 1812, in Warsaw. Died at the age of fifteen.

After Frederic's birth, Nicolas began to think seriously of moving to Warsaw. The Skarbek children were growing up, the eldest having already gone to Paris, where every young Polish aristocrat went while still capable of acting young. Nicolas wished to advance himself. If one was to believe Napoleon, Poland could look forward to better times. Was there hope? Nicolas was unsure. True, Napoleon had chased the Prussians out of Warsaw and announced that the city would once again become a cultural and political center. It was half deserted, and the Prussians had taken good care to destroy whatever they could destroy in a hurry—yet a Society of the Friends of Learning had already been formed. Learning was once more in the ascendancy. A new school, the Warsaw Lyceum, opened its doors, attracting young people from the provinces. Some of the rich returned.

In 1815, after Waterloo and the Congress of Vienna, Czar Alexander declared the "Restoration of the Kingdom of Poland." It was, to be sure, a kingdom dependent on the Czar's nod, but all the same Poland, and especially Warsaw, experienced a modicum of prosperity and more than a modicum of gaiety. Alexander called Warsaw his "third capital," and in that capital, Romanticism became a familiar visitor. Artists such as Hummel and Paganini arrived, on their way from Vienna to St. Petersburg. The Warsaw Opera gave performances more distinguished for scenic splendor than musical excellence, and concerts were occasionally presented, their programs "popular" and simple. More determinedly than before, the great Polish families imitated the French, their social evenings, called *assemblées,* ranging from balls and banquets to literary discussions and private perfor-

---

*The date has been disputed, some saying February 22, some 1809. March 1, 1810, is now the accepted date.

mances of plays. The first Polish performance of Beaumarchais's entic-
ingly dangerous comedy *The Marriage of Figaro* took place at the
palace of the Princesse de Nassau. When Alexander visited Warsaw,
the Czartoryskis entertained him at a costume ball for 2,500 guests, lit
by a thousand candles, the hostess greeting each guest with *"Mais,
vous êtes charmant d'être venu!"* She spoke in a hoarse voice. In Warsaw almost everybody suffered from frequent colds. Consequently
Warsaw society decreed that to have a cold was *bon ton:* it was smart
to be sniffly. A favorite fabric was called *le diable enrhumé.*

Amid the general euphoria, Nicolas retained his French skepticism.
All the same, when opportunity beckoned, he accepted the position of
instructor in French language and literature at the Lyceum and moved
his family to the capital. Soon he was so successful as a teacher that he
was able to establish a boarding school for the sons of well-to-do families.
His first pupils were two of the Skarbek boys and three of their cousins.
In due time the school expanded and moved to the fine Casimir Palace
on Warsaw's principal street, where Nicolas hired an assistant tutor and
Justyna hired a housekeeper. It became Warsaw's most fashionable
school, charging an annual fee of 4,000 zlotys (about $3,000 in today's
purchasing power), with hardly ever a place vacant. (A few scholarships
were given.) One of the students wrote in his memoirs that the boys
used to make fun both of Nicolas's foreign accent when he spoke Polish,
and of his stentorian threats to use "Madame Rozga" (the rod) if they
misbehaved. They all knew that he was too soft-hearted to carry out the
threat.

Music sounded in Nicolas's house—Thursday was chamber music
night—and the child Frederic had his choice of an extensive library,
mostly of French books. The children spoke both Polish and French. If
it was not a home of wealth, neither was it a home of poverty—and
certainly it was a home of culture. "Knowledge frightens the wolf
away," Nicolas used to say. He himself, "Professor of French Language
and Literature," now enjoyed a circle of scholars and writers—the rec-
tor of the university, Samuel Linde, who compiled the great *Dictionary
of the Polish language,* was one of his best friends—and the children
moved among them with the ease of knowing they were loved. The
serious talk was now and then relieved by games of whist or écarté, and
always accompanied by astounding quantities of food. It was absolutely
necessary to serve twice as much food and wine as could be consumed
and to urge the guest to eat and drink more than he wanted. Justyna

—or any Polish hostess—pleaded, "You don't like it?" if anybody around the table didn't help himself three times. Bread, always home baked, was the staple, and women vied with one another in the excellence of their product. Jam made of wild strawberries was a favorite delicacy, and so were the marvelous forest mushrooms, unique to Poland and parts of Russia, which were dried and threaded or pickled in a concoction of vinegar and herbs, each cook being certain that she alone possessed the one right recipe. On holidays Nicolas took the children to the woods; one could ride out of the city and in fifteen minutes find oneself among ancient trees, where they would search for strawberries. They much preferred "hunting the mushrooms" in dark, moist nooks.

All the children were early given piano lessons by their mother and all showed talent, though only Frederic also showed an indefatigable passion for music.* Louise indulged in a few romantic and edifying literary efforts, while Isabella, Emilia, and Frederic helped to polish her syntax. As the eldest, Louise was the leader. She was also the most gifted, and Frederic loved her best, as she loved him. The sisters chattered all day long (Polish sounds like rain splattering into a barrel), and Frederic used to call them "the drivelers." He didn't talk much, but he liked to curl up with a piece of chocolate and read. Soon he began to write little verses.

Polish life was much dependent on the seasons; the winters were long, the frosts obdurate, and the Poles invented an additional season, "pre-spring," which came late in March, when the ice began to melt on country roads and trading between the villages could be resumed. From then on until the last few days in August—when glistening loose threads of spiders' webs, called "the old woman's summer," floated in the sunny air—weather was a constant topic, and all his life Frederic's moods responded to good or bad weather.

Religion was almost as ubiquitous a concern, the two not unconnected when the peasants prayed to the Madonna for a good harvest. The "Black Madonna" of Czestochowa, with her wounded face, could help with the wheat; Our Lady of Ostrabrama could help with the potatoes. But Polish Catholicism was predominantly cheerful; it did not

---

*The inevitable sentimental anecdotes which embroider the childhood of a genius are told about him: how he cried when he heard music, how he sneaked into the room with the piano at midnight and began to play, etc. Not a shred of evidence exists to substantiate these tales.

wear the Spanish ruff. Rather, it was an excuse for a holiday at the drop of a cleric's hat, and for many a drinking and dancing party in honor of this or that saint. Nicolas was too convinced a Voltairean to believe it all, and Frederic was to believe even less, but Justyna was devout and dragged the boy to church and to confession.

Christmas—that was the year's most joyously observed festival, and all, believers and unbelievers, took part in it. It was a fast day: one did not eat until the first star rose (around 6 P.M.), symbol of the star which heralded the birth of the baby in the manger. Then the head of the family brought to each guest a wafer blessed by the priest, hugged and kissed all present, and wished them a merry Christmas. In turn, the guests kissed one another. The kissing done, they proceeded to the table, which was set for more people than were expected, to remember the absent. It was covered with the best tablecloth, underneath which a thin layer of hay had been spread, denoting the successful completion of the harvest as well as the Infant's crib.

Dinner began. And what a dinner! Twelve or thirteen courses, all traditional. First a clear mushroom soup with noodles or a borscht with tiny ravioli, followed by cold carp in aspic and three other fish, dumplings filled with cabbage, a *kulebiak* of cabbage, hard-boiled eggs, and mushrooms; and an assortment of sweets, a compote of prunes, noodles with poppy seeds, honey cakes. In the country the host would go to the stables after dinner and give the animals an extra ration of fodder.

When everybody had eaten and drunk himself as full as a Christmas stocking, the gifts would be opened. Then the singing began. The favorite carol was "Sleep, Baby Jesus"; Chopin was to use its melody in his Scherzo Opus 20.

Though "The Polish Question" hovered ever present, life in Warsaw after Waterloo remained for a time fairly stable. With caution, one could—and did—laugh.

Frederic's, then, was a happy childhood, free of want or dissension, with a respected and eminent father who, however dry by nature, recognized in the little boy that love for ordered sound, that absorption with melody, with which he followed his mother's playing, that quick grasp of all Justyna could show him, which testified to a talent stronger than the girls's. If Frederic's gift proved good enough to provide a career, Nicolas would be the first to encourage him. His son need not struggle. Furthermore, the profession of musician had become legitimate, and indeed, under Russian law (which was now Polish law), a "professor of music" was absolved from doing military service in peacetime.

Could so equable an ambience favor the development of genius? There was nothing here of Berlioz's revolt against his father, nothing of Brahms's childhood humiliation, nothing of Schumann's being forced to study law. Good fortune can no more halt the growth of talent than adversity can.

(2)

When Frederic was six years old—not all that young for a child prodigy —Nicolas knew that home instruction no longer sufficed. He chose a professional piano teacher named Albert Zywny, who lived around the corner, didn't charge much, and was willing to give lessons to both Louise and Frederic. Zywny was one of Warsaw's well-known eccentrics. He had begun as a virtuoso; was good but not quite good enough; was overly fond of vodka (a drink which in Poland at the time only the peasants favored); had at one time been court pianist to a Prince Sapieha; had lost that position in the partition of the country; and now trudged through Warsaw giving lessons from early morning until late afternoon, summer and winter wearing the same knee-high German boots, into which he stuffed his fees. Rumor had it that he was quite well-to-do, but he pleaded poverty, nobody was invited to visit him, and after giving a lesson he would hang around, hoping to cadge a meal. Since he was always in a good humor, not a bit sorry for himself, ready with the latest gossip, which he whispered in a mixture of Polish, German, Czech, and French, he was a welcome guest. The Chopin children were not in the least awed by this curious figure, clad in a long green coat, his head covered by an obvious blond wig, with an endless handkerchief protruding from his back pocket which, when he pulled it, scattered snuff over him and the keyboard. He was proud of his collection of old-fashioned waistcoats, which he had bought at auction; he claimed they had been made from the breeches of King Poniatowski. A classmate of Frederic's wrote: "Good old Zywny, he tried to teach me piano and never succeeded. He was probably the most mediocre music teacher in Warsaw. Chopin was his pupil, which proves that in order to become Alexander the Great one does not need Aristotle as teacher."

That is undoubtedly too harsh a judgment. The least Zywny had was enthusiasm. The long nose of his long face seemed to inhale the music he taught. Above everybody and everything, this Don Basilio loved Bach. At his shrine Zywny could worship: there were the head and fount of musical wisdom. And he transmitted that love to Frederic. When Chopin was eleven he dedicated to Zywny a Polonaise in A-flat major. (It is the earliest musical autograph of Chopin which has been preserved.) The man of sixty and the boy of seven recognized each other, Frederic absorbing, understanding, and before long presenting the teacher with ideas of his own. Zywny opened his eyes, took another pinch of snuff, drew a big pencil from his pocket, and wrote down the melodies the boy improvised.* Ignoring most of his other pupils, he concentrated on Frederic, visited the Chopin home day after day, lesson or no lesson, and spread the tale of "the new Mozart" all over town.

Frederic was far from that. Yet his gift was recognizable, and he began to be invited to the palaces of Warsaw's nobility, sometimes merely as a living toy, sometimes because a Czartoryski or a Radziwill felt sincerely interested in sponsoring the slight, self-confident boy, at once diffident and calm. He became accustomed early to the carpeted stairs and the gilt mirrors.

In school he was anything but diffident, his specialty being the caricatures he drew of classmates and teachers, which were passed around under the desks with full appreciation. (An especially unflattering portrait of the great Samuel Linde unluckily came to Linde's attention, but Linde had enough humor to return it to Frederic with a two-word comment: "Well drawn.") He showed no particular aptitude for any academic subject, but no gross incompetence either, and after passing the fourth- and fifth-grade exams—he was then fourteen—he was awarded a prize for "Good Conduct and Diligence."

The schoolboy did not at all fit the standard description of the budding genius. Far from being withdrawn and enclosed in himself, he was outgoing and popular with his classmates, and he made friends easily. Some of them remained close, first and foremost his "beloved Titus,"

---

*It was probably Zywny who wrote down a "Polonoise" [sic] dedicated to Countess Victoire Skarbek (bride of Frederic Skarbek), published in 1817. It attracted some attention from a literary journal, which "intended to demonstrate that under our sun, too, geniuses are born; only the lack of publicity keeps them hidden." This praise was almost certainly written by Frederic Skarbek.

Titus Woyciechowski; then Jan Matuszynski, who became a physician; and Julian Fontana.

Josephine Wodzinska—Chopin would become involved with her sister Maria years later—remembered their childhood days: "She [Maria] wasn't even nine, I was eight, and when we visited the Chopins all we had in mind was playing games. That Frederic was already considered to be the best pianist in Warsaw didn't mean nearly as much to us as that he was ready for jokes and fun . . . running, clowning, imitating people we knew—he did that best—sketching. . . . Sometimes he would sit at the piano, but because we were too young to take music seriously, he would play tricks or play dance tunes. . . . I remember, he was the gayest."

When Frederic was fourteen, the Chopin children spent their vacation with their mother in the village of Szafarnia, at the country home of a family named Dziewanowski, whose son attended Nicolas's boarding school. The village was famous for its lilac bushes, which showered blossoms that ranged from milky white to bloody purple, and Frederic loved these lilacs. During the past winter Frederic had grown too fast, Justyna thought, and had caught too many colds. He was too thin. The doctor prescribed a cure: four hard-to-swallow red pills a day to stimulate the appetite, linden tea after meals, six glasses of roasted acorn coffee during the day, lots of bread—but not the rough, crumbly peasant bread Frederic liked: he was to have only rolls baked of white flour, especially for him. Nicolas thought that what his son needed was good strong wine—"it builds blood"—but it had to be French wine. The boy loathed wine. Frederic obviously had a strong constitution to overcome such ministrations, and in no time he got well—because he enjoyed himself. Instead of writing letters home, he reported his doings in a one-sheet newspaper he called the *Szafarnia Courier,* writing as "Mr. Pichon" (anagram of "Chopin"). This "Courier" of his was a parody of Warsaw's leading newspaper, the *Warsaw Courier.* It carried "Foreign News" (happenings in the neighborhood), as well as "Home News." Three samples:

Aug. 11. Mr. Frederic Chopin goes horseback riding every day, with such skill that he regularly remains stationary—on his behind. (Passed by the censor L.D.*)

---

*L.D. was Louise Dziewanowska, a relative living in the house.

Aug. 12. The hen is limping, the duck lost a paw in a duel with the goose. The cow is grazing in the garden. Consequently an edict has been issued on the 14th inst. forbidding all pigs to enter the garden on pain of death.

Aug. 19. On 15 August, at a musical gathering at Szafarnia, consisting of a score or so of somebodies and nobodies, Mr. Pichon figured in the program, playing Kalkbrenner's concerto, which did not, however, make such an impression, particularly on the nobodies, as "The Little Jew" [a mazurka], performed by this same Mr. Pichon.

These read like the usual efforts of fourteen-year-olds. Seeing him there under the lilac bushes, one would have thought: lively and intelligent, yes; sensitive, perhaps; charming, certainly; but a genius?

He had made his first public appearance in his eighth year. It had come about through Zywny's vociferous propaganda, through the interest Mme. Skarbek had taken in the boy, and because prodigies give a touch of the kermis to affairs more social than musical. It was a charity affair, organized by a distinguished poet and playwright and sponsored by a member of the Czartoryski family. On February 24, 1818, titled society made its way to the Radziwill palace, the sleighs stopped, servants unwrapped the passengers, there was much greeting and kissing, and then, after the customary half-hour delay, the child (whose name was spelled Schoppin in the program) appeared on the stage. He was dressed in the standard uniform of the prodigy—the black velvet jacket, the lace-embroidered white collar, short trousers with white stockings. He played a concerto by the then popular Adalbert Gyrowetz, a composer of some thirty operas, nineteen masses, and sixty symphonies, a few of them good enough to have been attributed mistakenly to Haydn. Gyrowetz was himself a virtuoso pianist, and it is safe to assume that the concerto Chopin played was a virtuoso piece, intended to show an audience how well the pianist could play—without straining the intellectual capacity of the listeners. A sensible choice, in which one may discern the advice of Zywny, who was a good deal more nervous than his pupil and darted all over the hall, displaying a clean handkerchief for the occasion.

Chopin charmed the audience; his success was unequivocal, but he took it calmly. Justyna, prevented by illness from attending the concert, asked him what the audience had liked best. "The white collar you made for me," he answered.

How easy it would have been for Frederic to become the local wonder boy, the pint-size curiosity who is forgotten as soon as the little legs are long enough to reach the pedals! His father was too wise to let it happen. Frederic was allowed to build his talent quietly, nourished by the impressions made on him by the open countryside, youthful friendships, books, and talk. He did play for some of the artists visiting Warsaw, notably the famous Angelica Catalani, billed as *Prima Cantatrice del Mondo.* Her all-powerful voice provoked the story of a London music lover who, asked whether he was going to York to hear her, replied that he could hear her well enough where he was. When Frederic was ten she gave four concerts in Warsaw; he heard her, was enchanted by her, he improvised for her, and she, equally enchanted, gave him a gold watch. He kept that watch all his life.

Occasionally Frederic would be called for and taken to the Belvedere Palais, seat of the Grand Duke Constantin Pavlovitch, grandson of Catherine the Great, son of the murdered Czar Paul, and brother of Alexander I. Constantin had been appointed governor of Poland; he was feared because of his unpredictable rages, which sometimes caused him to gallop through Warsaw seated in his equipage with its four horses harnessed abreast; as he rode, he would shoot off his pistol right and left. Suspicious of everybody, especially the Polish intellectuals, "those café-sitting troublemakers," he hated himself as he hated his Polish wife and the Poles at large. From time to time, however, music could soothe that savage breast and he sent for young Chopin to play for him. "Why are you always glancing upward?" he asked Frederic. "Do you read your music on the ceiling?" Frederic said nothing; he had already learned to say nothing to a grand duke of Russia.

Most of the music he then "read" was by way of often tentative improvisation on melodies and turns of phrase picked up from the folk music around him. Nicolas quickly realized that his son needed not only technical instruction, but also a grounding in the forms and history of the art, and he insisted that Frederic receive both a general education and a specialized one.

(3)

Zywny himself said that he could teach Chopin little more and that a teacher experienced in formal composition was now required. Josef Elsner, born in Silesia but a long-time resident of Warsaw, was a man in his early fifties when he took Chopin under his wing. He was a well-known and prolific composer. Prolific? Grove's Dictionary states: "His works are legion—operas, ballets, melodramas, cantatas, church music, symphonies, and instrumental pieces of all sizes and kinds." All his work has been swept away by the river of time; but it is evident that his knowledge of the variegated forms of music benefited his young pupil. And Elsner was a cultivated man, broad-minded and perceptive. He wrote about Chopin: "Leave him in peace. If his method is out of the ordinary, so is his talent. What need has he of adhering rigorously to the usual rules? He follows rules of his own."

That came later. In the beginning Chopin did study the rules, the models of harmony and counterpoint, the classical sonatas, the choral Masses, first taking private lessons from Elsner, then enrolling in the conservatory which Elsner had founded in 1821 and of which he remained the director until the end of 1830. To that conservatory he attracted good teachers, his own dignity and devotion forming it into a first-class institution. Those kindly eyes beneath the large forehead watched over everything, and that kindly spirit was able to convey determination to others, because he himself was convinced of the usefulness of his work. As a composer he rarely rose above the merely competent; as a teacher he was inspiring. His wife, Caroline, was one of the stars of the Warsaw Opera and Frederic liked their daughter, Emilia. Indeed, Frederic entered into that family as more than a pupil, Elsner spending hours with the boy, discussing music and sipping tea. Those discussions were more nourishing than the regular curriculum, which, however, Frederic absorbed with increasing competence. The official evaluation was given in the yearly record:

1827. Junior pupil, first semester. Frederic Chopin, exceptionally gifted.
1828. Chopin Frederic, pupil, second form. Extraordinarily endowed. On leave for his health, temporarily.
1829. Pupil, third form. Szopen* Frederik, extraordinarily endowed. A musical genius.

Elsner lived to be eighty-five, outlasting Chopin by five years. Unlike many pupils, Chopin never forgot his teacher, asked him for advice when he got to Paris, and always addressed him with warmth and respect.

---

*They tried phonetic spelling that year.

Before and during the time Frederic came under Elsner's tutelage, he performed in a few private homes, and in a second public concert on June 10, 1825, when he played a movement of a concerto by Moscheles, who was later to become his friend and admirer. The previous week saw the publication of his first work, Opus 1, a little Rondo in C minor, dedicated diplomatically to Mme. Linde. It did not make much of a stir; it could have been composed by any earnest student. That year, too, he played for Czar Alexander I, who was visiting Warsaw. He played on a newly invented instrument called an aeolomelodicon, which was a combination of a small organ and a piano and which soon fell into disuse, being cumbersome to manage. The Czar rewarded him with the customary diamond ring—and then forgot the incident over graver matters of discontent in Russia and Poland. Chopin kept the ring, without feeling the slightest sentimental attachment to the occasion.

Alexander died that year. He had disappointed the Poles, granting little of the independence he had promised in his younger and more liberal days. Worse was to follow. His successor, Nicholas I, showed himself "as the very image of the autocrat and the champion of reaction." The Russian Decembrist uprising against him in the first year of his reign was ferociously crushed, and Nicholas then turned to Poland to abrogate its constitution and abolish what little autonomy it possessed. A winter cloud descended on Warsaw. Censorship became drastic. Young men were suddenly drafted into the Russian army, and the Grand Duke Constantin initiated an elaborate spy system. Every night the intelligence reports, meticulously calligraphed in French on elegant paper, were handed in to the duke; they covered all phases of Warsaw life—civil and military institutions, cafés, schools, homes, brothels. (They fill ninety-eight volumes, preserved in the Warsaw Archive.) Not only did they cast suspicion on this official or that writer, but they went into ridiculous details:

> Countess Zamoyska has ordered fabric for her dress [to be worn at Nicholas's Polish coronation] and she had to pay for the import duty alone 200 zlotys per pound of fabric.
>
> *May 2, 1829*

> The Rector advised the students that he hoped His Most Gracious Majesty would visit the University. Accordingly, he ordered that all students were to shave off their mustaches. This caused general indignation.
>
> *May 4, 1829*

The street banquet was well attended, though interrupted by a downpour. There were complaints of "not enough food." Too many potatoes, not enough meat. The meat had spoiled because of the heat; it had been doused with vinegar and onions, so that people wouldn't notice the smell.

May 28, 1829

Repression creates its counterforce. The young people, still vital and hopeful, plotted boldly, though in whispers, while they pretended to play chess and dominoes in the cafés. A favorite café was the Cinderella, so popular that its owner eventually made enough money on his cups of punch and his homemade caramels to buy one of the Radziwill palaces. Another was Honoratka, where politics were consumed along with the best pastries in town. Frederic frequented these cafés, staying out too late at night. Yet, warned by his father, he learned caution. Living among timid patriots and café revolutionaries, among nobles some of whom flirted with Russia while others brooded on change, he kept his balance. (This did not save him from suspicion later on, but nothing could be proved against him.) The reticence he showed in adult life may be traced to the political climate of his youth.

He began to long to leave the city from which freedom had been expunged.

(4)

In the summer of 1826 Justyna took Frederic, Emilia, and Louise to Reincrz, a spa in Prussian Silesia. Frederic had been ill during the winter, had lost weight and looked pale. Worse, Emilia was showing suspicious signs of a respiratory infection. Frederic took the prescribed —and nonsensical—water cure, two tumblers at 6 A.M. and two tumblers after lunch, and got better; Emilia got worse. By next spring she was much worse and Frederic for the first time experienced the touch of personal tragedy. He wrote to his school friend Jan Bialoblocki:

Warsaw [March 12, 1827]
We have illness in the house. Emilia has been in bed for the last month. She started to cough and spit blood, and Mamma became frightened. Dr. Malcz ordered bloodletting. She was bled once—twice; then countless leeches, blisters, sinapisms, herbal remedies, all sorts of nonsense. During the whole time she ate nothing; she got so thin that you would

not have known her, and only now is she beginning to recover somewhat. You can imagine what a state things have been in. Imagine it if
you can, for I am not equal to describing it. Carnival time came to a sad
end.

A month later Emilia was dead. Frederic, mourning, saw his father
weeping, his mother pale in her black dress. In the same month Nicolas
lost not only his youngest child but one of his oldest friends, Jacob Benig,
who had worked with Nicolas at the tobacco factory and who had been
Isabella's godfather. The Chopin household was reduced to whispers.

But Frederic could not whisper for long. He was seventeen, he was
eager, he was in a hurry, the talent within him pushing him on indomi-
tably. It was then that he worked out the *Don Giovanni* Variations.

A year passed. Frederic had become a young man whose charm and
humor, not his talent alone, made him liked by his father's friends, as
well as by his contemporaries. In 1828, a friend of Nicolas's, Felix Jarocki, a professor of natural history at the University of Warsaw, was
invited to attend a congress of naturalists in Berlin, the chairman of
which was the famous explorer and naturalist Alexander von Hum-
boldt. Jarocki suggested that Frederic go with him to Berlin, so that the
young man might make the acquaintance of such panjandrums of music
as Spontini and Mendelssohn. Nicolas willingly consented. Jarocki took
the congress very seriously and dragged the young man to various
scientific meetings and to the Zoological Institute, when all Chopin
wanted was to go and hear music. He did manage to hear five opera
performances, at that. He saw Spontini, Mendelssohn, and Zelter, Goethe's friend and Mendelssohn's teacher and the head of the Berlin
Singakademie, but he did not speak to any of them, "because I was too
timid to introduce myself." Nevertheless, he had not lost his sense of the
ridiculous: he made caricatures of the scientists and observed Teutonic
self-importance. He wrote to his family:

> Berlin [September 27, 1828]
> On Tuesday, the day before the congress broke up, there was a banquet
> accompanied by suitable songs. Everybody present sang, and those who
> were at table drank copiously and beat time to the music, Zelter con-
> ducting. Near him stood a huge gilt cup on a scarlet pedestal as a symbol
> of his supreme musical rank. They ate more than usual, and for the
> following reason: the worthy scientists, particularly the zoologists, had
> been concerning themselves principally with the improvement of
> meats, sauces, broths, etc., and they had made great progress in the
> science of eating during the few days of the congress.

Practically, the voyage to Berlin proved useless: Chopin left as un-known as when he came. Psychologically it proved useful: for the first time Chopin had the opportunity to observe the life of a metropolis. And a fairly prosperous life it was under Friedrich Wilhelm III. The young visitor commented on the geographical and intellectual open-ness; he was impressed by Berlin's "cleanliness and the order which reigned everywhere"; and he wished for such a frame within which to display his art.

On the return journey, an incident is supposed to have occurred which, first reported by Maurice Karasowski in his biography of 1877, has been repeated by all biographers. In the village of Sulechow (Zülli-chau), the travelers' carriage stopped for a change of horses. Fresh horses were not ready. Chopin alighted with the other travelers, made a tour of the village, where there was precious little to see, returned to the station, found that it would still take some time for the horses to arrive, and at the inn discovered a piano in reasonably good condition. He sat down to play. By and by the other travelers gathered around him, he played on, everybody was mesmerized, and when the coach-man suddenly announced that the horses were ready, nobody wanted to leave; they begged him to go on playing, the innkeeper's wife brought cakes and wine, and an old man who had been silently smoking a pipe announced that he was the local organist and said to Chopin, "I know something about music and I tell you that if Mozart had heard you he would have shouted 'Bravo!' " Chopin had to continue playing until, exhausted, he was carried by the coachman to the coach, while the people at the inn shouted and waved good-bye.

Well, is it a true story? Probably not. Travelers want to travel and get it over with; they would not willingly brook delay if Orpheus him-self were to play his lyre, and Chopin would have been the last artist to volunteer to perform, especially on the kind of instrument to be found at a local inn. Furthermore, the anecdote is not mentioned by any of Chopin's contemporaries.

Chopin himself was anxious to get home and resume his studies with Elsner. No sooner settled, though, than he became restless, and at the end of 1828 he wrote to Titus, reporting (in bad Italian) some scandal about a governess who had been seduced and became pregnant (the local gossip had it that Frederic was the father, but he was innocent, he said, because "she did not attract him"), then telling Titus what was new in the Warsaw French and Polish theaters, and conveying to his friend his groping dissatisfaction:

Warsaw, December 27, 1828

The score of the *Rondo à la Krakowiak* is finished. The Introduction is original—more so than I look in my felt greatcoat. But the Trio [Opus 8] is not yet ready. Upstairs a room has been put at my disposal; the stairs lead up to it from the wardrobe room. There I shall have an old piano, an old desk, and a den of my own. My orphan Rondo for two pianos [an unimportant piece, published posthumously as Opus 73] has found a foster father in Fontana. . . . He has practiced it over at Buchholtz's [a piano manufacturer] to see how it *might have* sounded. I say "might have" because the two instruments were not in tune. We did not achieve the proper expressiveness and the thing did not go well in all those little details (you know what I mean) which give *nuance* to any piece of music. For the last week I have written absolutely nothing. I am running around from one place to another. I rarely alight upon ideas like the ones which came easily to my fingers when I used to play in the mornings on your piano. . . . *I have been wasting my time and trouble* [in Latin].

(5)

We cannot know the *real* first works of an artist; we know only "Opus 1." Between the ages of seven and fifteen, when his Opus 1, the Rondo in C minor, appeared, Chopin covered a mountain of notepaper. Some of the efforts at which he tried his 'prentice hand we know merely by contemporary testimony—such as a March he composed for Constantin which the grand duke had scored for a military band; then several Variations, Polonaises, a Waltz, etc.—the music itself being lost. Other early tries, such as the Polonaise in A-flat major, composed at eleven and dedicated to Zywny, are extant and were published posthumously when scraps by the famous composer were being collected. Yet what we know is less than half the story: Krystyna Kobylańska, who in 1977 published a catalogue of his works, believes that some fifty compositions preceded Opus 1 and that some of them will surface in the future, as in the recent past several Chopin "discoveries" have been made.

His early fame derived from Opus 2, the Variations for piano with orchestral accompaniment on "Là ci darem la mano" from *Don Giovanni.* He composed these when he was seventeen and dedicated them to Titus. What musician has not received profound inspiration from Mozart's realm of jest and menace, one of the half-dozen greatest of all works of art? Gounod had himself portrayed holding the score of *Don Giovanni*. When Rossini was asked which of his own operas he preferred, he answered at once, *"Don Giovanni."* Schubert and Brahms, Mendelssohn and Mahler, loved the work. Chopin succumbed to it early and returned to its study all his life. (He later transmitted his love to George Sand, who wrote at length about *Don Giovanni* in *Le Château des Désertes*.)

Chopin's Variations stick closely to the melody; they are, so to speak, all too respectful and the orchestra does little more than link them together. It is difficult to understand why these rather conventional thoughts elicited the excitement they did and why the young Schumann rushed to hail them with the often quoted admonition: "Hats off, gentlemen, a genius!" Schumann's article appeared in the Leipzig *Allgemeine Musikalische Zeitung* of December 7, 1831—a year after the publication of the Variations—and it marked Schumann's debut as a writer as well as the debut of his imaginary *Davidsbündler*, Florestan and Eusebius. This is the beginning of the essay by "K. [sic] Schumann":

> Eusebius dropped by one evening, not long ago. He entered quietly, his pale features brightened by that enigmatic smile with which he likes to excite curiosity. Florestan and I were seated at the piano. He, as you know, is one of those rare musical persons who seem to anticipate everything that is new, of the future and extraordinary. This time, however, there was a surprise in store even for him. With the words, "Hats off, gentlemen, a genius!" Eusebius spread out before us a piece of music. . . .
>
> "Well, let's hear it," said Florestan. Eusebius obliged, while we listened, pressed against each other in the embrasure of a window. He played as if possessed, conjuring up countless figures of the most vivid actuality. It was as if the enthusiasm of the moment had given to his fingers a dexterity far beyond their normal endowment. Florestan's applause, to be sure, not counting a serene smile, consisted of nothing more than a statement that the variations could have been by Beethoven or Schubert, had either of them been a great piano virtuoso. But then he looked at the title and read: *Là ci darem la mano, varié pour le Pianoforte par Frédéric Chopin, Œuvre 2*, and we both exclaimed incredulously, "An Opus 2!"
>
> We all started talking at once, our faces flushed with excitement. The general tenor was: "Something decent, at last—Chopin, never heard of him!—Who can he be?—A genius in any case!"

Schumann's panegyric was companioned by a second review, unsigned, which called Opus 2 nothing but a "bravura piece," a "parade horse."

But that wasn't all. Earlier, a third article had been published in Kassel, and it was on this article that Chopin commented in a letter to Titus:

> December 12, 1831
>
> I received a few days ago a ten-page review from a German in Kassel who is full of enthusiasm for them. After a long-winded preface he proceeds to analyze them bar by bar, explaining that they are not ordinary variations but a fantastic *tableau*. In the second variation he says that Don Giovanni runs around with Leporello; in the third he kisses Zerlina while Masetto's rage is pictured in the left hand—and in the fifth bar of the *Adagio* he declares that Don Giovanni kisses Zerlina on the D flat. [Count Ludwig] Plater asked me yesterday where her D flat was, etc! I could die laughing at this German's imagination. He insisted that his brother-in-law should offer the article to Fétis for the *Revue Musicale*, and Hiller, a good fellow with enormous talent (a former pupil of Hummel, whose concerto and symphony were played with success two days ago—he's a man of Beethoven's type, but full of poetry, fire and spirit)—well, Hiller only just managed to protect me by telling Mr. Brother-in-law that, far from being clever, the idea is very stupid.

He wrote this from Paris in a mood half amused, half angry. And from then on he used "D flat" as a code word for sex.

"The German in Kassel" has been proved to be Friedrich Wieck, Schumann's future father-in-law. He and his daughter Clara were in Kassel while Clara, aged twelve, was making her first concert tour. The "Mr. Brother-in-law" was the brother of Wieck's second wife.* Despite Hiller's efforts, Wieck's article was published in two German publications, *Caecilie* and *Komet*, and in the *Revue Musicale*. It could have done Chopin no harm.

---

*We owe these facts to the musicologist Henry Pleasants.

(6)

Chopin's creative genius ripened rather slowly, in contrast with his early mastery as a pianist and his youthful prowess at free improvisation. The composer followed, as it were, in the footsteps of the performing artist. Such a sequence is not usual. At eighteen Schubert wrote "Heidenröslein" and "Erlkönig," Mendelssohn the Overture to *A Midsummer Night's Dream,* and to speak of Mozart's output in his eighteenth year is to speak of the improbable. At that age the great Chopin was not yet; he emerged only two years later, when he began to compose the first two of the Twelve Etudes (Opus 10). With that work, published when he was twenty-three, he did shine forth in a light which has illumined keyboard music for almost a century and a half.

Before that he undertook what was almost an obligatory task for the pianist-composer of the period: the creation of "grand" compositions for piano and orchestra. These were considered important demonstrations and they were useful to the virtuoso himself, because they gave him a chance to appear at orchestral concerts within a larger frame, and often for a larger public, than did solo recitals. "Grand" was the key word. At eighteen Chopin produced a "Grand Fantasy on Polish Airs for Piano and Orchestra" (Opus 13) and his "Krakowiak Grand Rondo de Concert" (Opus 14), both of them very successful when he played them and both of them now forgotten.

At nineteen he worked out his first Piano Concerto, the one in F minor (Opus 21), which is called his second concerto because it was not published until 1836, due to Chopin's losing the orchestral parts somewhere between Warsaw and Paris. This is still part of the living repertoire, along with the E-minor Concerto (Opus 11), the "first." Today they still appeal to the romantic spirit in us, because they are melodious and impassioned, as are Schumann's, Grieg's, Tchaikovsky's, and Rachmaninoff's. These are the *Lucias* and *Bohêmes* of the piano world. Chopin's two concertos are as indispensable as the others—especially the F minor, with its nocturnal slow movement—though they are not "Chopin *in excelsis*" (Huneker's phrase), being essentially solo flights with timid orchestral accompaniment. Berlioz had a point when he wrote:

When they [the orchestral instruments] play *tutti,* they cannot be heard, and one is tempted to say to them: why don't you play, for heaven's sake! And when they accompany the piano, they only interfere with it, so that the listener wants to cry out to them: be quiet, you bunglers, you are in the way!

Emerging from his teens, Chopin had sufficient "equipment" to show himself as composer and pianist to a larger world. Where should he go? Boldly he chose as his first testing ground the city of Vienna.

CHAPTER

II

TRIAL IN VIENNA

THE SUMMER OF 1829 proved to be the usual Viennese summer, hot and sticky, the leaves of the Prater turning brown, buildings and trees peppered by the pellets of dust thrown up by carriages rushing over unpaved streets. Yet few even of those who could afford the refuge of lakes or woods had left the city. Austria was experiencing the problems of a world power; that summer Emperor Franz II remained in Schönbrunn and Metternich stayed with him. The Hungarians were restive, seeking independence, the Czar had turned nasty over the Polish question, the students in Prague were protesting against censorship, secret conclaves were being held in Milan. One had better stick close to home.

If so, one needed diversion, and music furnished it. At the Kärntnertor Theater, performances of Italian opera, chiefly Rossini, were helping audiences to forget the heat and in the suburbs rowdy crowds were guffawing over dialect comedies spiked with rough songs. Vienna was now a city of musical memories, drawing on a glorious past. Beethoven had died barely two years before, and twenty thousand Viennese had turned out to watch his funeral procession. Even now hundreds made the long journey to the outskirts of the city to place a flower on his grave. Not even a full year had passed since Schubert died, and slowly the Viennese, who often treat their great men with indifference while they are alive, only to build monuments to them after death, were realizing what they had lost.*

No new composer had come upon the scene to continue the tradition, but the tradition was still strong. Vienna was still considered the city of music. A few men were alive who had known Mozart personally, many who had known Beethoven. Though the only music the Emperor really cared for was the Austrian national anthem, he knew his Viennese and he appropriated a sizable sum of gulden for the subvention of the opera and the ballet.

To this city which made musical reputations, in which Liszt and Czerny and Herz and Thalberg had performed early in their careers, Chopin came that summer. A scrap of fame preceded him: a few musicians had heard of the Polish prodigy and were curious. He arrived well provided with letters of introduction from the benevolent Elsner. The organist Wilhelm Würfel, who had given Frederic some lessons in Warsaw and who was now a conductor at the Vienna Opera, welcomed him and shepherded him around to the musical bigwigs. Chopin met the violinist Ignaz Schuppanzigh—"My Lord Falstaff"—Beethoven's good friend and devoted interpreter, now jollier and fatter than ever and married to an equally jolly waddling wife. He warned the young visitor to beware of Vienna's musical politics: jealousy was as ubiquitous as the dust. He met Johann Andreas Stein, who, impressed by what he heard when Chopin played privately, offered to send one of the pianos of his make to Chopin's lodging. Most important, he met Tobias Haslinger, the music publisher, who had several times felt the brunt of Beethoven's anger and yet had loved him well.

Haslinger invited Chopin to dinner and told him he was going to publish his *Don Giovanni* Variations within a week's time. Chopin was sensible enough to doubt this, and in point of fact, it took seven months before Haslinger issued them. He never did pay Chopin; wasn't the prestige enough? At Haslinger's he was introduced to Count Wenzel Robert Gallenberg, whose wife, Giulietta Guicciardi, was the "dear and enchanting girl" whom Beethoven had loved and to whom he dedicated the "Moonlight" Sonata. (She was once considered Beethoven's

---

*That very summer discussions began about raising money for a tombstone on Schubert's grave. Grillparzer, Austria's national poet, made several suggestions for an appropriate inscription. The monument was erected the next summer. The poet's inscription reads: "The art of music here entombed a rich possession, but even far fairer hopes."

"Immortal Beloved.") Gallenberg had become director of the Kärnt-nertor Theater, and as a shrewd impresario, he urged Chopin to make his public debut there—without, he was quick to specify, asking for a fee. Chopin was encouraged as well by old Adalbert Gyrowetz, who knew that Chopin had played one of his concertos in Warsaw; and by Ignaz Xaver Ritter von Seyfried, a prestigious conductor at Schi-kaneder's theater, to whom we owe a good many personal reminis-cences of Beethoven and of Mozart, whose pupil Seyfried had been.

The conversations at the dinners, in the coffeehouses, and at Haslin-ger's shop revolved around Beethoven, mighty as a memory; Chopin found these glances into the recent past, these sighs after glory gone, excessive. Of Schubert, who had died leaving possessions worth about ten dollars and a few "worthless" manuscripts, little was said, though Chopin met the conductor Franz Lachner, Schubert's friend, who urged that the young man show himself as a performing artist, not merely as a composer: such had been Schubert's mistake.

The long and short of it was that jealousy and jockeying notwith-standing, several men of music in music's town were animated by help-fulness and good will toward the personable newcomer. To be sure, none of them was a pianist.

In the first part of his stay Chopin enjoyed himself, indulging his love for opera. He heard Boieldieu's *La Dame Blanche,* Rossini's *Ceneren-tola,* Meyerbeer's *Il Crociato,* Méhul's *Joseph.* In Warsaw and now in Vienna, later in Paris, still later in London, an opera performance could lure him out of the house. The Viennese performances greatly sur-passed anything he had previously heard; he was all enthusiasm now, a warm mood stoked by the fuss his new acquaintances made over him. He was youth away from home, full of hope and adventure, walking in a lordly and lively city, a city which ruled an empire.

What of the concert? Chopin showed the hesitancy to appear in public with which a writer regards a blank page. He would forever be reluctant to enter a concert hall; he was to become the great pianist of the small room. To his parents he wrote that "they" (his Viennese acquaintances) "were trying to persuade me. Everyone says that it would be a great loss to Vienna if I left without being heard. I simply don't understand it." He pretended to himself that he had a choice, but wasn't he just treading water? For what purpose would he have come to Vienna, spending his father's money, except to further his career? He knew he had to play.

On Saturday he was standing in front of the opera house. Gallenberg
came up, pointed a finger at him, and said, "You play—Tuesday." No
nonsense about it. Thus Chopin was pushed into a decision which he
himself half feared and half desired. Between a Saturday and a Tuesday
(August 11, 1829), Gallenberg got the orchestra alerted, furnished a
singer, arranged for a ballet, put out notices of the event, had the
program printed. Considering on how short a notice the concert was
given, it is not surprising that the house was not full; it is remarkable
that *anybody* attended a debut in the heat of August. Chopin intended
to play the Variations, of course, and his *Krakowiak* Rondo with orchestra, but during the rehearsal it appeared that the orchestral parts were
copied badly, and the musicians could not or would not play the second
piece. So Chopin substituted an improvisation. The concert began with
the overture *The Creatures of Prometheus* by Beethoven—Beethoven
was *de rigueur*—was interspersed with songs and arias, and ended with
a comic ballet, called "The Masked Ball"—"music by various composers." The usual hodgepodge.

The day after the concert, he wrote his parents a long, disorganized,
and overwrought letter.

> Vienna, August 12, 1829
>
> From my previous letter you learned, my dearest parents, that I had
> allowed myself to be persuaded to give a concert; and so yesterday,
> Tuesday, at seven o'clock in the evening, I made my bow on the stage
> of the Royal and Imperial Opera House! . . .
>
> As soon as I appeared on the stage they started clapping; and the
> applause was so great after each variation that I could not hear
> the orchestral *tuttis*. [Chopin was on the stage, the orchestra down
> in the pit.] At the end they applauded so loudly that I had to come back
> twice and bow. Although my free Fantasia did not turn out particularly
> well, they clapped still louder and I had to take another bow. I came out
> the more willingly since the appreciation of these Germans is worth
> something. . . .
>
> The journalists have taken me to their hearts; perhaps they will give
> me a few pinpricks, but that is necessary so as not to overdo the praise.
> Mr. Demmar, the stage manager, is particularly kind and pleasant to me.
> Before I went on he encouraged me so much by his reassurances and
> so took my mind off things that I had no trace of stage fright, especially
> as the theater was not full. My friends and colleagues distributed them-
> selves among the audience in order to hear the various opinions and
> criticism. Celinski [a fellow music student] will tell you how little was

said against me. Hube [a teacher] heard the worst: "It is a pity the young man looks so unimpressive"—so declared one of the ladies. If that is the only fault they could find with me I have nothing to worry about. My friends swear they heard nothing but praise and they did not once have to give the sign for applause. I improvised on a theme from *La Dame Blanche.* Then the stage manager begged me to choose another Polish theme—he liked my Rondo so much at rehearsal that after yesterday's concert he shook my hand warmly and said, "Yes, the Rondo must be played here"—so I selected "Chmiel,"* which electrified the public, unaccustomed as it is to this kind of melody. My spies on the floor of the house declare that people were jumping up and down in their seats. . . .

The general opinion is that I play too quietly, or rather too delicately for those accustomed to the banging of the Viennese pianists. I expected to find such a reproach in the newspaper in view of the fact that the editor's daughter bangs the piano frightfully. It doesn't matter. There must always be some kind of "but . . ." and I should prefer it to be that one rather than have it said that I play too loudly. . . .

So there you have my debut, all the more successful since it was unexpected. . . .

I am curious to know what Mr. Elsner will say to all this; perhaps he is displeased that I have played? But they really insisted so much that I could not refuse. Besides, it seems to me that no harm has been done. Nidecki** was extraordinarily obliging yesterday; he looked over and corrected the orchestral parts and was sincerely delighted at my success. I played on a Graff† piano. Today I am wiser and more experienced by four years. How surprised you must have been to notice that I sealed my last letter with a seal taken from a bottle of Madeira! But I was so absent-minded that I picked up the first decent seal that came to hand —left behind by a waiter—and hastily stuck it on my letter.

At once not only the professionals but the patrons of music became interested. Prince Moritz Dietrichstein of the imperial court, director of the Imperial Library and a member of one of Austria's august families,‡ had attended the debut. The day after, Chopin was invited to tea

---

*A drinking song which used to be sung at Polish weddings when the bride's sisters placed a marriage cap on her head.

**Thomas Nidecki, another pupil of Elsner, who was in Vienna on a government grant.

†He thought the Graff was better than the Stein piano.

‡He was entrusted with the task of watching over L'Aiglon, the son of Napoleon and Franz II's daughter, Marie Louise.

at the palace of Count Moritz Lichnowsky. That was tantamount to the highest approval, Lichnowsky's palace, rivaled only by the Lobkowitz Palais, being the center of musical and literary society. It was Lichnowsky who five years previously had collected signatures for a petition which was to convince Beethoven to accord Vienna the honor of the premiere of his Ninth Symphony. The countess and her daughter praised and petted the young virtuoso. Under these touches Chopin's self-esteem expanded; his confidence, however mixed with diffidence, bubbled to the surface, and he unabashedly reported home that "my way of playing pleases the ladies." He decided to play a second concert, no doubt because he wanted to, but giving as his reason the fact that "they in Warsaw" could not say, "What! He played only once? Perhaps the concert was a failure." The second concert took place a week later. His letter home shows that he had gained more than a little certainty; it exhales a joyful boldness:

Vienna, 19 August 1829

If I had a good reception the first time, it was even better yesterday. There were three bursts of applause when I appeared on the stage; there was a bigger audience, too. Baron what's-his-name, the business manager [Gallenberg], thanked me for the cash takings, saying that "if the audience was so large it was certainly not on account of the ballet, which is already known." I have won over all the professional musicians thanks to my Rondo.* From Kapellmeister Lachner down to the piano tuner, they all admire the beauty of this composition. I know that I have pleased the ladies and the artists. Gyrowetz, who was standing near Celinski, clapped and shouted Bravo! What I don't know is whether I satisfied the out-and-out stone-faced Germans. Yesterday one of them came in from the theater as I was sitting at supper. The others asked him how he had enjoyed his evening. "The ballet was quite nice," he replied. "How about the concert?" they asked. It was easy to see that he had recognized me, although I had my back to him, for he started to talk of something else. I felt that I ought not to hinder the outpouring of his feelings, so I went to bed, saying to myself:

"Unborn is he for whom mankind
Naught but words of praise can find."

---

*The *Krakowiak* was played at the second concert, the parts having been cleanly copied.

I have played twice and been even better received the second time, so things are going *crescendo*—just as I like. Since I am leaving at nine o'clock this evening, I must spend the morning paying farewell visits. Yesterday Schuppanzigh reminded me that as I am leaving Vienna after such a brief stay I must return very shortly. I answered that I will come back here to study, whereupon the baron retorted, "In that case there is no reason at all why you should come": an idea which others confirmed. These are just compliments, but it is pleasant to hear them. They all refuse to look on me as a *pupil*. Blahetka said that nothing surprised him so much as to find that I had learned all that in Warsaw. My answer was that with Messrs. Zywny and Elsner, the greatest ass would learn. . . .

[Later] I have just come back from saying good-bye to Schuppanzigh and Czerny. There is more feeling in Czerny himself than in all his compositions. My bag is packed; I have only to go to Haslinger's and then to the coffeehouse opposite the theater, where I shall find Gyrowetz, Lachner, Kreutzer, and Seyfried. After three nights and two days we shall reach Prague. The express coach leaves at nine o'clock tonight and I shall have a marvelous journey in delightful company.

No reviews of the concert had as yet appeared, and Chopin wondered whether they would be "pleasant or disagreeable." The first was published in the *Wiener Theaterzeitung* the day after he had left. It was decidedly pleasant and not unperceptive, the critic praising him because "he takes it into his head to entertain a large audience with music as music." Yet his "execution conquered difficulties the overcoming of which could not fail to astonish even here, in the home of piano virtuosos." In November appeared another review in Germany's important periodical, the *Allgemeine Musikalische Zeitung*, which judged that his compositions "bear the mark of great genius," surely a premature judgment. Chopin had every reason to be satisfied.

Such, then, was his first professional appearance away from home, his first experience with an audience which did not regard him with the tolerance extended to the local boy, his first self-measurement against the judgment of musicians in a city which considered itself the appellate court of music. Yet, though he passed the test and took pleasure in his success, the two concerts did not free him from a deep dislike of exhibiting himself to the anonymous crowd, an agoraphobia which it would be simplistic to call stage fright. Its cause was an instinctive aloofness, a constraint which was at variance with the performer's reaching across the footlights. It got worse as he got older. Liszt quoted him as saying: "I am not fit to give concerts: the crowd intimidates me, I am asphyxiated by its irregular breathing, paralyzed by the curious stares, mute before the strange faces. You, instead, are destined for it. Even if you do not conquer the public, you dominate it." The language sounds more like Liszt than Chopin, but the thought is substantially authentic.

(2)

He left Vienna in high spirits, traveling with three Polish friends and reaching Prague "after many bumpings and joltings." There he met Friedrich Wilhelm Pixis, the renowned violinist, and August Klengel, a famous organist, who played fugues of his own composition for more than two hours. "I had expected better," was Chopin's comment. They wanted him to give a concert but he refused, offering his family the excuse that "the Czech critics write with razor blades; even Paganini was booed here," and he contented himself with sightseeing. He spent three days in Prague, and though he enjoyed the beauty of the city, his head was occupied with music, for he was putting the finishing touches on his F-minor Concerto.

> I have always something on my mind, which explains how, in the day before I left, I came out of the toilet not properly buttoned up and walked straight into somebody else's room. I was right inside when an amused traveler said in amazement, "Good morning!" "I beg your pardon," said I, rushing out. You really could not tell one room from another.

From Prague he drove to Teplitz, the famous resort which Beethoven and Goethe had visited, where he was invited to the palace of Prince Karl Clary, a scion of Austria's widespread Clary-Aldringen family, members of which were active in the government until World War I. Prince Karl was immensely wealthy: he was said to own "practically all of Teplitz." His four daughters, all pretty and gifted girls, had been given the unusual (for Austria) names of Eufemia, Leontine, Mathilde, and Felicia. (Eufemia and Mathilde later married two sons of Prince Anton Radziwill, at whose palace Chopin would stop in the fall of that year and to whom he dedicated the Trio Opus 8.) Now Chopin "put on his white gloves, which had already performed excellent service at the Vienna concerts," and in company with a Polish friend, was driven to the palace. Of course he was asked to play. Chopin suggested that the company, which "was not numerous but most select," and which included three of the four daughters, choose a theme on which he might improvise. The girls giggled, whispered, *"Un thème, un thème,"* couldn't agree, consulted "the teacher of the son of Princess Clary," who proposed, to everybody's high satisfaction, a theme from Rossini's *Moses.* Rossini—of course; who didn't love Rossini? Chopin improvised. General joy! The company couldn't get enough of his playing: he had to seat himself at the piano four times. He did so willingly—he liked the girls. Eufemia kept a diary. She noted—in terrible French:

> Le cousin de Mad. Lubienska, qui est ici depuis quelque tems, a amenée le soir un jeunne homme qui nos afuit grand plasir en jouant declavesin, des Variations et des Fantasies sur de charmants thèmes qu'il a choisi: de Mosè, Barbier, des Airs Polonais. Il jeue bien joliment, d'une manière fort brillante, et avec beaucoup d'enpression.
>
> [The cousin of Madame Lubienska, who has been here for some time, this evening brought a young man with him who gave us great pleasure with his playing of variations and fantasies on charming themes he had chosen: from *Moses,* the *Barber,* and Polish airs. He plays beautifully in a most brilliant manner and with much feeling.]
>
> *August 25, 1829*

Apparently Eufemia couldn't remember the young man's name.

The girls begged him to stay. He declined; he wanted to push on; and he and his traveling companions hired a private coach, dividing the expense. They left Teplitz at five o'clock in the morning and reached Dresden at four in the afternoon. But these long journeys did not disconcert him. The very next day he made his duty calls, wandered through Dresden's famous picture gallery, the Zwinger, looked at the gardens, visited a horticultural exhibition, and at half-past four stood in line to get into a special festival performance of *Faust*—Goethe's eightieth birthday was being celebrated—with the great actor Karl Devrient as Faust. The performance lasted from six to eleven. What could he have made of that philosophic poem, in a language with which he was but half conversant? As usual, he had little to say: "It is a frightening but a powerful fantasy." Yet he remained for the full five hours, thanks to his eager curiosity, on a day which would have exhausted the most inexhaustible traveler. He was as responsive to the pictorial arts. "If I lived here," he wrote, "I would go to the gallery every week, for there are paintings there at the sight of which I imagine music." He had expressed himself with like enthusiasm about the paintings in the Belvedere of Vienna.

Having been introduced to a few of the leading personalities of Dresden, he thought he had earned a country holiday; he made a short tour through Saxon Switzerland, enjoying lakes and woods entirely different from his native landscape, and then returned to Warsaw and work. His *Wanderjahre* were but *Wandermonate,* yet as the diligence carried him home, his heart beating high, he knew he had gained in worldliness.

(3)

A young artist may have already obtained a degree of stability in his work, he may already have created valid productions, while in behavior and emotional reactions he appears still to be an adolescent. Shelley at nineteen lost the girl he loved (because he was imprudent enough to confess to her that he was an atheist). "Is suicide wrong?" he wrote. "I slept with a loaded pistol and some poison last night, but did not die." Of course he did not die, but three months later met Harriet, with whom he eloped, only to fall in love with Mary Godwin two years after. Couldn't they all live together? he proposed. Yet while he acted so ingenuously, the poet finished *Queen Mab*, revealing a world view which seemingly only an older man could have obtained:

> Power, like a desolating pestilence,
> Pollutes whate'er it touches . . .

Similarly, Chopin had finished his F-minor Concerto and was thinking of the E-minor Concerto, both of which, though imperfect, indicate a degree of maturity. Had we met him then, we might have considered him—away from the piano—an unformed romantic fledgling, beset by the usual longings for he knew not what. Like Shelley at the same age, Chopin at nineteen was in love, or thought he was, with a young singer, Constantia Gladkowska. It was a daffodil love. He never told Constantia: "I have found my ideal whom I have served faithfully, though without saying a word to her, for six months." He wrote Titus that she inspired the Adagio of the F-minor Concerto. More probably he wrote the slow movement—marked "Larghetto" in the final version, not "Adagio"—because a slow movement was needed. He also composed "a little waltz" while dreaming of Constantia (Opus 70, No. 3); it is not one of his best. The brief *Schwärmerei* was but a sign of his search for love, a state aggravated by the absence of Titus, who was studying agriculture some two hundred miles away from Warsaw and whom Chopin now overwhelmed with letters of such longing that amateur psychoanalysts have deduced an element of homosexuality in them. That is to misread the language of Romanticism. "I know you don't like to be kissed—but let me today kiss you for once," Chopin wrote to Titus. Such phrases must be judged in the context of nineteenth-century expression. And men did kiss. Beethoven, after a quarrel, wrote his friend Wegeler: "I am coming to see you, to throw myself into your arms." Berlioz to Liszt: "I love you so, Liszt." Delacroix, the most virile of men, wrote similar letters in his youth.

In the very year when Chopin's letters to Titus were most fervid, Schiller's *Don Carlos* was performed in Warsaw. Carlos greets his friend Posa:

> CARLOS: Is it possible?
> Is it true? Is this reality? Is it you?
> Oh—it is you!
> I press you to my soul and I sense your august spirit melt in mine.
> In this embrace my sick heart is restored.
> I lie at the breast of my Roderick.

Chopin's effusions to Titus, though they often seem to overstep the bounds of man-to-man communication, are simply a reaching for a kindred soul.

> October 3, 1829
> You wouldn't believe how depressing Warsaw is for me just now. If it were not for my family's devotion I could not put up with it. How awful it is to have no one to go to in the mornings, no one with whom to share one's joys and sorrows. It is dreadful, when something weighs on your mind, not to have someone to whom you can unburden yourself. You know what I am referring to.

March 27, 1830

A single glance from you after each of my concerts would have been more to me than all this praise from journalists or people like Elsner, Kurpinski [a composer], Soliva [conductor at the opera], and so on. . . .

I will send you my portrait as soon as I possibly can; you want it and shall have it, but no one else. Well, I *might* give it to one other person, but not before you, who are dearest to me. No one but myself has read your letter. Now, as always, I carry your letters about with me. In May, when I go for a walk outside the town, thinking of my approaching journey, what a joy it will be to take out your letter and learn again beyond doubt that you love me, or at least I can look at the handwriting of one to whom I am absolutely devoted!

April 17, 1830

What a sense of relief I feel in the midst of my unbearable melancholy when I receive a letter from you; I needed one especially today for I have never been so depressed. I wish I could throw off the thoughts which poison my happiness, but I take a kind of pleasure in indulging them.

Yet, without Titus and while looking with moist eyes at Constantia, whose talent he himself confessed was not altogether overwhelming— by coincidence just at this time Henrietta Sontag gave several recitals in Warsaw, adorable Sontag, whom Beethoven had chosen as soloist for the Ninth Symphony; and Chopin heard the difference, writing that "she breathes a scent of freshest flowers over the theater"—he knew it was imperative for him to carry on his work. His family expected it. Warsaw expected it. The *Warsaw Courier* had something to say about that:

December 23, 1829

After the warm welcome he received abroad, our compatriot has not let himself be heard in our city. Such modesty, however praiseworthy a trait it may be in a talented artist, is not altogether to be condoned. Does the talent of Mr. Chopin not belong to his fatherland? Is Poland unable to appreciate him adequately?

A public concert was announced, after he had played to a private audience in his home. At once people responded, and three days before the event not a ticket was to be had. It took place on March 17, 1830, at Warsaw's National Theater. Again the program strikes us as an indigestible mixture: it began with an overture by Elsner, then Chopin played the first movement of the F-minor Concerto, after which he ceded the stage to a man named Görner, who performed a "Divertimento for the hunting horn." Chopin reappeared to play the other two movements of the Concerto, then came the intermission. The second part began with an overture by Kurpinski, followed by a singer rendering variations by Paer; and Chopin closed the affair in bravura style with a "Potpourri on national melodies."

His success was clamorous. He was called "the Paganini of the piano," and one Warsaw newspaper went overboard:

> The night before last represented a true thrill for all those who love the great art. Our compatriot, Mr. Chopin, demonstrated with his Concerto that he had the courage to disregard that weakness—so frequently found here—of imitating blindly those masters who, thanks to the people who are supposed to determine our tastes . . . sit on the musical thrones of Europe. . . . Though Chopin is still an adolescent, he follows the road of genius laid out by his predecessors, marching with virile fortitude to the temple of Euterpe . . . but treading a new path of his own. . . . [The "predecessors" mentioned are Bach, Handel, Gluck, Haydn, Cherubini, Beethoven—no less!]

A second concert was announced, which was attended by an audience of nine hundred. Even that was not enough; a third was demanded, but Chopin refused. Again he enjoyed the acclaim, yet again that enjoyment was outweighed by the agonies he suffered before he walked onstage. It is a feeling many artists share and any artist understands. Vladimir Horowitz has said that the longest walk in the world is between the wings of Carnegie Hall and the piano stool.

"Fate has given us Poles Chopin, as it gave Mozart to the Germans." Remarkably enough, he maintained a cool self-estimate, despite such exaggerated praise. He wrote to Titus:

> March 27, 1830
>
> Well, then, my first concert, although it was sold out and there was not a box or seat to be had three days beforehand, did not make on the general public the impression I thought it would. The first Allegro of my concerto, which relatively few could grasp, called forth applause, but it seems to me that people felt they had to show interest ("Ah, something new!") and pretend to be connoisseurs. The Adagio and Rondo produced the greatest effect and exclamations of sincere admiration could be heard. But the Potpourri on Polish Airs did not in my opinion fully achieve its aim. They applauded because they felt they must show at the

end that they had not been bored. . . . Elsner regretted that the tone of my piano was too woolly and prevented the runs in the bass from being heard. That evening everybody up in the gallery and those standing at the side of the orchestra were satisfied, but the audience in the stalls complained about my playing too quietly—and I would like to have been at "Cinderella's" to hear the arguments that must have raged about me.

He was now ready to set out for Vienna and proceed to Milan. But he was not. He vacillated from day to day, now impatient to leave boring Warsaw, now unable to confront what lay ahead. "I am departing," he wrote to Titus in one letter, only to postpone the date in the next, then once more determining to go. During early July he did find brief encouragement by visiting Titus; then he rejoined his family, who were staying at the summer residence of the Skarbeks, and returned to Warsaw in time to hear Constantia make her operatic debut in Paer's *Angela,* a debut which created something short of a furor. July was gone, August passed, and early in September 1830 he wrote Titus:

I am still here—I have not the strength to fix on the day for my departure; I believe that when I leave it will be to forget home forever; I feel that I am leaving home only to die—and how awful it must be to die far away from where one has lived! How frightful it will be for me to see some cold-hearted doctor or servant by my deathbed instead of my family. Believe me, I have sometimes thought of coming to find peace of mind with you; but I go out, I wander moping about the streets and come home again—to what purpose? merely to kill time. I have not yet had a rehearsal of my concerto; but whatever happens, before Michaelmas I shall cast aside all that is dear to me and find myself in Vienna, condemned to eternal regrets. What is all this nonsense I'm writing! You who know so well what a man's strength is, explain to me why it always seems today that things will happen *tomorrow.* The only answer that comes to my mind is: "Don't be such a fool."

Many years later George Sand was to write of him: "Chopin is always leaving—tomorrow."

About three weeks later, having finished the Second Concerto, he wrote in a lighter mood:

September 22, 1830

For the last few weeks my father has not really wanted me to leave, on account of the disturbances which have broken out all over Germany. Apart from the Rhineland provinces and Saxony (where they already have a new king), Brunswick, Kassel, Darmstadt, etc., we heard that in

Vienna also a few thousand people have started a rebellion—something to do with flour. I don't know what flour has to do with it, but I do know that there has been trouble. In the Tyrol, too, there has been a row. Italy is at boiling point and one may expect to hear about trouble there at any moment. . . . I have done nothing yet about my passport, but everyone declares that I shall get one for Austria and Prussia—not a hope for Italy and France. And I know for a fact that several people have been refused passports altogether, but surely that could not happen to me. Thus I shall certainly be leaving in a few weeks' time for Vienna via Cracow. . . .

My second concerto is finished and I feel like a novice, just as I felt before I knew anything of the keyboard. It is far too original and I shall end up by not being able to learn it myself. . . .

The Rondo is effective and the first-movement Allegro is impressive. Oh, this cursed self-admiration! But it is you, the egoist, who are to blame, if anyone, for this conceit of mine: one picks up one's manners from one's friends. There is, however, one thing in which I do not imitate you: the making of swift decisions. Nevertheless I have made up my mind, quietly and without a word to a soul, to clear out on Saturday week, without so much as by-your-leave, in spite of all weepings and wailings and implorings on bended knee. And so, with my music in my knapsack, my ribbon next to my heart and my soul slung over my shoulder, I shall jump into the stagecoach. Tears as large as peas will flow from King Sigismund's column to Blank [next to the Royal Palace], but I, cold and as dry-eyed as a stone, shall only smile at my poor sisters, who will take such an emotional leave of me.

Chopin then decided to give a farewell concert, no doubt because, after playing it in private, he wished to test the effect of the new concerto in public. He invited Constantia and her friend Anna Wolkow, a pretty and flirtatious singer, to participate. Six days before the concert he resolved to leave directly after the event: "My trunk is bought, my outfit is ready, my scores are corrected, my handkerchiefs are hemmed, my trousers are tailored. Now—only to say good-bye."

Though this concert, too, was successful and he was quite aware that it was, Chopin still did not muster enough courage to confront the world away from home. It took him until November 2 to bid farewell to his city and his family. Elsner and a group of his friends accompanied him a little way and serenaded the hometown genius with a short cantata composed by Elsner for the occasion.* Titus, to Chopin's de-

---

*The oft-repeated story that they gave him a silver goblet filled with Polish earth is almost certainly a sentimental invention.

light, decided to join him on the journey. Many and many a tear was shed—and not alone by his mother and sisters—and many an embrace exchanged. He was to retrace his steps to Dresden, then to Prague, then to Vienna—and then he was not sure where. Into the competing world, Milan, Paris, London, to return triumphant to his native land? He was never to see that land again.

(4)

He was now to undergo two experiences, both disillusioning, the first showing him the blunder of anticlimax, the second demonstrating the difference between compliments and cash.

In Vienna Chopin was no longer a fresh sensation. The Viennese had seen and heard him, and in a city where illustrious pianists came and went with the regularity of post chaises, the sated public was no longer curious. He was not unique in experiencing such disappointment: in the seven months Robert Schumann spent in Vienna, to which he had been lured by glowing promises, he inveighed in vain against the public indifference, and Clara Wieck, hailed with wonder on her first visit, was ignored on her second, when in fact she had arrived at the zenith of her art. Chopin's second visit was also, through no fault of his, ill timed: Schuppanzigh was dead, Lachner had been promoted and was so busy he had no time to spare, and Gallenberg was no longer head of the Kärntnertor Theater, his post having been taken by a former member of the ballet, Louis Duport, who "wouldn't dare risk a florin." Würfel, who did welcome him anew, was very ill with tuberculosis. Haslinger "treats me with courtesy, but also with a certain amount of nonchalance, perhaps because by doing so he thinks he'll obtain my compositions for nothing. I've finished with unpaid work. Now, pay up, you beast!" Chopin called on Czerny, who asked if he had *fleissig studiert* and then told him proudly of an overture he had arranged for eight pianos and sixteen pianists. When he called on the banker Geymüller, he received a frosty welcome:

December 1, 1830

I went to Mr. Geymüller's since Titus has his deposit of six thousand florins there. Having taken note of my name, without troubling to read the rest of the letter, he declared "that he was pleased to make the acquaintance of such an *artiste* as myself but he would not advise me to appear in public, for there are so many good pianists here that one needs to have a great reputation in order to achieve anything." He ended by adding "that he can afford me no assistance as times are so bad, etc. . . ." I had to swallow all that with my eyes popping out of my head! I let him finish his tirade and then told him that I really did not know whether it was worth my while to appear, since I had not had time to call on any of the important people or on the Ambassador, to whom I had an introduction from the Grand Duke [Constantin] in Warsaw, etc. You should have seen his face at that moment! I left with apologies for having interrupted him in his business. Just wait, you J[ew?] d[ogs?]!

The Jews were always at fault.

A special reason lay behind this cold reception. Five days after Chopin's arrival in Vienna, the Polish insurrection had broken out. No longer able to bear Russian oppression and, specifically, Constantin's tyranny, a group of Polish patriots attempted to kidnap the grand duke. Incredibly maladroit, they didn't know that he had left Warsaw, and succeeded only in killing a few Czarists. But Warsaw was now seething, its citizens in open rebellion, ready to "Pluck down forms, windows, anything." Poland now seemed as dangerous a spawning ground of revolution as Paris. Conservative Austria, which had viewed the July revolution in Paris with trepidation, dreaded trouble at its northern border. Any moment the Czar might call for help; that meant sending Austrian soldiers. The air of Vienna smelled of peril—and the Emperor, never the most courageous ruler, was aging.

The members of the imperial court, Lichnowsky, Schwarzenberg, Dietrichstein, thought it prudent not to show sympathy with the Polish cause and, indeed, to pretend that it didn't exist. In a word, the Poles were anything but popular just then. In a restaurant Chopin heard two men discussing the situation, one saying, "The good Lord made a mistake when He created the Poles," the other replying, "Nothing is to be found in Poland," opinions which echoed Metternich's aphorism, *"In Polen ist nichts zu holen."*

On the other hand, Chopin did have the good fortune to become friends with a marvelous man. Suffering from a prolonged cold and a swollen nose, he consulted Dr. Johann Malfatti. The two liked each other instantly; perhaps the fact that Malfatti was married to a Polish woman had something to do with that, but his love for music surely counted for more. Malfatti was a physician of world reputation, one of the men who were to establish the preeminence of Vienna's medical school, and he was now official physician to Emperor Franz.* This man, filled with love, saw Chopin's perplexity and invited him to his house often, serving the Polish dishes of which Chopin was fond. Frau Malfatti was a good cook, one of her specialties being *bigos,* a stew of at least three kinds of meat and sausages cooked with sauerkraut and fresh cabbage (it took three days to make this).

When he was not with Malfatti, Chopin felt alone and confused. Spurred by patriotic fervor, Titus left Vienna to join the soldiers in Warsaw; impulsively Chopin decided to follow him. He hired a carriage to try to overtake his friend, did not reach him, perhaps didn't really *want* to reach him, gave up, and returned to Vienna. His father wrote him that he would make a mighty poor soldier and that his duty lay in music, and deep down within himself he was too much the artist to let the patriot push the composer aside. He could write to Elsner:

> January 29, 1831
> From the day on which I learnt of the events of 29 November until now, I have experienced nothing but distressing fears and melancholy, and it has been useless for Malfatti to try to convince me that every artist is a cosmopolitan. Even if it were so, as an artist I may be still like a child in its cradle, but as a Pole I am a man of twenty. So I hope that, knowing me as you do, you will not think ill of me for having so far done nothing about a concert. Today, in every respect, incomparably greater difficulties stand in my way. Not only does the continuous round of mediocre piano recitals spoil this kind of music-making and frighten off the public, but in addition the events in Warsaw have changed my situation here for the worse, to the same extent as they might have improved my chances in Paris.

Or he could write: "If it were not that I should be a burden to my father, I would return at once," but it was not true. His anxiety over and hope for Poland's future were genuine, though of course he had to express them cautiously, all letters being censored, yet his anxiety and hope in regard to his own career absorbed his more vital energies. The

---

*Beethoven had been in love with his niece, Therese, and Malfatti had fully valued the deaf and difficult man ("He is perhaps the greatest of all geniuses"), although Beethoven would never obey the doctor. Nevertheless, in Beethoven's last days Malfatti was prevailed upon to come for a consultation. He had not seen Beethoven for ten years; now the dying man threw his arms around Malfatti and wept. Malfatti realized that the case was hopeless, threw out the medicines, and prescribed frozen punch. The ice cooled the fever and the alcohol acted as an anesthetic.

artist is, and must be, an apportioned being, letting the world around
him crack while his symphony is written, his canvas painted. So Chopin
remained in Vienna month after month, and as each month passed
frustration mired him. His own lack of success seemed to parallel his
country's failure. The concert which was to demonstrate his maturer
powers never took place, though he did take part in at least two unimportant smorgasbord charity affairs, which slipped by almost unnoticed.
Nor was his Second Concerto published. He remained for eight months,
the pessimism of youth, which is darker than the pessimism of age,
deepening his irresolution. On Christmas Day 1830—it was a Sunday—
he sat in his room, "all alone in my dressing gown, gnawing at my ring
and writing" a long letter to his friend Jan Matuszynski in Warsaw. In
it he gave expression to his longing for Constantia; he spoke of pretending to be calm in company, "but on coming home I vent my rage on
the piano"; he described the uselessness of the round of dinners, from
which he would return never later than midnight, "play the piano, have
a good cry, read, look at things, have a laugh, get into bed, blow out my
candle and dream always about all of you. . . ." Thoughts of death came
to him:

> How am I to make the journey [to Milan]? My parents leave the choice
> to me, but I can't choose. Should I go to Paris? . . . Shall I return home,
> or stay here, or kill myself?

And again: "To live or die—it is all the same to me. . . . Why am I
abandoned?"

He earned no money during this time and he now began to hate the
city he had loved a year ago. He could not even appreciate the new
waltzes of the senior Johann Strauss, though one would have expected
that he would respond to their charm:

> Best known among the many Viennese entertainments are those even-
> ings in the beer halls where Strauss or Lanner . . . play waltzes during
> supper. After each waltz the applause is terrific: but if they play a
> "quodlibet," i.e., a potpourri of opera tunes, songs and dances, the audi-
> ence are so delighted that they can scarcely contain themselves. It just
> shows you how corrupted the taste of the Viennese public is.

There was no woman in his life. Did he approach any of those
accessible Viennese beauties? Almost certainly not. He imagined himself still in love with Constantia: in his letters he stammered puerile

phrases such as: "Const— I can't even write that name, my hand is not worthy!" But five months later, in May 1831, he confessed: "Her image appears before me; I don't think I love her any longer, yet I cannot forget her." He forgot her soon after.

Yet he retained the consciousness of his mission. He had to rouse himself. Away from fruitless, fickle Vienna! But it was June before he could get himself to act, and although he had decided that his destination would be Paris, when he applied for a passport visa, he pretended, on a friend's advice, that he wished to go to London. The Russian embassy looked askance at Poles going to Paris. Nor did Chopin have an entirely clean political bill of health in the embassy's view: they knew that he corresponded with one or two Polish patriots who were suspect. Whatever their reasons, they claimed they had mislaid his passport, and it took the better part of two months—it was late July— before he could travel. By that time he had so little money left that he had to apply to a Viennese bank for a loan. He hated to do it. He felt guilty and asked his father to sell the Czar's ring. "I am already costing you quite enough."

He had composed little during this period of inanition, but that little included the Scherzo in B minor (Opus 20), which he finished later. "Scherzo" is a misnomer, for this is tragic, agitated music—its opening chords, somebody said, are Wagnerian before Wagner—its lyric melody shattered by fury.

He left for Munich with a Polish friend, Alfons Kumelski—like Wagner, Chopin needed company—and his spirits were buoyed as soon as he lost sight of the Stephansdom. They reached Munich after a pleasant journey, and there he waited several weeks for the money from his father. While he waited, his belief in himself grew stronger again, and he used the interval to appear at a concert, a first-class affair by the Philharmonic Society. He played his new E-minor Concerto and a Fantasy on Polish Airs (Opus 13) with a good orchestra, and enjoyed not only a personal success but the satisfaction of having the two works intelligently discussed in the periodical *Flora*. Then the letter with the money arrived from Nicolas: not a syllable of reproach, not a whisper of "Behold my sacrifice"; just "Go ahead and do what is best for your talent."

Stuttgart was his next stop. There he learned of the failure of the Polish uprising. The Polish leader Chlopicki had been inept—the revolutionary leadership had changed three times—but even had the campaign been conducted steadfastly it stood little chance against Russian might and against the determination of the Czar: "I am King of Poland.

At the first shot fired by the Poles I shall annihilate them." One hundred fifty thousand Russian soldiers faced eighty thousand Polish soldiers, and the Russian general bombarded Warsaw with three hundred cannons. By September 7 it was all over—except for the arrests and the reprisals, the torture and the executions.

Chopin was alone in Stuttgart when this news reached him, his friend having traveled on. Now his sorrow over Poland, his worry over the fate of his family, and most of all, perhaps, the recollection of his failure in Vienna, flooded over him. For the first and only time in his life he let out his tension not in music but in words. His journal affords us a momentary glimpse into his tumultuous and angry state of mind. Awkwardly though it reads, it is a moving document; though it echoes the language of Werther, it is an honest cry uttered by a deeply feeling soul.

> How strange! This bed on which I shall lie has been slept on by more than one dying man, but today it does not repel me! Who knows what corpses have lain on it and for how long? But is a corpse any worse than I? A corpse too knows nothing of father, mother or sisters or Titus. Nor has a corpse a sweetheart. It cannot speak in its own language to those around it. A corpse too is pale, like me. A corpse has ceased to live, and I too have had enough of life—enough! Why do we live on through this wretched life which devours us and only serves to turn us into corpses? The clocks in the Stuttgart belfries strike the midnight hour. Oh, how many people have become corpses at this moment! Mothers have been torn from their children, children from their mothers—how many plans have come to nothing, how much sorrow has sprung from these depths and how much relief!

It continues with a recollection of Constantia:

> She was only pretending—or is pretending. Ah! What a puzzle to be solved! Yes, no, yes, no, no, yes—she loves me, she loves me not—I've lost count. . . . Does she really love me? Really? Let her please herself. At present I have loftier, far loftier feelings than mere curiosity in my soul.

And then:

> Father! Mother! Sisters dear! All you who are most dear to me, where are you? Perhaps corpses? Perhaps the Russian has played a foul trick on me! Oh, wait, wait! What's this? Tears? How long is it since they have flowed! . . .

I wrote the above lines not knowing that the enemy has reached my home! The suburbs are stormed—burnt down.

Oh, God, art Thou? Thou art, but Thou avengest not! Hast Thou not seen enough of these Russian crimes—or—or art Thou Thyself a Russian? My poor kind father! Perhaps you are hungry and cannot buy bread for Mother. My sisters have perhaps fallen victims to the unleashed fury of the Russian scum. Paskiewicz, that hound from Mohilev, is master of the residence of the first monarchs in Europe! The Russian is lord of the world. Oh, Father, is this the joy reserved for your old age? Poor, suffering, tender Mamma, did you survive your daughter [Emilia] only to see the Russians trample her bones underfoot and reduce you to slavery? Oh, churchyard of Powanski [where Emilia was buried]! Have they respected her grave? They have trampled on it—a thousand other corpses are piled on it. They have burnt down the town! Oh, why could I not slay even a single Russian! Oh, Titus, Titus!

The journal ends with:

Oh, God, God! Make the earth tremble and let this generation be engulfed! May the most frightful torments seize the French for not coming to our aid!

One would find all this a tasteless effusion, if one did not read it as part of a very young man's travail. Let it be understood as an expression of his loneliness and frustration.

He cursed the French. Yet he did not turn northeast from Stuttgart to join his country and his family, but went straight west. His irresolution over, he was ready to confront the intellectual center of Europe. On to Paris.

CHAPTER

III

PARIS

LATE ONE EVENING toward the end of September 1831, a traveler arrived in Paris. His spine ached and his head hurt, he was so weary as to be unable to feel just how weary he really was, and he longed for a bath. He had come all the way from Stuttgart, having spent the greater part of two weeks on the road, starting out each morning while the autumn frost still bespattered the bushes, and continuing till the setting sun signaled a halt for that day. Not being able to afford a carriage of his own, he had used public diligences, into which as many as fifteen passengers were stuffed. He had eaten strange meals in strange inns and slept in strange beds. He had communicated with strange fellow travelers, first in German, which he spoke haltingly, and then in French, which he spoke fluently though with a Slavic accent. He had been treated kindly at the French border because he was a Pole and the French felt friendly toward the Poles. Now at last he had arrived. Paris was dark, its obscurity broken only by the light of a weak gas lamp—a recent innovation—or the glimmer of a candle shining from a silent window and reflected in the silent river. He alighted at the first inn he saw and tumbled into bed.

The name on his passport was Fryderyk Franciszek Szopin,* and for the rest of his life he would be known as Frédéric Chopin, with two acute accents.

---

*Judging by a passport issued in 1837, which is owned by Arthur Rubinstein.

Vigorous, twenty-one years old, driven by an ambition in which self-confidence mixed with fear, his desire to excel not unmindful of the excellence he would have to compete with, he needed only one long night's sleep to recover from the dusty journey. The next morning, buttoned up in his unstylish greatcoat, he started out on a triple errand: first, to find a lodging suitable to his modest means but good enough to allow him to enjoy his stay, however long or short; second, to acquire a gazing acquaintance with the great city; and third, to make use of the letters of introduction and recommendation he carried in his pocket.

He found a room quickly enough, at 27 Boulevard Poissonnière, a broad, tree-shaded avenue on the right bank in a quarter the cleanliness of which left something to be desired. But the room was "handsomely furnished in mahogany"—or what Chopin then thought "handsome"—and had a little balcony "from which I can see from Montmartre to the Panthéon." To reach it he had to climb five flights of dark stairs; it didn't matter.

As soon as he had bestowed his few belongings, he climbed down again. He needed to rent an inexpensive piano, and he wanted to orient himself, using the map he had brought along.

The Paris Chopin set out to explore was, in Goethe's words, "a city where all the best of the realms of nature and art of the whole earth are open to daily contemplation, a world-city where the crossing of every bridge or every square recalls a great past, and where at every street corner a piece of history has been unfolded." The pieces of history which interested Chopin most were of fairly recent origin: over the portals of the public buildings ran the legend: "Liberty, Equality, Fraternity, or Death"; it was to be read even above the cages of the lions and tigers in the Jardin des Plantes, and though Chopin knew that the proud motto had become devalued, it still served as an inspiration to somebody who had come from a country that knew no liberty, no equality, and plenty of death.

Though Napoleon's mortal remains lay on a far distant island, there were reminders of the man all around: he had built sixty new streets, including those near the Tuileries and the Louvre. New bridges spanned the Seine, called Austerlitz and Iéna. He had planned two triumphal arches to face each other across a wide prospect; the smaller one, the Arc de Triomphe du Carrousel, was by this time a standard meeting point for lovers walking in the Tuileries gardens, but the larger one, the Arc de Triomphe de l'Étoile, which though designed as an imitation of Rome's Arch of Constantine, was to surpass its model in architectural grandeur, was as yet a bewildering aggregation of stone blocks; workmen in blue smocks were swarming over the place. As a boy Chopin had heard of the Vendôme column, which told the story of Napoleon's victory at Austerlitz and was surmounted by a statue of the Emperor, cast from the bronze of cannons captured from the nations of Europe. The statue was no longer there. Public opinion had to change before it could be restored. (It was restored in 1833, and Victor Hugo wrote an ode for the occasion.)

The construction of the Church of the Madeleine had been started some seventy years before, in 1764; Napoleon wanted to turn the church into a "Temple of Glory," and the building was still far from finished. Chopin saw its completion eleven years after his arrival and saw it become the most fashionable church of Paris. The obelisk of Luxor on the Place de la Concorde, the column of the July Revolution on the Place de la Bastille, were being raised. Wherever Chopin walked, he saw building activity, pride in and hope for the city's future. Paris was like a beautiful actress rehearsing a new part and then spending her time at the dressing table trying on ornaments and hairdos.

Chopin inquired where the halls might be in which he could exhibit his skill. He learned of a small one, called the Salle Pleyel. The Conservatoire, the powerful musical institution, presided over by the seventy-one-year-old Cherubini, the famous composer of *Médée* and *Les Deux Journées,* contained a larger hall, but it was available only to such musicians as were approved by the school—which meant by Cherubini. Opera was performed at two buildings: one was the Opéra, which everybody agreed was superannuated (Paris had to wait until 1875 for a new opera house), the other the Salle Favart, which served opéra comique. Paris had as yet no opera house to compare to La Scala in Milan. Good theaters there were aplenty, the Théâtre Français, home of the Comédie Française, and the Théâtre de la Nation, soon to be known as the Odéon, being the most impressive. At the theater Cirque Olympique a big spectacle was being given, complete with live horses, entitled "Historic Happenings in Poland" and written by one Auguste Lepoitevin de l'Egreville Saint-Ahne, alias Vieillerglé (under which name he collaborated with Balzac), alias Prosper. The Parisians flocked to it partly because of the horses, partly because of their sympathy for Poland.

Everywhere Chopin went he could see signs of the July Revolution of 1830, which had driven out the Bourbon king and begun a new era. Notre Dame was being restored to its ancient beauty by the great architect Viollet-le-Duc, but in front of the church lay ugly rubble, testimony of recent hatred. The portal of St. Denis was damaged by the stones the embattled citizens had thrown from its top, the front of the Louvre was pockmarked by gunshot, the old Hôtel de Ville showed black streaks of burning, the Rue St. Honoré was still torn up.

Chopin walked for hours, comparing Paris to Warsaw and Vienna. He observed the quick gait of the young men, looked into their faces, and caught snatches of their talk, which changed speed as often as a steeplechase. Optimism prevailed. It had been the young liberals who in three hot days of July 1830 had packed Charles X off to England and installed Louis Philippe as constitutional king, fit for modern times. How exhilarating! They had got rid of the *perruques*—or so they believed—they had opened the windows of government bureaus, and they were sure that, in Chateaubriand's words, they could "achieve reality by way of dreams."

The dreams centered on the great city, Balzac's "beloved hell." Already in the seventeenth century Pascal had said of his fellow Parisians that "they could least endure to be by themselves." As a result, the Boulevard des Italiens offered a choreographic diversity. Here strolled the *flâneurs*, the dandies, in false-bottom shoes, tall top hats, gold-buttoned waistcoats, and condescending smiles . . . bare-headed artists of serious mien in short black jackets, green trousers, a white kerchief carelessly slung around the neck . . . paunchy government officials scowling through a pince-nez . . . veterans of Napoleon's wars, their medals, dangling from their tight uniforms, still as polished as pieces in a jeweler's window . . . boys rushing to deliver packages . . . *grisettes* walking with a staccato gait . . . waffle vendors . . . and not infrequently Louis Philippe himself, the new "Citizen King," ambling with an umbrella under his arm and nodding to the left and right. On the side of the procession a juggler threw coins in the air, made them adhere to each other, and caught them in his vest pockets. The pencil seller "L'illustre Mangin" intoned an oration stuffed with allusions to Virgil and Tacitus; he was dressed in a scarlet cloak, on his head a brass helmet crowned with black feathers. A "tooth doctor" at a stall offered to extract teeth for five sous. The parade changed continuously in color and tempo. The French said that when God in his heaven got bored, he opened a window and looked down at the boulevards of Paris.

Yet the city had its dark side. By day it was safe enough to stroll; by night it was dangerous. Filled with light though Paris seemed, the shadows covered vice. An Englishman, Thomas Raikes, who lived there during the 1830s and kept a journal, wrote:

> January 18, 1836
> The police here, so busily attentive to political offences, is most culpably negligent as to other crimes; robberies and murders in the streets are frequent, and a passenger on foot who may be out late in the evening runs a serious risk of his life; most of the young men carry arms in their pockets to defend themselves.

Chopin understood Paris almost at once and almost at once loved it. The spell the city was to exert on him intellectually and artistically began with the delight he felt in its physical beauty. Coming from a city where almost everybody knew almost everybody, Chopin was not in the least intimidated by the *laissez-faire* of the metropolis, which produces either loneliness or free-breathing or both. To Titus he wrote:

> December 12, 1831
> Paris is whatever you care to make of it. You can enjoy yourself, get bored, laugh, cry, do anything you like, and no one takes any notice because thousands here are doing exactly the same—everyone goes his own way. Well, I really don't know whether any place contains more pianists than Paris, or whether you can find anywhere more asses and virtuosos.

A lot of asses and a lot of pianists—but there were as well a lot of attractive girls moving about. As a young man with normal instincts, he sensed the venery of a city famous for its "tender-hearted young ladies." Again he wrote to Titus:

> December 25, 1831
> As soon as it gets dark all you hear is street vendors shouting out the titles of the latest pamphlets, and you can often buy three or four sheets of printed rubbish for a sou, such as "How to Get and Keep a Lover," or "Priests in Love," or "Romance of the Archbishop of Paris and the Duchesse de Berry," and a thousand similar obscenities very wittily put together.

To N. A. Kumelski, who had been with him on part of the journey, Chopin had earlier reported:

November 18, 1831

You find here the greatest splendor, the greatest filth, the greatest virtue and the greatest vice; at every step you see posters advertising cures for ven[ereal] disease—there is shouting, uproar, rattle, and mud past anything you can imagine. One gets lost in this swarm and that's convenient: no one inquires how anyone else manages to live. You can walk about in winter dressed like a tramp and yet frequent the best society. One day you may eat the most copious dinner for thirty-two sous in a restaurant full of mirrors and gilded moldings and lit by gas—and the day after you may go for breakfast to a place where they'll give you just about enough to feed a bird, making you pay three times as much. This sort of thing happened to me to start with, until I had paid for my lesson. And what numbers of tender-hearted young ladies! They chase after you, although there are plenty of sturdy Azazels [lecherous men; Biblical?] about: I regret that the memento left by Teresa (notwithstanding the efforts of Benedict [a doctor?] who [word erased] considers my misfortune a mere trifle) does not allow me to taste the forbidden fruit. I have got to know a few lady vocalists—and singers here, even more than those Tyrolese singers, would willingly "join in duets."

Evidently Teresa was a girl he had slept with, who had left him with a venereal infection. If there had been an infection—it may have been misdiagnosed—it was soon cured and he never again exposed himself to such danger.

Paris was a hostess who knew how to attract and stimulate artists, thinkers, schemers, idealists. The city also offered a welcome to political refugees from all parts of Europe: thousands, literally thousands, came to it—those who had been denounced by Metternich's police, or had fought Austrian soldiers in Milan, or had committed some indiscretion against the royal house of Spain, or had spoken an imprudent word against the Czar.

In Paris the *élan vital* surged more copiously than in any other European city; the place seemed to be awake around the clock. "Here nobody sleeps, it is not the way," Thomas Gray had written in 1763. Large ideas and tiny epigrams, clamorous controversy and endless discussion, gossip and philosophy, theories about art and scandals about the artists, kept one awake.* Chopin was soon to be plunged into the whirlpool of words.

---

*The Norwegian writer H. Steffens recalled that when he met the Danish poet Oehlenschläger, they discussed Romanticism for sixteen continuous hours.

First, however, he needed to use his letters of introduction, one of which was addressed to Ferdinando Paer, an Italian composer initially summoned to Paris by Napoleon and now, sixty years old, the conductor of "Royal Chamber Music." Paer's forty-three operas are forgotten; one remains a historical curiosity. He used the same subject Beethoven did *Eleonora ossia l'amore coniugale.* (Chopin had heard the opera in Warsaw.) The letter to Paer had been written by Dr. Malfatti, and it proved an open sesame to Chopin: Paer showed himself more than kind; at once he wrote a note to an official of the passport bureau saying that "this young man has been warmly recommended to me and I ask you to protect him. He is Polish, deported during the Warsaw revolution, went to Vienna, where he was highly appreciated by the press and society. He has quality and is well educated." Because of this letter Chopin was granted permission to remain in Paris "until further notice . . . to exercise his art." Paer did more, introducing Chopin to Cherubini and Rossini, and later to Mendelssohn, and what was of more immediate importance, to Friedrich Kalkbrenner.

Kalkbrenner represented to the piano what Cherubini represented to the opera. A teacher at the Conservatoire, allied with the piano firm of Pleyel, he was, and certainly considered himself to be, the authority of ultimate appeal, the last word in matters pianistic. Basing his method on the work done by Clementi, Czerny, and Cramer, he developed a technique which demanded playing with the body perfectly still, wrists and hands horizontal, fingers placed vertically on the keyboard, all power to be transmitted by the fingers, each finger developed to independent agility. He invented a *guide-mains,* a wooden barrier that he placed in front of the keyboard, which forced the pupil to keep his arms steady. No doubt he was a fine pianist, his style smooth and elegant—"as polished as a billiard ball," one of his pupils said—his execution punctilious. But if he possessed these attributes of the true artist, he possessed as well what Carlyle called "the sixth insatiable sense," vanity. He was a self-applauding braggart, a sycophant, pretending to be a *grand seigneur,* and he walked about as if he were turned out "by a confectioner, almost but not quite concealing Berlinisms of the lowest order," as Heine wrote. In a later year Chopin, along with Liszt, Mendelssohn, and the pianist Ferdinand Hiller, were to play a trick on him. Dressed in dirty clothes as Parisian beggars, they accosted him in an elegant café, hailed him as a long-lost boon companion, and mortified him to speechlessness.

Now, however, the young Chopin stood before him and recapitulated in a few words his musical schooling. Sit down and let me hear you play, said Kalkbrenner. Chopin played. After a few seconds of indifference, Kalkbrenner listened; after a few minutes he listened with astonishment. Strange though this young man's playing seemed, "incorrect" to Kalkbrenner's eyes and ears in posture and fingering, the sound was warm and fresh. No question, here was somebody exceptional, a true musician. Here was somebody worth taking in hand. Kalkbrenner had enough talent to recognize talent.

Chopin was quite carried away by the force that emanated from this four-square personality. He deemed Kalkbrenner "the only one whose shoelaces I am not fit to tie," the others being but "blusterers who will never surpass him." Perhaps the fact that the older man took an interest in the younger (Kalkbrenner was more than twice Chopin's age) influenced his judgment. Chopin's letter to Titus rises to eloquence:

> December 12, 1831
>
> If Paganini is perfection itself, Kalkbrenner is his equal but in quite a different field. It is impossible to describe his *calm,* his enchanting touch, his incomparable evenness and the mastery which he reveals in every note—he is a giant who tramples underfoot the Herzes, Czernys and of course me!
>
> What happens? On being introduced to Kalkbrenner he invites me to play something. Willy-nilly, not having heard him beforehand but knowing how Herz plays, I sit down at the piano, having put aside every shred of conceit. I played my E-minor Concerto, which the Rhinelanders—the Lindpainters, Bergs, Stunzes [conductors]—and all Bavaria could not praise highly enough. I surprised M. Kalkbrenner, who at once questioned me as to whether I was a pupil of Field, for he found that I have the style of Cramer and the touch of Field. I was terribly pleased to hear that—and even more pleased when Kalkbrenner took his seat at the piano to show off to me but got lost and had to stop. But you should have heard how he took the repeat—I never imagined anything like it. From that time we have been seeing each other daily, either at his house or mine, and now that he has got to know me well he proposes that I should become his pupil for three years and he will make of me something very, very . . . !
>
> I have told him that I know how much I still have to learn but I don't want simply to imitate him, and three years is too long. Meanwhile he has convinced me that I can play splendidly when I am inspired but abominably when I am not—something that never happens to him.

When he had observed me closely he declared that I had no "school," that I am going along fine but might take the wrong turning. He added that after his death, or when he retires, there will be no representative of the great school of piano-playing left. He says I cannot, even if I wanted to, create a new school since I haven't mastered the old one. He sums me up thus: I have not a perfect *mechanism* and the free expression of my ideas is thereby cramped; my compositions have a personal stamp on them and it would be a pity if I didn't become what I promise to be, etc. So far as that goes, if you yourself were here you would say: Learn, my lad, while you have the chance!

Many people advise me against it, judging that I play as well as he, that he is only doing it out of vanity so that he may later on describe me as his pupil, etc. That is nonsense. You must realize that if everyone, absolutely everyone, respects Kalkbrenner's talent, they can't stand him as a man—for he is not a bit hail-fellow-well-met with every imbecile. I swear on my love for you, he is superior to all the pianists I have ever heard. I have written to my parents about this. They seem to agree, but Elsner thinks it's a question of jealousy.

Elsner was wise. He felt that the young man needed to develop without didactic pressure. No, he wrote Chopin, don't submit yourself to a three-year course. Much as I admire Kalkbrenner, I think he is wrong in determining "immediately after seeing and hearing you for the first time how long you will require." A packet of pleading letters arrived, all in one envelope, from his father, from Elsner, from his sister Isabella, and an interminable one from his sister Louise. She quoted Elsner as saying: "I know Frederic, he is a good fellow but lacks confidence . . . he lets himself be dominated." Elsner sensibly pointed out what was important: "The ability to play an instrument perfectly—as Paganini does the violin or Kalkbrenner the piano—with everything that this ability implies . . . is still only a means to arrive at the expression of thought. The fame which Mozart and Beethoven enjoyed as pianists has long evaporated." In short, be a composer.

Luckily, Chopin heeded the advice, which conformed to his own ambition. Kalkbrenner has been accused of self-serving counsel: it has been suggested that his desire was not merely to take on another pupil (he had all he wished) but to promote his personal glory by molding this obviously gifted musician in his own image. Kalkbrenner might, to some extent, have forced the burgeoning talent into a Procrustes bed. Yet the accusation is unjust: in Kalkbrenner's view, Chopin's playing *did* have faults, and there was some truth in his critical view of the concerto Chopin played for him. Back in Warsaw they were of course "infuriated." Louise wrote:

> Warsaw, November 27, 1831
> What infuriated Elsner immensely was what he called Kalkbrenner's audacity and arrogance in asking for a pencil to cross out a certain passage when he had merely glanced at the score, never having heard the complete effect of the concerto with orchestra. He says that if Kalkbrenner had offered you some advice, as for instance, to try to write a shorter first movement the next time—*that* would have been different. But to instruct you to suppress what was written, *that* he cannot forgive . . . and he adds, "What about Kalkbrenner's own concertos? Aren't they too long? But not half as good. . . ."

When Chopin refused both lessons and compositional advice, Kalkbrenner did not turn away. He offered to give him lessons for nothing—his usual fee was twenty-five francs a lesson (equivalent to fifty dollars in today's purchasing power)—and he promised to make the Salle Pleyel available to him the following spring. He even invited Chopin to play one of his own compositions, "just a short one," at a concert Kalkbrenner was organizing for Christmas Day. He kept these promises. And though Chopin later moderated his enthusiasm for the pedagogical virtuoso, a cordial relationship developed between the two men. Three years later, Kalkbrenner sent a note to the now much preempted and popular Chopin:

> December 28 [1834]
> My dear Chopin: Why don't we see each other these days? No doubt the innumerable pleasures and distractions of Paris make you forget your old friends. Come then to dine tomorrow; you'll find here Litsz [*sic*] and some other friends who, like ourselves, will be very happy to see you. Addio.

And Chopin dedicated the E-minor Concerto, the composition he had played for him in that first interview, to Kalkbrenner.

His decision, then, was to pursue his path by himself, and by practicing his art, to perfect it. But how was an artist to become known in that artistically overstuffed city? How should he begin?

Chopin knew that he would need the approval of the Parisian aristocracy; his father had so advised him. The duchesses and baronesses, the princesses and countesses and their husbands, no longer functioned as direct employers: there were no Esterhazys to hire a Haydn, no

Lobkowitzes to grant a stipend to a Beethoven. Yet it was within the circle ensconced in the Faubourg St. Germain that reputations were made and, between tea and ices, between dusk and midnight, an artist's desirability assayed. It was the Beauveau, the Montalembert, the old Talleyrand-Périgord and the younger Rothschild, the Comte d'Argout and the various descendants of Napoleon, such as Charles Lucien Jules Laurent Bonaparte, those who sported at least two first names and compounded family names, who functioned as the Guermantes of pre-Proustian times. Their homes offered either a Pleyel or an Érard piano, covered by an Aubusson throw and surmounted by a Sèvres vase which held artificial lilies. Yet sumptuous though these homes were, they were no longer palaces. After the revolution the aristocracy of France had become a salon society, its mark not the marble column but the silk divan. Quite a few of the hostesses and patrons were not Parisians or were Parisian only by adoption or marriage—the pallid and exquisite Cristina Trivolzio Barbiano de Belgioioso, the dark-eyed Delfina Potocka, the superbly talented Princess Marcellina Czartoryska of the Radziwill family, famous Prince Anton Radziwill himself, a fine cellist and an amateur composer.

Within the walls covered with red damask, artists were not only welcome, they were vied for, the more so if the artist was young, lean of figure, pale of countenance, his long locks carefully combed, his gaze abstracted into a world whose beauty was visible to him alone. (It must be added, however, that neither Balzac, an obvious upstart who was fat and ugly, nor the elder Dumas, who became fat and rambunctious, had any trouble becoming accepted in aristocratic homes—and aristocratic bedrooms.) The day when the artist was considered a subservient member of society had passed. The rope separating him from the titled had fallen—literally, at one aristocratic affair. He was no longer expected to use the back stairs; he entered by the front portal, while the prince's servant bowed. In Paris, above all cities, one spoke of the "aristocracy of genius." That is not to say that the artist's work was always understood—Berlioz's certainly was not and Delacroix's often was not. Three years after Chopin's arrival in Paris, de Vigny in his preface to *Chatterton* still spoke of the "perpetual martyrdom and immolation of the poet." He was exaggerating. If nothing more, the artist amused a bored society, reviving the dream in men and women who, having lived through the cruelty of revolution, had forgotten how to dream.

(2)

The Romantic Movement, into the center of which Chopin was transported and some of whose music he was soon to provide, not only freed the artist from the image of the unkempt and starving night bird, but made new allowances for individuality, creative strength, and what Isaiah Berlin calls the right "to live and act in the light of personal, undictated beliefs and principles." It represented, as Jean Paul Richter defined, "the renaissance of the spirit of wonder in poetry and art," and in France it arrived as a double import, both from England and from Germany. It was an émigré who became as completely French as a *croissant* (which came from Vienna). Goethe's *Werther* (published in 1774, fifteen years before the French Revolution) started it; the sorrows of the young hero were felt by all who in their youth suffered much extremity for love. Young Parisians dressed à la Werther—blue coat, yellow trousers, jackboots—and mooned and moped over the novel. Soon after, Madame de Staël, in *De l'Allemagne,* depicted what she herself wanted to see, a Germany of romantic vistas, a country of oaks, fir trees, waterfalls, and poets . . . poets galore: Schlegel, Jean Paul, Hölderlin, and Novalis, who created "the blue flower," the flower which could not be plucked and which became the symbol of the German Romantics.

Yet the wave which lifted French Romanticism to the heights flowed not across the Rhine, but across the Channel. That wave was stronger and saltier. The French, accustomed to the classicism of Racine, discovered Shakespeare. They had long had a nodding acquaintance with Shakespeare, of course, but to the Romantics he became friend and preceptor, the man to be imitated. Dumas hailed the experience as "the freshness of Adam's first sight of Eden." Berlioz, aside from falling in love with Harriet Smithson—in 1827 she played Ophelia so movingly that the audience, though listening to unfamiliar English, wept—wrote: "I saw, understood, and felt that I was alive and that I must 'arise and walk.'" Victor Hugo, Delacroix, Sainte-Beuve, Mérimée, Stendhal—who published *Le Rouge et le noir* the year after Chopin's arrival—now looked on Shakespeare as the teacher of, or as an excuse for, the freedom of form, the uninhibited force, they sought for their own work. Vigny made a translation of *Othello* which, when it was performed in 1829, caused the conservatives to burst into unmannerly booing: never before had so commonplace a word as *mouchoir* been heard at the Théâtre Français. But the young leaders "shuddered with emotion."

Another Englishman, Byron, loomed even larger. He had died while on his mission to Greece, in 1824, when Chopin was fourteen. The boy had read his poetry in a Polish translation (preserved in the Chopin Museum) and been thrilled by it. Byron had met, it seemed to Chopin's Polish contemporaries, a sacrificial end:

> The land of honourable death
> Is here: —up to the field, and give
> Away thy breath.

To the Poles, engaged in political struggle, this was a precept. "Byron's fame in his native country was insignificant if we compare it with the near worship surrounding him in Slavic countries," wrote Czeslaw Milosz in *The History of Polish Literature*. The new French artists—more than the British—responded to his *"inquiétude méta-physique,"* his search for self-knowledge. In his life and in his work Byron represented the Romantic ideal. Six years after Byron's death, Thomas Moore's *Life and Letters of Byron* not only revealed the poet as a writer of brilliant prose, but shed further light on his turbulent life, his unhappy marriage, his relation with his half sister, and his last attachment to Teresa Guiccioli. His restlessness, his *Wanderlust,* combined with disillusion and disdain for social convention—all were attributes of the Romantic hero.

Chopin found himself in an ambience which favored a breakaway from classicism, from measured threnodies and severe Alexandrines, from David and Gérard, and gave pride of place to the heart over reason. De Quincey had said that sublime beauty "could only be understood by Reason." The Romantics said that it could only be understood by feeling. That creed aided Chopin's talent.

Another influence smoothed his path. A new solidarity had arisen among the artists. Though they were often self-conscious and posturing, their belief in themselves yet braced all those they admitted to the union, Chopin becoming one of them in a remarkably short time. The Parisian Romantics formed themselves into a band of mutual admiration. When de Vigny read his "Moïse," there were Mérimée and Dumas and Musset listening. Hugo first read his play *Marion de Lorme* to an audience of Sainte-Beuve, Vigny, and Balzac, and Balzac described the occasion. When Berlioz gave a concert, Liszt or Gautier or Delacroix—and soon Chopin—were in the stalls. At the *vernissage* of a Delacroix, Heine and Nerval and the journalist Jules Janin examined the painting and discussed it. They were always visiting one another and, together or separately, they were to be seen in the homes of the "advanced" aristocracy, being entertained and entertaining. Liszt, Musset, Dumas, Hugo, were aware of their own stellar radiance. "If I had not been present," Dumas said of a dinner he had attended, "I might have found it rather boring." When Sainte-Beuve challenged the editor of the *Globe* to a duel, and when they met in a forest outside Paris while the rain was coming down in torrents, Sainte-Beuve put up his umbrella. Everybody protested such a breach of etiquette, but Sainte-Beuve said, "I have no objection to being killed, but I do not wish to get wet."

The year before Chopin reached Paris, the premiere of Hugo's new play, *Hernani,* took place. It was a historic event. To be sure, it was an engineered event. Hugo had assembled a squad of young people, students of course included, who, whether they liked the play or not, were going to demonstrate to the old patrons of the Comédie Française that a new era had dawned. His adherents, dressed in Spanish cloaks and huge Rubens hats, were at their posts hours before the performance began, each bearing a red card with the Spanish password *Hierro* (Iron) on it. The young Gautier in his pink waistcoat and the young Gérard de Nerval (translator of *Faust*), exquisitely cravated, served as group lieutenants, under the generalship of Mme. Hugo. The whole evening had been conceived as a battle, the *perruques* versus the firebrands, who were hellbent to unshackle French drama from Racine. The very opening line of the play, the seemingly prosaic announcement, "It will soon be midnight," was hissed by one group, applauded by the other. The changes of locale, the broken lines, were all offensive to the *perruques,* all delirious to the rebels, as were such grandiloquent phrases as Hernani's:

> Ah! Would it be a crime
> To pluck the flower as I fall into the abyss?
> Go, I have breathed its perfume! That is enough!

The evening ended in noisy victory for the new. *Hernani* became a rallying point, not alone in poetic drama but in painting and music as well. Some sober judgments, such as Balzac's and Stendhal's, perceived its posturing and implausibility. Berlioz didn't like it all that much. Yet, as he wrote his sisters, "Hugo has destroyed the unities of time and place and for that I take an interest in him as a daredevil who risks death to set a mine under an old barrier." Berlioz himself was setting a mine under a musical barrier, and Chopin was soon to give new intensity, often in broken lines, to piano expressiveness.

One art spilled over into the other. During Chopin's first year, Balzac produced *La Peau de chagrin* (which made him famous), *Maître Cornelius,* and *L'Auberge rouge.* Hugo published *Notre Dame de Paris.* Meyerbeer's *Robert le Diable* was given at the Opéra (it made *him* famous), Berlioz finished the *Symphonie fantastique.* Daumier was drawing his caricatures for *Charivari* and Delacroix exhibited *Liberty Leading the People.* It was not difficult to see the connection; theirs was a similar perception, a kinship of feeling.

This kinship explains why Chopin was made welcome not only by musicians such as Liszt and Hiller, but by writers such as Théophile Gautier, Heine, Sainte-Beuve, and the leader of the movement, Victor Hugo. He expressed in sound what de Musset penned in poetry and what Hugo created in the figure of Esmeralda, the gypsy girl. Chopin set the *Zeitgeist* to music—and that explains why, daring though his music often was, it was eagerly listened to in the salons. His compositions of the first two Paris years show that he had become a member of "The Circle" in good standing. The sentimental school of biography would have it that "these compositions were not understood"; that is unadulterated nonsense. He published no manifesto, yet he was very much a part of the Romantic revolution. The Nocturne Opus 9, No. 2, one of his most beloved pieces, or the twelfth Etude of Opus 10, called the "Revolutionary," or the Ballade Opus 23 (composed later), are products of the great movement, as different from anything written previously for the piano as Musset's *On ne badine pas avec l'amour* is from *Phèdre.*

Yet such is Chopin's genius that in his best works he combines the Romantic with the classical. That combination holds steady the keel of his unique talent. His classical bent saves him from being wholly the child of his time. Even when he waxes sentimental, Mozart and Bach —his "gods"—seem to be around administering a gentle slap on the wrist. Compare his piano music to that of Liszt, who was composing for the same instrument at the same time and was just a year younger. To be sure, Liszt outlived Chopin by thirty-seven years and enlarged his field to include the orchestral tone poems and the *Faust* Symphony. Yet a considerable part of Liszt's work suffers from the *folie de grandeur* (Heine's phrase) which was a transitory characteristic of the Romantic Movement: the thunderstorm in the dark forest, the Caspar Friedrich moonlit ruin, the Hungarian Rhapsodies which pretend to be folk music but are not; Liszt's early music thus seems more "dated" than Chopin's.

To understand Chopin we must understand this classic-romantic amalgam. Although very much a part of the Romantic Movement, he rose above it, distilling the best of its sentiment but shedding its excesses, tempering emotion with elegance and often with irony.

He was not an isolated artist, borne up by the wings of night. He lived in the world, his mind open to the ideas around him.

IV

A WORLDLY YOUNG MAN

AFTER LIVING IN PARIS for a while, Chopin began to look like a Parisian. The moist air which rose from the Seine and the clouds which drifted across the Channel rubbed pale the color of his complexion; no trace remained of the outdoor look set there by Polish fields. His hair—thick, fair, and silky, much like that of his father—was now smoothed to formal elegance. His smile, as described by one of his pupils, had "an inexpressible charm," but would occasionally assume that ironic twist with which certain French phrases are spoken. His eyes were dark brown, almost black,* "more cheerful than pensive," and covered by waferlike lids. Often, when he played, he lowered them, but one could guess the intensity underneath. His forehead was extraordinarily high. His hands were thin, strong, their skin milk white, and he "would often rest them on his knees with a certain ostentation." His feet were very small, his figure lithe—he weighed no more than a hundred pounds and was only about five feet five inches tall—and he walked at the pace young Parisians adopted, with quick, determined, small steps. His face had a fine oval shape, but his nose—how he disliked his nose (as Mozart did), which was too prominent and aquiline. His voice was soft and subdued, but with that voice he could say some very cutting things. He was a poetic-

---

*Liszt in his biography of Chopin described him as "a convolvulus balancing his azure-hued cup upon a very slight stem, the tissue of which is so vaporous that the slightest contact wounds and tears the delicate corolla." Nothing less! But he got the color of his eyes wrong, saying they were blue.

looking yet vigorous young man during those first Paris years. In a sense he resembled the other French Romantics; they were bound not only by spiritual affinities but by a certain physical resemblance. Musset, Heine, Liszt, the young Hugo, and the very young Dumas had that "Byronic look"—all wore the stiff collar which hugged the chin, or what had been Byron's costume in Greece, the wide-open shirt with a cape flung picturesquely over the shoulders. Chopin preferred the collar. They all prized personal beauty, Gautier defining the ideal as being "beautiful, young, and free." They were all vain, Chopin not the least. His nature despised bohemianism in whatever form. Being unkempt and beflecked with dandruff was no sign of talent. Good manners, a tone of aristocratic reserve, not only came naturally but were cultivated by him.

The artist existed in equilibrium with the hedonist. Chopin was not meant to live in a garret. He had to live in finely furnished rooms; he had to have fresh flowers in these rooms. His handkerchief had to be perfumed.

He shared the love of luxury with most of the French Romantics, who, if they were not wealthy, fabricated for themselves the illusion of wealth. The successful ones earned good money—and away the money went, leaving hardly an impression in the pocket lining. To avoid his creditors, Balzac holed up in the cellar of a house where he lived under an assumed name; the bailiff came and took away Dumas's furniture and his carriage and even his stuffed animals; George Sand wrote the night through and was forever asking her publisher for an advance. Always optimistic (when they were not in the depth of despair), they spent their earnings at once, ignoring any prognosis of drought. Chopin, because of his bourgeois upbringing, was not quite so contemptuous of husbandry as most of them, and he rather feared to fall into debt, but he could not help being attracted to an existence of which the *pâté* of today seemed more important than the *pain* of tomorrow.

Several biographers have described his early days in Paris as a time of penury and desperation. Was it so? A rags-to-riches story enlivens a biography, but the truth is less dramatic. His father sent him enough money to get by, he never starved, nor did he have to visit a pawn-broker. Nicolas took it as understood that a young artist in a foreign city needed support; he never doubted that such aid was necessary, he never questioned the outcome, he never said to his son, "Come home." On the contrary, his encouragement was unwavering. In addition, his mother sent him, perhaps secretly, a gift of 1,200 francs in the spring of 1832. Chopin was aware that this subsidy was intended for his food and rent; all the same he wanted, and he needed, more than necessities.

He loved the opera and he had heard much in Warsaw and in Vienna. The Parisian performances, vastly more resplendent, enchanted him and he went again and again, usually paying for his ticket. Two and a half months after he had arrived in Paris, he confessed that he had spent twenty-four francs (forty-eight dollars in today's equivalent—surely an extravagant sum in his circumstances) for a performance of Rossini's *Otello;* he regretted it because that particular performance, with Schröder-Devrient as Desdemona and Malibran as Otello (a soprano in a tenor part and in blackface), did not please him; "Malibran is small while the German lady is huge—it looked as if *she* would stifle Otello." Of other performances he gave Titus an enthusiastic report:

December 12, 1831

Never have I heard the *Barber* as last week with Lablache, Rubini, and Malibran, nor *Otello* as with Rubini, Pasta, and Lablache; or again, *Italiana in Algeri* as with Rubini, Lablache, and Mme. Raimbeaux. Now, if ever, I have *everything* in Paris. You cannot conceive what Lablache is like! They say that Pasta has gone off, but I never saw anything more sublime. Malibran impresses you merely by her marvelous voice, but no one *sings* like her. Miraculous! Marvelous! Rubini is an excellent tenor. He sings true notes, never *falsetto,* and sometimes his ornamental runs go on for hours (but sometimes his decorative passages are too long and he deliberately uses a tremolo effect, besides trilling endlessly—which, however, brings him the greatest applause). His *mezza voce* is incomparable. . . .

The opera nourished Chopin musically, but he enjoyed its social pleasure as much, the promenading on the polished parquet, the inhaling of that unique scent compounded of candle smoke, grease paint, and perfume, the marmoreal shoulders of the *Parisiennes.*

Though he ate sparingly and was constantly watching his diet, he enjoyed dining and treating his friends at fashionable restaurants—the Café de Paris, the Café Riche, the Café des Anglais. He drank only a glass or two, but it had to be the best vintage wine.

As soon as he began to earn—and even before—he spent. For what? For glacé gloves made to measure—gloves were a symbol of being well dressed: they had to be immaculate and were cleaned at special shops —for walking sticks, for cuff links, for the silkiest of shirts and the softest velvet waistcoats. He conferred with Chardin the perfumer, Rapp the bootmaker, Feydeau the hatter, and Dautremont, one of the best Parisian tailors, who would make a redingote for sixty francs, but made one for Chopin with gold buttons which cost 140 francs. His patent-leather boots, his black cape lined with gray satin, his jacket of royal blue, were all expensive. He hired a horse and carriage with a liveried driver; that cost him 450 francs monthly, though taxis could be had for single trips at 1 or 2 francs. He later bought his own barouche for one thousand francs.

A young man making his career in the city of elegance had to be elegant. Balzac in *Le Père Goriot* knew it all. Vautrin counsels the young Rastignac:

> You would show yourself unworthy of your destiny if you spent no more than three thousand francs with your tailor, six hundred in perfumery, a hundred crowns to your shoemaker, and a hundred more to your hatter. As for your laundress, there goes another thousand francs; a young man of fashion must of necessity make a great point of his linen; do not look any further.

Chopin had practical reasons for his extravagance, or so he told himself. He realized almost immediately that his compositions could not earn him a sufficient income and that his best chance of making a livelihood was as a teacher of wealthy pupils. If he was to attract such pupils and if he was to be received in rich homes, he had to look rich. Yet even in later years, when his fame had no need of show, he remained a follower of *la mode,* paying great attention to his personal appearance and studying the latest fashions.

(2)

Even as a very young composer, at twenty-two or twenty-three, he was quite certain of the direction he wanted to take. His musical will was of hammered iron. To be sure, he was not doctrinaire, not an expounder. He was not what Heine ironically called Liszt: "Doctor of philosophy and demisemiquaver." As a composer he limited himself severely. His contemporaries—as well as his biographers—were puzzled. At a time when Victor Hugo produced not only plays, poems, novels, essays, but was simultaneously engaged in politics, at a period when Berlioz was experimenting with a symphony based on a poetic idea *(Fantastique)*, a mastodon of an opera *(Les Troyens)*, a combination of symphony and song *(Roméo et Juliette)*, a programmatic concerto *(Harold en Italie)*, Chopin would have none of these. He was angry at the great Polish poet Mickiewicz because he insisted that Chopin compose an opera. With all his admiration for Rossini and Bellini, no. There was a practical reason why a composer ought to write operas. If successful, an opera earned more money than a symphony or a piano piece, just as a play, if popular, earned more money than a novel. Hugo earned four times as much from *Hernani* as from *Notre Dame de Paris.* But Mickiewicz wanted Chopin to write an opera not for money, but "for the glory of Poland"—on a Polish subject. A symphony? Chopin did not even experiment with one. In his later years he never attempted another concerto. Only the solo piano, then.*

His discoveries were made, so to speak, without a compass. If he had a theory, he did not write it down. Berlioz wrote brilliantly about music, Schumann often perceptively though fancifully, Liszt yet more fancifully; but Chopin wrote next to nothing, and when he did, what he wrote was flaccid. What he had to give he gave in sound, not in words. No composer walked his way with firmer steps or lost himself on fewer side paths.

That the piano was his means of expression helped him to gain recognition, since the piano was the Parisians' favorite instrument. Around its graceful curves Parisian society draped itself in graceful attitudes. Girls of good family started to practice scales about the same time they learned to recite La Fontaine's fables. Countesses played and so did many a baker's daughter, though their playing was longer on sentiment than on accuracy. Heine commented: "The heavenly powers have bequeathed us a gruesome gift. 'Pianoforte' is the name of the instrument of torture on which our society is put to the rack."

Competition among pianists ran keen, and when there are a lot of exciting pianists around, the public's interest in piano music is stimulated. Discussions as to the comparative merits of Liszt, Herz, Pixis,

---

*His few songs are not of the highest quality. He did compose a very good sonata for piano and cello (Opus 65), and a little weak chamber music.

Kalkbrenner, Thalberg, were lively, and soon Chopin was being discussed. Heine witnessed it:

> The triumphal march of the piano virtuosi is especially characteristic of
> our time and testifies to the victory of the machine over the spirit.
> . . . Like locusts the pianists invade Paris every winter, less perhaps to
> earn money than to make a name for themselves here, from which they
> can then profit all the more richly in other countries. Paris to them is
> a huge billboard where their fame is lettered in giant letters. . . . The
> virtuosi practice with virtuosity the trick of exploiting the journals and
> journalists. They know how to get around them, even those who are
> hard of hearing. . . . One hand washes the other, the one less clean being
> seldom that of the journalist. . . .
>
> When I was still enjoying the favor of the director of the *Gazette
> Musicale*—alas, I lost it through youthful impudence—I was able to
> observe how these people kowtowed to him and fawned on him, just so
> that they might obtain a few lines of praise in his journal. . . . In his office
> I once met an old man, dressed in a shabby torn suit, who announced
> that he was the father of a famous virtuoso and who begged the editor
> to print an article dealing with the noble deeds of his son. It seems that
> the illustrious boy played a benefit in the south of France, of course with
> enormous success, to aid the reconstruction of a Gothic church which
> threatened to give up the ghost. Then he helped a water-damaged
> widow, then a seventy-year-old schoolmaster who had lost his only cow.
> . . . I suggested that he next give a benefit concern for the shiny trousers
> of his progenitor.
>
> *Lutezia II*

Chopin never practiced the trick of "exploiting the journals and
journalists." Though he was sensitive to criticism, he never kowtowed
to critics. He gave no interviews. Unlike Meyerbeer, he did not invite
the gentlemen of the press to dinner on Sunday night. He formulated
no creeds, left no "method"; though later in life he began to sketch a
teaching manual; he gave it up after a few paragraphs. The French
Romantics filled the air with recruiting cries and published their truculent statements of intention, using slogans as ballistics, theaters as rallying points, and salons as forums. Liszt wrote "On the Situation of Artists" (1835), which with all its self-serving arguments was an important
sociological document. Chopin said not a word. Nor did he publicly
discuss a picture, a book, or a play.

As a result of his reserve, it came to be believed that Chopin hardly ever visited an exhibit, was not to be seen at the Odéon Theater, and cared not two straws about the visiting English actors.* He has been called an "unconscious genius," a man whose ideas came to him in midnight revelations, an "unintellectual creator" who sank a bucket into the well of his instinct to draw up melodies and harmonies almost as if in a trance. Aside from the fact that a work of art—*any* work, but surely Chopin's highly organized achievement—cannot be altogether instinctive, these characterizations fit Chopin less than other artists.

No, Chopin did not live exclusively within a terrain bounded by the lowest bass note of the piano and the highest in the treble. Even as a boy he responded to poetry, both Polish and French. He liked to write verses and once he gave detailed instructions for furnishing his home, written entirely in verse. His interest in the pictorial arts and his understanding of painting were less definite; yet he owned a few good pictures and he was constantly sketching, mostly quite telling pen portraits of his friends. Nicolas had instilled in him a curiosity for literature. He was not a voracious reader, but he liked to read late at night and books were always on his night table. In short, he was by no means a unilateral young man with whom it was difficult to hold an intelligent conversation.

He readily joined the talk at the Austrian ambassador's reception or at supper at the Czartoryskis', whose house was a meeting place for the intellectuals. His was a very worldly world, and he much preferred the *palais* to the ivory tower.

(3)

Women were attracted to Chopin, as he was attracted to them. In spite of those gushy letters to Titus, in spite of George Sand's playfully calling him "the girl friend," in spite of his lack of aggressiveness, he was a normal man, and his supposed "psychic duality," of which much has been written, was no more pronounced than it is in many another quiet personality. No evidence exists which would suggest homosexual tendencies, conscious or unconscious, in him. It is pointless and presumptuous to bid a dead man lie down on the psychoanalyst's couch. A vignette

---

*He did write on the manuscript of the G-minor Nocturne (Opus 15): "After a performance of *Hamlet.*"

written by Eugenius Skrodzki (pen name Wielislaw), the son of a professor at Warsaw University who lived in the same building as the Chopin
family, indicates Chopin's early interest in the female sex:

> A few hundred students went in and out of the university buildings.
> That is the reason why I can no longer identify the girl who deeply
> preoccupied Chopin when he was a fifth or sixth grade student at the
> Lyceum. He seemed too serious and mature for his age, clad in his
> uniform, which he sometimes wore unbuttoned—strictly against regula-
> tions. . . . Today I can't even recall the features of this girl.
>
> I used to spend summer evenings in the acacia row of the Botanical
> Garden. Usually a group of girls would appear, most of the time chaper-
> oned, but sometimes without an escort. Chopin would turn up. They
> would all sit down on a bench and Frederic's hazel eyes would light up.
> I could hear loud talk and soft sighs, then teasing, joking, and laughter.
> . . . I would see Frederic strolling alone with one of the girls. I [still a
> small child] would bring him worms and May bugs, ask him about them,
> and I would pick flowers for the girl. Frederic used to smile and give me
> caramels extracted from his pocket.
>
> One day the stern professor, Frederic's father, appeared in the gar-
> den. Recognizing me, he began to question me. "Tell me"—he said—
> "my dear boy, does my son Frederic happen to be here?" I could tell
> from his expression that he was intending to scold Frederic. I lied. "No
> —I haven't seen him." "But he does come here, doesn't he?" asked the
> father, looking severely at me. "I haven't seen him" —and feeling my
> face turn purple, I turned away and started to play ball. Frederic's father
> lingered for a minute, grumbled, tapped his cane on the ground, and
> then left. When I was sure he had gone, I ran to find Frederic and told
> him what had happened. He winced, blushed, and said to me, "You did
> well, Gene, you did well," and he pulled out a handful of caramels.

His upbringing, supervised by the "stern professor"—he was not all
that stern—acted as a brake to the giddy carrousel of easy morality on
which Chopin found himself in his first Paris years, where the *ménage
à trois* was a commonplace; Balzac juggled his affairs with four or five
mistresses; Liszt, though in love with the beautiful Marie d'Agoult,
could not resist invitations for the night; and de Musset picked up
streetwalkers in Venice. Chopin took sex seriously; he was as fastidious
about it as he was about his gloves. He had first to fall in love, but when
he did, he did so body and soul. In that respect the worldly young man
was not very worldly—not in comparison with the French and Polish
aristocracy, or the Romantic artists.

Yet Chopin's response to women sounds as an overtone—gentle, unostentatious, but evocative—in his life. The better part of his nature was enriched by the better part of the eternal feminine. He was happy, or as happy as he could manage to be, in their company. He would rather play to a female audience than to a hall full of men. He preferred, in the main, his women pupils. The countesses and princesses who walked with a light step, exhaling their perfume, bestowing their smiles, their silken skirts swishing, formed the cast of coryphées among whom Chopin worked, and to whom he dedicated some of his best music. Many of these relationships were held fast by nothing more than the bonds of admiration. He possessed none of the flamboyance of Liszt —who was more handsome than he—nor the fascination of Wagner's ugliness or Bellini's cynical insouciance. Heine described him as "a charming trinity," his personality, his playing, and his compositions "so much in harmony as to be three aspects of one apparition." That "apparition" was, with all his ability to laugh, essentially serious; it would hardly appeal to a giddy female, but to a serious and profound woman.

Princess Würtemberg, Countess Emilia Perthuis, Baroness Carlotta Rothschild—all prominent in Parisian society and all gifted women— were delighted to be on friendly terms with this strange, mercurial, and talented young man, so different from the bowing and chattering popinjays who peopled their salons. In turn, Chopin delighted in knowing them, sprinkling over his life a bit of the powdered sugar of flirtation. After a while Chopin could have dined at a different house every day of the week. But even as a young man he knew when to shut himself away; much of his composing seems to have been done in the deep of night.

V

THE TEACHER

THE POLES had tried again. And again they had failed. In the autumn of 1830 they attempted a *coup* with too much fervor, too little finance, and too few soldiers. The troops of Czar Nicholas I rode over the fields, easily overwhelming patriotism by cannon. Poland was now a sorrowful fief of Russia. Many sympathized with her plight, but no more than does a casual acquaintance at a funeral. Warsaw capitulated, and some of its best citizens were summarily shipped to Russia and Prussia, some to prisons there, some to menial labor. And no fewer than eight thousand Poles fled, seeking asylum: many found it in France, a country which knew the cost of a revolution. Those who were able to get to France and could maintain themselves away from home included some members of the ancient Polish families—and those who had been farsighted enough to invest their capital with the Rothschilds. Between 1832 and 1836, the flow of emigration was particularly heavy, representing a cross section of the entire population, from prince to poet.

Many of the aristocratic Polish émigrés intermarried with the newer French nobility created by Napoleon; these comfortable fugitives found little difficulty in becoming part of the Parisian scene. They constituted an enclave in which patriotism mingled with Gallicism, true intellectual pursuits with support of the Romantics because it was the fashionable thing to do, a real love for the arts with flirtation with the artists. The wealthy émigrés were welcomed in the most desirable salons of the genuine Parisians, because they carried about their persons an aura of strangeness—with their unpronounceable names, their noble bearing, their unhappy history, the siren voices of their women, the flamboyant colors of the uniforms the men wore.

La Pologne héroïque was regarded sentimentally in all Western Europe, men such as Musset, Tennyson, and the Scottish poet Thomas Campbell espousing her cause. The French prefecture of police was less enthusiastic, as was the Russian ambassador in Paris, Count Pozzo di Borgo. The emigrants were watched and Nicolas Chopin cautioned his son "to stay away from the militant exiles," advice his son ignored.

General Joseph Bem was in Paris at this time. He traced his ancestors back four centuries, and his intense eyes, too large for his small wooden face, looked with disdain on all who were less knowledgeable in science than he. After the collapse of the uprising, he had aided the evacuation of Warsaw, had twice been incarcerated, twice escaped, and now devoted his life to technical inventions—specifically, ways to perfect steam engines. He hoped eventually to raise a Polish army of liberation. He was not in the least musical, yet shortly he became a friend and admirer of Chopin.

There was also Julian Ursin Niemcewicz, now in his seventies, once president of Warsaw's Royal Society of Science, critic, historian, poet, novelist, biographer (he had written a biography of George Washington), who represented to the exiles a symbol of the "ancient motherland." When Chopin was eight years old, Niemcewicz had befriended the little boy in Warsaw. From then on Chopin was thoroughly awed by him, but the older man laughed and told Chopin he would be remembered only as a footnote in Chopin's biography.

Count Vladislav Plater held open house on Thursdays. With his elder brother Ludwig, he founded and edited a short-lived newspaper, *Le Polonais*. The artistic world gathered at his Thursday receptions, and Ludwig Plater's wife, who loved music, said, "Were I young and beautiful, I would choose the pianist Hiller as a friend, Liszt as a lover, and wonderful little Chopin as a husband." Their daughter Pauline became Chopin's first pupil, and he dedicated the Four Mazurkas (Opus 6) to her.

The same crowd gathered on Mondays at the Hôtel Lambert, one of the most beautiful mansions of the city. (It is still standing and is still beautiful.) It was the residence of the leader of the Polish colony, Prince Adam Czartoryski, who bore a name woven into the history of his country since the fourteenth century—the early Czartoryskis had been king-makers—and was the possessor of estates whose extent he could not measure. Adam was as handsome as he was wealthy: he looked as Byron would have looked had he lived longer, eyes veiled, a chin of softest sweep, a sensuous mouth, all quite at variance with what he really was—a worldly wise statesman. His youth had been spent in Russia, and in his memoirs he recalled how he had waited many months for an audience with the great Catherine, how he had gradually become a friend of the young Czar Alexander I, who called him "my mentor" and praised him as an "exceptional political brain," and how, believing that a rapprochement between Russia and Poland could be possible, he had served Alexander as minister of foreign affairs, while he served Alexander's Czarina as lover. Three times he proposed plans to Alexander for a Europe based on the principle of nationality, a "natural equilibrium" which would lead to peace. He designed a new liberal educational system for Russia and represented Russia at the Congress of Vienna.

When Alexander married—it was a wholly political marriage—husband and wife had signed a paper giving each freedom in their personal behavior. Alexander knew of the Czarina's love for Czartoryski, and was at first indifferent to it. But later he began to resent it and a split opened between the two men. It became wider as Alexander turned from a liberal ruler to a morbid despot, much under the influence of Metternich, and Czartoryski had to stand by while Metternich offered Poland as a spoils of war. Yet he continued to harbor hope. He believed that the rebellious Poles could be directed from a foreign center, that pressure could be brought to bear on France and England, that Western Europe could be made to realize the danger of Russia's growing might. Hidden in the Hôtel Lambert, in a small office behind the sumptuous ballroom and exquisite little drawing rooms, amid constant comings and goings, a kind of government in exile spun plans and proposed schemes.

It was all a chimera. However warmly French sympathy for Poland flowed in words, practical support amounted to nothing. Hugo wrote of France that "The immense heart of the world beats in her breast." But under the cautious Louis Philippe "the heart of the world" beat quietly. The King was afraid of the Czar. The émigrés themselves were as divided as men of good will often are, Czartoryski, essentially a conservative, being at odds with the radicals who wanted to unsheath the sword at once. And in time Czartoryski became to them "a symbol of a monarchic and aristocratic regime . . . an adversary and even a foe." So the

émigrés talked and they argued and they quarreled, and by and by all
the noble plans petered out and the guests of the Hôtel Lambert were
reduced to a band of well-groomed dilettantes, concentrating on the
"higher life" when not occupied by sex or gossip or the inventions of
Brillat-Savarin. The evening gatherings continued in splendor, Adam's
wife, Princess Anna, always present as the most adroit of hostesses.
Heine said that she was beautiful enough to be painted by Giorgione's
brush; Chopin dedicated to her one of his early works, the *Krakowiak*
Rondo.

Count Wojciech (Albert) Grzymala belonged to a slightly lower social rank. Like many Poles, he had believed in Napoleon's promise to
liberate his country, and in 1812 he had fought for Bonaparte. After
Napoleon's defeat he joined the subversive Polish "Patriotic Society"
and was promptly imprisoned. In prison he was comforted by one of his
two mistresses, the actress Sophia Kurpinska, wife of the director of the
Warsaw National Theater, who came to him disguised as a laundress.
His other mistress, Princess Zajaczek, twice his age, was the wife of the
pro-Russian governor general. Between them, the two women—one
popular, the other powerful—managed to obtain his release. He then
went to London to plead the Polish cause, and after the collapse in 1831
he moved to Paris. Having lost the greater part of his fortune, he still
had enough left to be able to open his house to, and to aid, the Parisian
artists. His special enthusiasm belonged to Delacroix and he bought a
number of his paintings. For Chopin he acted as a substitute father:
time and again the composer turned to that tall, lusty, benevolent man
with a trust that he vouchsafed to few. Twelve years after Chopin's
death, Delacroix wrote to Grzymala:

January 7, 1861

With whom else can I speak of that incomparable genius Chopin, whom
heaven grudged to us on earth and of whom I think so often now that
I can no longer see him in this world, nor hear his divine melodies?

(2)

Chopin played at the houses of the Polish émigrés—often at the Hôtel
Lambert and at Grzymala's—as well as at the Parisian salons, and,
initially, the welcome he received was tendered to him as a performer
more than as a composer. By the time he came to Paris he had com-

posed a variety of works—Waltzes, Mazurkas, Polonaises, Nocturnes—though he had published little. He would not submit his compositions to the finality of printing, but—performing them—he revised them again and again, filing, condensing, and bringing them closer to the intensity of feeling for which he strove. Sometimes he set them aside for years.*

He performed mostly his own music, although he did play a little Mozart or an occasional piece by Liszt, and his artistry as a pianist was enhanced by his marvelous improvisations. When his fantasy flowed as a summer shower sprays a field of wheat, he could move his listeners to tears, tears more sweet than salty—all who heard him agree to that. Yet in detail the descriptions differ. One pupil spoke of his pianistic "delicacy," while another asserted that he could command "an immense tone." He could be playful, a miniaturist even, daubing bright, coquettish colors, but he was capable as well of "dark moments, when the keyboard was too small, his ideas too big for utterance."

Fourteen months after his arrival in Paris, he could write to a friend in Berlin:

> I have entered into the very best society; I sit between ambassadors, princes, ministers—I don't know by what miracle it has come about, for I am not a climber. But today all that sort of thing is indispensable to me: those circles are supposed to be the fountainhead of good taste. At once you have more talent if you have been heard at the English or Austrian embassies; at once you play better if Princess Vaudemont has patronized you. I can't write "patronizes," for the poor old thing died a week ago. . . . She used to entertain at court and did much good, giving shelter to many aristocrats during the first Revolution. . . . She always had a host of little black and white bitches, canaries, parrots, and was the owner of Paris high society's most amusing monkey, which used to bite the other countesses at her parties. . . .
>
> If I were even more stupid than I am, I would think that I have arrived at the summit of my career. However, I see how far I still have to go, and I realize it all the more from mixing intimately with the first artists and observing how far each of them falls short of perfection.
>
> Shame on all this rubbish! I have bragged like a child or someone with an uneasy conscience, who defends himself before being attacked.

---

*Grand Fantasia (Opus 13)—six years; Waltz in A minor (Opus 34, No. 2)—seven years; Ballade in G minor (Opus 23)—begun in 1831, published in 1836.

.I would erase it all, but I haven't time to write a second letter. Besides, you have perhaps not yet forgotten what I am really like; so remember then that I am just as I used to be, except that I have one side whisker only, the other simply won't grow. I have five lessons to give today. You will imagine that I am making a fortune—but my cabriolet and white gloves cost more than that, and without them I should not have *bon ton*. I am all for the Carlists, I hate the Louis Philippe crowd; I'm a revolutionary myself so I care nothing for money, only for friendship, which I entreat you to give me.

> *To Dominic Dziewanowski, second week of January, 1833*

This jaunty letter, perhaps slanted to picture his situation as rosier than it actually was, was preceded by days of frustration and dejection. A cholera epidemic swept Paris in 1832; in the spring of the year the workers of Lyons rose against their employers after the employers had violated a collective agreement. Blood was shed. In Paris the workers sympathized with the Lyons uprising and so did the followers of the social philosopher Saint-Simon. A good deal of unrest prevailed in a nation under a do-little government. People worried over graver issues than the fate of a young pianist. Yet it might have been that no outward cause was responsible for his melancholy. A pupil who showed that she had not learned her lesson could plunge him into the conviction of his own failure; a bunch of violets, arriving at his house in the morning, would fly him to the stars; hours of struggle with one harmonic progression would leave him limp with exhaustion, but the next minute he would run out to a party, stay up half the night playing dance music for the gathering, caricature the mannerisms of other pianists, play tricks on the piano. He hid much of what he felt or thought. He confessed that he "would not admit anybody to [his] sphere of feelings," that he was a "hypocrite, emotionally." His letters are rarely self-revelatory. In April 1832 he wrote to the pianist Josef Nowakowski, a friend in Warsaw who was planning to come to Paris:

> It's very difficult to get pupils here and harder still to give concerts. . . . The public is indifferent and bored with everything. There are various reasons for this, but the political situation is chiefly to blame. . . . So I advise you to put off your visit until May—at any rate until the French opera returns from London. Otherwise you will miss *Robert le Diable, William Tell,* and *Moses.* I hope you understand French (I'm sure you do) so as to be able to fend for yourself, and then I guarantee that you will have a pleasant time in Paris. I'll introduce you to the

leading European personalities: you shall make the closer acquaintance of those divas who appear less formidable the nearer one approaches them.

It doesn't sound as if Chopin was altogether forlorn. Yet at about the same time Anton Orlowski, a Polish violinist living in Paris, reported to his own family:

Dear Chopin sends you warm greetings. He has been so depressed during these last few days that sometimes when I go to see him we haven't the heart to say a word to each other. He is homesick. But please don't mention it to his parents: it would worry them.

The story goes that Chopin was so discouraged that he thought of emigrating to America. He was ready to leave when he met Prince Valentin Radziwill on the street and Valentin urged him to go to a party at the Rothschilds' that night; "all Paris" would be there, he could play and gain new influential friends. Chopin let himself be persuaded, he went, he played—and he played with such fervor that one and all were moved and Chopin was overwhelmed by requests for lessons, so many indeed that the terrified artist did not know whom to accept and whom to refuse. The tale does not ring true, though it is given in virtually all the biographies. Many of Chopin's letters to his family were destroyed by Russian soldiers in 1863; along with his piano, the letters were dumped into a courtyard and swept away.* The only biographer who saw any of the original letters was Maurice Karasowski, and Chopin's fleeing to America would have been just the sort of anecdote Karasowski would have used; he mentions no such thing. We do have the letters of Chopin's family to him: they contain not a word about America. Surely he would have told them and Nicolas would have scolded or approved. Nor is the matter mentioned in the reminiscences of any of Chopin's friends, such as Liszt or Hiller. As to the Rothschild evening —it is entirely possible that he played there, but hardly as an unknown, having already given a successful public concert. (Would the Rothschilds have invited an unknown to entertain at their party?) Nor would he have been propelled from obscurity to popularity in one evening:

---

*The poet Cyprian Norwid described this act of barbarism in a long poem, written in 1864, "The Piano of Chopin." He depicts the city of Warsaw, the arrival of the Cossacks, the burning of the building, and the hurling down of piano and letters. To Norwid this act was a symbol of the impulse "which arouses men from slumber . . . to destroy what disturbs them."

such meteoric streaks occur only in the theater, and there more often in fiction than in fact. It is probable that Chopin's ascent took a normal, though relatively rapid, course. In September of that year the Polish poet Julius Slowacki, one of the émigrés, wrote his mother of a dinner at Count Plater's, where Chopin played, calling him "the famous pianist."

He was called famous after appearing in only two public concerts in that unquiet year of 1832. The first of these had had to be twice postponed, the second time because Kalkbrenner fell ill and it was he who was to be the chief attraction. The program of Chopin's concert of February 26, 1832, in the Salle Pleyel shows the usual potpourri of light and serious pieces,* the usual ill-assorted mixture of artists. Yet it is significant that these artists were by no means nonentities: the violinist Pierre Baillot was a leading light of the Conservatoire, Henri Brod a famous oboist, Hiller and Mendelssohn celebrated pianists, and Kalkbrenner the *ne plus ultra*. Chopin was worthy of appearing in such company. Camillo Stamati, a pupil of Kalkbrenner's, substituted for Mendelssohn at the last minute. The printed program read:

FIRST PART

1. A Beethoven Quintet [unspecified which] with Baillot
2. A Duet for female voices [composer unspecified]
3. [F-minor] Piano Concerto, composed and played by Chopin
4. An Aria for female voice [composer unspecified]

SECOND PART

1. *Grande Polonaise,* preceded by an "Introduction" and "March" composed for six pianos by Kalkbrenner and to have been played by Mendelssohn, Kalkbrenner, Hiller, Osborne, Sowinski, and Chopin
2. Aria for female voice [composer unspecified]
3. Oboe Solo played by H. Brod [composer unspecified]
4. *Grand Variations in brilliant style* of a theme by Mozart, composed and played by Chopin [Opus 2, the *Don Giovanni* Variations]

What orchestra accompanied the concerto Chopin played? No conductor or orchestra is mentioned. It is possible that the other instrumentalists helped out.

---

*At that, it wasn't as bad as some. At the premiere of Beethoven's Violin Concerto, Franz Clement, the violinist, inserted a piece of his own played "on one string with the violin turned upside down" between the first and the second movements of the concerto.

Notwithstanding the stellar line-up and notwithstanding Kalkbren-ner, who was "box office," the Salle Pleyel was only one-third full. The sparse attendance may have been due to a fear of the cholera or to Kalkbrenner's immodesty in charging ten francs for a ticket. (For nine francs one could buy a seat at the Opéra; for 7.50, at the Opéra Comique; for 6.50, at the Théâtre Français.) All the same, it was an occasion, as is evidenced by the facts that not only Liszt but François Joseph Fétis came. He was the leading music critic, founder and editor of the *Revue Musicale,* a towering theorist and scholar—"one can learn much from him," said Chopin—and he recognized the talent:

> Here is a youngster who . . . disclosed, if not a complete renewal of piano music, an abundance of original ideas to be found nowhere else. . . . If his future works will fulfill the promise of his debut, he will undoubtedly achieve a deservedly brilliant reputation.

As to his playing:

> He plays with elegance, grace, ease; he is both brilliant and neat . . . [though] he produces little sonority from his instrument.
> *March 3, 1832*

This was a push from a forceful hand, yet it did not immediately advance Chopin's cause. He had to wait almost three months for the next opportunity to perform, and then it was at a charity concert orga-nized by the Polish crowd under the sponsorship of the Princess Mos-cova, the widow of Marshal Ney. That concert, on May 20, 1832, was a lackluster affair, the cholera epidemic now representing a real threat to public gatherings. This time Fétis was not quite so enthusiastic:

> Chopin played the first movement of the Concerto which he had per-formed at the Pleyel and with which he had there obtained a brilliant success. This time it was not quite so well received, because of its orches-tration and the slight sonority Chopin was able to draw from the piano. All the same it is evident that the music of this artist is becoming better known.

Orlowski reported jubilantly: "Our dear Frederic gave a concert that earned him great reputation and a bit of money. He killed all the local pianists. All Paris is stunned."

The "slight sonority" of which Fétis complained, and not only he, and not only then, was not a symptom of frailty. Chopin was not so feeble as to be unable to strike a fortissimo, nor is the dynamic mark *ff* missing from his scores. To believe that he whispered because of weakness is to ignore his range. His style may have begun, if only half consciously, as a turning away from the mighty expletives of Beethoven's chords and as a return to the Mozart he worshiped. It was Beethoven who had demanded greater force and sonority from the pianoforte —"it is still the least studied and least developed of instruments; often one thinks one is merely listening to a harp," he wrote to the piano manufacturer Johann Streicher—and while this demand was necessary to the conveyance of Beethoven's thought, it had brought in its trail a certain pounding of the instrument. Even the pianists who did not play the *Appassionata* (and few as yet played Beethoven sonatas) played loud. Herz, Thalberg, Pixis, and above all Liszt, brought the house down with flaming paraphrases of operatic melodies—*very* loud. Chopin was as great a virtuoso as any of these—except Liszt—but his sonorities were gentler, suited to the essence of his thought and not, or at least not in his years of health, because his arms lacked muscle. How often since then have his works been played as if their composer drank nothing but weak tea!

In the letter to Dziewanowski quoted earlier, he calls himself "a revolutionary"; that is exactly what in his political outlook he was not. He had been indoctrinated early with a belief in "established order."* As a man his bent was toward the conservative; only as a composer was he revolutionary. Mendelssohn called Chopin "radically original," but his originality was evolutionary, growing from and nourished by his great predecessors. That is characteristic of whatever is both new and of enduring value.

---

*Though as a young man Nicolas had joined Kosciuszko, he had taught his son that the throne was a bulwark against disorder. Hereditary monarchy was the natural form of government, democracy a dangerous illusion. The French Revolution had been a tragic and anarchic mistake. In his father's house Chopin had read Joseph de Maistre's *Essai sur le principe générateur des constitutions politiques,* a famous work published in 1810, which postulated that unsocial man must be turned into a social being through the authority vested in an aristocratic organization, headed by a monarch. If Chopin did not accept all of Maistre's prescription, he probably did believe much of it.

(3)

The Polish nobles, Czartoryski in the vanguard, helped to smooth Chopin's path. The intellectual influences which pressed on and enlarged his genius came at him from two sources: one was the French Romantic Movement—and this source was to grow ampler as he grew older—the other derived from the work of Poland's greatest poet, Adam Mickiewicz. He too was an émigré, he too lived in Paris, he too never lost a nostalgic longing for his homeland, to which he, like Chopin, was never to return.

Mickiewicz's work is virtually unknown outside Poland. Not only the cadence of his language, but his way of thinking and feeling, cannot be translated into a Western idiom. George Sand spoke of him as "the only great ecstatic I know." His poetry grows from an earth veiled in fog; his world was a world "on which the moon shines with but half an eye." His major work is a huge, amorphous dramatic poem, *Forefathers' Eve* —its four parts only loosely connected—whose love story is set in a frame of philosophic animadversions, as in *Faust,* which influenced him. His epic poem, *Pan Tadeusz,* is more easily assimilated, being tighter and more coherent. With lyric sweetness and mockery, it describes the life of manor and village, raising the most commonplace scenes to the level of ritual. The love he bears his country permeates every line: "No frogs sing so beautifully as those of Poland."

He dedicated two works to the service of his country, *The Books of the Polish Nation* and *The Books of the Polish Pilgrims.* It would have been better, he said, for the Polish soldiers to let themselves be buried under the stones of Warsaw than to cross into Prussia and lay down their arms. One of the generals at the Hôtel Lambert retorted wryly: "You think so, I suppose, so that you could have one more ruin on which to sit and sing mournful songs."

This man with his coal-black eyes, his huge black brows, and his mournful songs, a man filled with both passion and erudition—he knew twelve languages and their literature—stood in a curious relationship to Chopin, half mutual artistic admiration, half personal disapprobation. Chopin loved his poetry; a volume of Mickiewicz was always on Chopin's table and he reread his two major works time and again. He wrote to Grzymala:

Marseilles, March 27 [1839]

My own one [George Sand] has just finished a most excellent article about Goethe, Byron, and Mickiewicz. You must read it: it will rejoice your heart—I can see you enjoying it. It is all so true, so deeply penetrating, so wide-ranging, written from the heart without distortion or the desire merely to praise.

To the fastidious Frederic, the poet's rumpled nature seemed too demonstrative, too like a prophet Ezekiel. On the other hand, Mickiewicz could not understand Chopin's wish for elegance or his enjoyment of luxury. His own life was tragic. He had been profoundly in love with the daughter of a well-to-do landowner; her parents forbade the union, and the girl obeyed her parents. Mickiewicz never got over it, in spite of numerous affairs. When he was thirty-six, he married a girl of twenty-two, who became insane two years later. They lived in straitened circumstances, until he was appointed professor of Slavonic literature at the Collège de France. His lectures there were attended by Chopin, along with George Sand (whom the students greeted with more applause than they did the professor), Sainte-Beuve, Lamartine, Montalembert. But soon the poet-professor got weary of lecturing and introduced political propaganda into his classroom. He was dismissed, fell under the influence of a half-mad mystic, Andrei Towianski, a kind of poor man's Rasputin, and was then reduced to earning a livelihood as a librarian, his creativity choked in the dust of books. During the Crimean War he went to Constantinople to try to organize a Polish legion, contracted cholera, and died there in 1855, at the age of fifty-seven.

A biography of the poet written by his son records an incident reported by Anton Dessus, a friend of both men:

I went to visit Chopin and found him in his salon. Complying with a request by your mother [Mickiewicz's wife], he went to the piano and played with great feeling. When he had finished, your father ran his hand through his hair and began to shout at Chopin so violently that I really did not know where to hide myself. [Mickiewicz said:] "Instead of developing that great gift you have of touching people's hearts, why are you content with strutting, like a peacock, on the Faubourg St. Germain? You could uplift the masses and instead you take such pains to please the nerves of the aristocrats." The angrier he became, the more silent fell Chopin. At length Mickiewicz ceased speaking and Chopin began timidly to play popular [Polish] songs. Your father's forehead smoothed out.

Another testimony:*

[Mickiewicz said:] Chopin expresses himself with inspiration. He sees
the world with the eyes of Ariel. Liszt, when he appears in public, is an
eloquent demagogue; certainly he is vulgar and strives for effect. But as
for myself, I prefer the demagogue.

On the other hand, George Sand remembered in *Impressions et
souvenirs* an occasion when Chopin was playing at her house, and her
son and Delacroix were present. Suddenly Mickiewicz entered:

He shook everybody's hand affectionately and, sinking into an easy chair
in a corner of the room, he begged Chopin to continue. Suddenly a
servant ran in in great fright: the house was on fire. We ran to investi-
gate. Indeed a fire had broken out in my bedroom, but we arrived in
time to extinguish it rapidly. All the same, the matter took a good hour.
After that we asked, "Where is Mickiewicz?" We called him, he didn't
answer. We went back to the salon, but couldn't find him at first. Yet
there he was in the same corner where we had left him. The lamp had
gone out, but he didn't notice it, nor had he noticed all the hubbub and
confusion two steps away from him. He had not heard anything, he
didn't even ask why we had left him alone. He had been listening to
Chopin—and he continued to "listen."

However tenuous the two men's personal relationship, Mickiewicz's
poetry profoundly influenced Chopin. Each man in his way summoned
recollection to nurture his work, while he lived where another language
was spoken. Each man's work is tinged by a Poland fantasized. Dipping
into *Pan Tadeusz* was for Chopin what dipping the madeleine into his
tea would be for Proust. That is not to say that Chopin's music is Polish
by quotation. His "Polish themes" and rhythms are transmuted into
music which owes as much to Bach or Mozart or Handel—and which
comes out "Chopin."

Mickiewicz on his part remembered the essence of Chopin's art long
after the composer's death. We may guess what it meant to him from
an incident recounted by Mickiewicz's cousin:**

Fontana played some pieces by Chopin which were published posthumously. Adam listened, standing by the door. But the execution did not
satisfy him and he showed his displeasure; every strongly hammered

---

*Told by Manfred Kridl in *Adam Mickiewicz, Poet of Poland* (New York, 1951).
**T. Lenartowicz, *Letters About Adam Mickiewicz* (Paris, 1875).

note annoyed him. He asked Marcellina Czartoryska to go to the piano. She played.

He exclaimed, *"That* is Chopin. . . ."

(4)

Marcellina Czartoryska . . . She played Chopin's music with the profoundest understanding. Born Princess Radziwill, she married Adam Czartoryski's son, Alexander, uniting in that marriage, which seems to have been a happy one, "two houses, both alike in dignity." Music was her passion and she had been taught the piano by no less an authority than Czerny. George Sand called her "an angel," Delacroix called her "exquisite," remarked on "the mischief in her eyes," and said that as a painter he was unable to do her justice. Raphael could have painted her, for she resembled his Madonnas, her profile a peaceful line, her eyes clear and open with the look of honesty, her head, round and small, set on a column of a long white neck, which by contrast made her black hair look blacker. Though she was wealthy and pampered, she was not in the least self-important and, as a matter of fact, was a lot more democratic than Chopin.

Shortly after he appeared on the scene, she began to take lessons from him, she recognizing his genius and he her talent, and this led to a deep, unclouded friendship which was to last to his last conscious hour. She was seven years younger than Chopin and lived to the age of eighty-one.

Their friendship never became a love affair, their devotion to each other remained undisturbed by physical passion. She understood him as man and artist and was there whenever he needed her. Even during the George Sand years she remained steadfast, and Sand came to hold her in high affection. During his lifetime he gave her life meaning and substance, and after his death, she became the elegant evangelist of his music. As Anton Rubinstein said, "One can learn to love Poland when one listens to the princess playing Chopin's Mazurkas."

It was undoubtedly her early enthusiasm which within a few months brought to Chopin a procession of pupils—most of them young and female, and titillated by anticipation, caused as much by the teacher as by the teaching. Chopin's appointment book began to read like a condensed *Almanach de Gotha:* in addition to the Polish, international names abounded: Countess Apponyi, wife of the Austrian ambassador; the Baroness d'Este; Countess Adele Fürstenstein; Princéss Ludmilla Beauveau; Princess Elisabeth Czernycheff; Countess Esterhazy; Count Perthuis, adjutant to Louis Philippe, who tried time and time again to induce Chopin to compose an opera; Elisa Peruzzi, wife of the Tuscan ambassador, who was said to be almost as gifted as Marcellina Czartoryska; Baroness Stockhausen, wife of the Hanover ambassador, to whom Chopin dedicated one of his masterpieces, the Barcarolle Opus 60; the Norwegian Thomas Telleffsen, who later carried on the Chopin tradition and himself became a teacher. None of these pupils were beginners. Chopin did not usually teach beginners, nor did he teach children. Each pupil possessed talent, though none, except Marcellina, reached the heights. Perhaps Chopin was too strong an artistic personality to be a flexible teacher. One pupil did show exceptional endowment: "little Hungarian," Karl Filtsch. During an evening at Marie d'Agoult's house, when Filtsch played, Liszt said, "When that little fellow starts concertizing, I'll shut up shop." The English critic J. W. Davison esteemed Filtsch highly when he played in London as a boy of ten. But Filtsch died of tuberculosis at the age of fifteen.

Chopin was a conscientious teacher, generous with the clock. When he felt the pupil worthy, a lesson could go on for hours. He would appear punctually at eight o'clock in the morning—and this perhaps after a social evening lasting until a late hour—and at once get down to business. Strict business. On these early mornings he looked to his student George Mathias like a "gentleman to the tip of his hair . . . graceful, elegant, impeccably dressed in a jacket of pale violet or blue or hazel, buttoned to his chin, his feet small and narrow, always finely shod in shoes of bright leather which shone like a mirror."

When he was pleased, he would say, "You are an angel." When he was displeased, he could lose his temper, tear his hair, his hands, which seemed so elfin, breaking pencils as if they were straws. A singing tone was his criterion. "What is this?" he would say when somebody would play percussively. "A dog barking?" "Don't listen to other pianists," he would plead. "Listen to the great singers, then you'll learn how to phrase."

The English writer J. C. Hadden, who wrote a short biography of

Chopin around the turn of the century, got in touch with a lady* who took some lessons from him in 1846. In a letter to Hadden dated March 27, 1903, she reminisced:

In compliance with your request that I should tell you something about Chopin as a teacher, I can only speak from my own experience, and after the lapse of fifty-seven years my memory is naturally rather hazy, though I can recall some incidents distinctly.

My first interview with Chopin took place at his rooms in Paris. Miss Jane Stirling had kindly arranged that my sister and I should go with her. I remember the bright fire in his elegant and comfortable *salon.* It was in this very month of March, 1846. In the center of the room stood two pianofortes—one grand, the other upright. Both were Pleyels, and the tone and touch most beautiful.

In a few moments Chopin entered from another room and received us with the courtesy and ease of a man accustomed to the best society. His personal appearance, his extreme fragility and delicate health have been described again and again, and also the peculiar charm of his manner. Miss Stirling introduced me as her *petite cousine* who was desirous of the honour of studying with him. He was very polite, but did not give a decided assent at once. Finally he fixed a day and hour for my first lesson, requesting me to bring something I was learning. I took Beethoven's Sonata in A flat (Op. 26). I need hardly say I felt no slight trepidation on taking my place at the grand piano, Chopin seated beside me. I had not played many bars before he said: *"Laissez tomber les mains."* Hitherto I had been accustomed to hear: "Put down your hands," or "Strike" such a note. This *letting fall* was not mechanical only: it was to me a new idea, and in a moment I felt the difference. Chopin allowed me to finish the beautiful air, and then took my place and played the entire sonata. It was like a revelation. You are doubtless well acquainted with the celebrated *Marche funèbre* which of late has so often been played on mournful occasions in public, in conjunction with Chopin's own most beautiful and pathetic composition. He played that *Marche Funèbre* of Beethoven's with a grand, orchestral, power-fully dramatic effect, yet with a sort of restrained emotion which was indescribable. Lastly he rushed through the final movement with fault-less precision and extraordinary delicacy—not a single note lost, and with marvellous phrasing and alternations of light and shade. We stood spellbound, never having heard the like.

---

*She wished to remain anonymous. She must have been near or over eighty when she wrote the letter.

My next lesson began with the sonata. He called my attention to its structure, to the intentions of the composer throughout; showing me the great variety of touch and treatment demanded: many other points, too, which I cannot put into words. From the sonata he passed to his own compositions. These I found fascinating in the highest degree, but very difficult. He would sit patiently while I tried to thread my way through mazes of intricate and unaccustomed modulations, which I could never have understood had he not invariably played to me each composition —nocturne, prelude, impromptu, whatever it was—letting me hear the framework (if I may so express it) around which these beautiful and strange harmonies were grouped, and in addition showing me the special fingering, on which so much depended, and about which he was very strict.

He spoke very little during the lessons. If I was at a loss to understand a passage, he played it slowly to me. I often wondered at his patience, for it must have been torture to listen to my bungling, but he never uttered an impatient word. Sometimes he went to the other piano and murmured an exquisite impromptu accompaniment. Once or twice he was obliged to withdraw to the other end of the room when a frightful fit of coughing came on, but he made signs to me to go on and take no notice. . . .

Another testimony was left by Friederike Müller, a pupil recommended to him by Countess Apponyi. Though she had given a few successful recitals, she had "much, much to learn," especially about the interpretation of Chopin's own works. "Oh," he replied, "it would be too bad if they couldn't be played without instructions from me." . . . "Well, *I* couldn't." . . . "Let us see: play for me." Presently he put her at her ease, asked her if she was comfortably seated, let her finish the piece without interruption, and then very gently remarked that the rhythm was not steady enough. He agreed to take her on and she took lessons for three years:

Many a Sunday I began to play at Chopin's at one o'clock, and only at four or five o'clock did he dismiss us. Then he also played, and how splendidly; but not only his own compositions, also those of other masters in order to show the pupil how they should be performed. One morning he played from memory fourteen Preludes and Fugues by Bach, and when I expressed my joyful admiration over this unparalleled performance, he replied: "That, one never forgets," and, smiling sadly, continued: "For a year I have not studied one entire quarter hour. I have not the force, not the energy. I always wait for a bit of health in order to take all that up again, but—I am still waiting. . . ." His playing was always noble and beautiful, his tones always sang, whether in full forte or in the softest piano. He took infinite pains to teach a pupil this legato, cantabile manner of playing. "He—or she—does not know how to link two notes," was his severest censure. He also demanded adherence to the strictest rhythm, hated all lingering and dragging, misplaced rubatos, as well as exaggerated ritardandos. "I beg you to seat yourself," he would say on such an occasion, with gentle mockery.

Yet it must be said that he chose his pupils not entirely for their talent, but also for their social rank. While he had a few pupils whose names did not carry the prefix "de"—plain Mathias or Mikuli or Gutmann—he turned his studio more and more into an academy for aristocrats. He moved from his first lodging to a small furnished apartment in a more fashionable neighborhood, Cité Bergère 4, but this soon proved inadequate for his needs—or his desires—and at the end of 1833 he rented an apartment at 38 Rue de la Chaussée d'Antin—a beautiful tree-shaded avenue*—which he began to furnish with the appurtenances of comfort and the bric-a-brac of the age. Now he had a residence worthy of his pupils. His father, who had written him admonishment after admonishment about not being extravagant—"Keep a pear for the day when you are thirsty"—understood: "So now you are settled with your own furniture and, I take it, not without some little luxury. I realize that you had to have it since you give your lessons at home, and now, as always, people judge by appearances."

How many pupils made their way to his studio? More than a hundred are known, but Ludwig Bronarski in *Les Elèves de Chopin* states that there were probably more. At first Chopin struggled with a corpulent and opinionated duchess or two, but he soon got rid of her likes, for he demanded that the pupil follow *his* opinion, and he could soon afford to refuse pupils. His valet was adept at turning them away, with the usual "Maître is not at home" ploy. The valet knew that his employer could not abide an ugly woman and that he disliked anybody who was slovenly in dress. It was for neither of these reasons that he declined to teach the sister of Alfred de Musset, although the writer's mother implored Chopin to take charge of the girl:

---

*Under the Second Empire it was called Rue du Mont Blanc.

No doubt you are marveling after your positive and hopeless refusal of
yesterday to see me today reopening the subject and returning to my
request. . . . From infancy on my daughter was being spoiled by those
fine lessons given her by Liszt* and now she won't heed the council of
the very best teachers. Only you, whose original and fascinating talent
she appreciates and admires almost fatally—only you could inspire in
her the ardor for the work necessary to surmount the great difficulties
that the study of the piano entails. . . . My daughter returned yesterday,
desperate, discouraged, having studied all summer in the hope that you
would welcome her devotion . . . only to receive a rigorous and implaca-
ble refusal [and so on, at some length].

A year later:

[1840?]

I hear that your health is greatly improved this year and therefore I
harbor a tiny hope that perhaps you would now be willing to add my
daughter to the list of your pupils. . . . If this note remains unanswered,
I will understand that you wish to spare me the pain of a refusal.

EDMÉE DE MUSSET

The note remained unanswered. Did Chopin not want to have anything to do with the family of the man who had been George Sand's
publicized lover? Or did he resent that remark about the "fine lessons
given her by Liszt"?

Professional pianists came to Chopin for consultation, seeking advice on special problems of interpretation. One of these was Wilhelm
von Lenz, a year older than Chopin, who was a better "theoretical"
master of the piano than a practical one. Born early enough to have
heard old John Baptist Cramer (who so impressed Beethoven), he
chased through Europe listening to the virtuosos, and lived long enough
to listen to Bülow. He left a record of his adventures in a book which,
though it may now and then be colored by dramatic touches, is a
compendium of historical importance.**

Lenz asked Liszt for a recommendation to Chopin, but Liszt merely
gave Lenz a card reading: "Let pass . . . Franz Liszt." Lenz presented
himself at Chopin's apartment; the valet said that Chopin was not at
home. In Boswellian style, Lenz would not accept this refusal and in-

---

*Liszt dedicated to her his *Rossini Fantasy* (Opus 3, No. 2).
***Die grossen Pianofortevirtuosen aus Persönlicher Bekanntschaft* (Berlin, 1872).

sisted that at least the card be taken in to the man who was not at home. In a few moments Chopin appeared, the card in his hand, but did not invite Lenz to sit down.

"What do you want? Are you a pupil of Liszt's? Are you an artist?"

"I'm a friend of Liszt's and I'm hoping to learn the Mazurkas under your tutelage. I have already studied some of them with Liszt."

I suddenly realized that I had committed a faux pas. It was too late.

"In-deed," replied Chopin, drawing out both syllables, but with great courtesy. "Then what do you want of me? Play me what you practiced with Liszt. I have still a few minutes to spare"—and with that he drew a tiny watch from his pocket—"you must excuse me, but I was just on the point of leaving and I told my valet not to admit anybody."

Lenz now played a Mazurka, with a variation he had learned from Liszt. Chopin stopped him and asked calmly:

"This variant—it isn't yours, is it? It is he who taught it to you? Because he puts his hand in everywhere. . . . All right, all right. I'll give you a few lessons, but only twice a week, not more; it is difficult for me to spare even three-quarters of an hour."

Once more Chopin looked at his watch. Suddenly he asked:

"What do you read? What are your interests in general?" I was not at all prepared for that question! "I prefer George Sand and Jean-Jacques [Rousseau] to all other writers," I exclaimed without thinking.

He smiled. At that moment he was truly handsome. "It is Liszt who suggested that to you," he said. "Well, I perceive you are initiated. So much the better. Be punctual, my studio is a pigeon house."

Lenz also told of an incident which took place one afternoon at George Sand's. Chopin played his E-minor Concerto while young Filtsch marked the orchestral portion on a second piano. Lenz, who had never been impressed by the concerto, now thought it "marvelous." After playing, Chopin escaped as soon as he could, and he, Filtsch, and Sand went to the music publisher Schlesinger, where Chopin purchased a copy of the *Fidelio* score. He presented this to Filtsch, saying, "You gave me great joy today. . . . My dear little friend, accept this gift of a masterpiece. Study it as long as you live, and from time to time think of me." (So much for Chopin's supposed failure to appreciate Beethoven, though it *is* true that he was not entirely in sympathy with Beethoven's last works.)

It was inevitable, since "Pupil of Chopin" conferred such prestige, that some pianists appropriated the distinction with no right whatever. Surprisingly, Chopin seemed indifferent: "I don't know him and I never gave him lessons, but if it helps the poor fellow, leave him in peace, let him be my pupil."*

The "pigeon house" of the Rue d'Antin became a meeting place for golden pigeons. When the pupil departed, she or he left the fee, twenty francs, in a sealed envelope on the mantelpiece. The recipient was supposed not to glance at the envelope—until later.**

Nicolas was worrying over his son's working too hard and being too much caught up in the "so-called Great World which is very small when one looks at it closely."

December 7, 1833

I see by your letter that you are extremely busy. At your age occupation is necessary and leisure often harmful. But do take care lest the work fatigue you. You must think of your health, and surely your work is not routine. I won't reproach you for frequenting high society, I fear only that your evenings last too late. You need rest.

Rest was what he didn't get. And didn't want.

(5)

As a composer Chopin's path did not ascend in a straight line, as did Beethoven's or Verdi's. Though the intensity of feeling and form deepened in later years, some of the compositions of his first Paris years are masterly, while others are less than that. One may conjecture that he composed several pieces for the use of his pupils, or some to serve in his own career as a virtuoso, a career he had not as yet abjured. Whatever the cause, the quality goes up and down. In 1831 he wrote the

---

*Quoted by F. Hoesick.
**A bit of hypocrisy widely used with members of a profession. One handed the doctor his fee in an envelope (in cash) and the doctor pretended to ignore it. As to what the twenty francs represented—as Arthur Loesser mentions in *Men, Women and Pianos* —a member of the Chamber of Deputies was paid twenty-five francs a day in 1848, a sum supposedly sufficient to maintain a bourgeois standard of living. Chopin, according to the report of a young pianist, Carl Hallé—who later became Sir Charles Hallé, conductor of the Manchester Symphony—gave eight or nine lessons a day, but surely that is exaggerated. Even if he gave but half that number, his income was enviable.

Grand Valse Brillant in E-flat major (Opus 18), just a bravura piece, the only waltz of his which could be danced to as a change of diet from Johann Strauss—and not as good—yet in the same year he composed the Nocturne in F-sharp major (Opus 15, No. 2), one of the most poetic and magical products of his pen, greater than anything he had done before. In 1832 came the Rondo in E-flat major (Opus 16), a dull, vacant concoction. But the same year marked the completion of Etude No. 3 of Opus 10 in E major, a revelation of new beauty, an astonishing masterpiece: it is simple, free of technical complexities, and yet requires a great pianist, such as Horowitz or Rubinstein, to disclose it. He worked on the Ballade in G minor (Opus 23) for four years, beginning in 1831, and it turned out to be one of the cornerstones of piano literature—but what should one say of the shaky Boléro (Opus 19), composed around 1833?

The valuable works appeared often enough to outshine the minor ones. The Twelve Etudes (Opus 25), dedicated to Marie d'Agoult, and composed between 1832 and 1836, fill a rich canvas with the strangely modern A minor; the G-sharp minor, which foreshadows Debussy; the sad and songful C-sharp minor (misnamed "The Cello"). The last three —the B minor, the A minor, called "The Winter Wind," and the C minor, "The Ocean"—are gigantic in concept, powerful in their working through, virile in tone, and often wild in sound. No faint mind, no dreamer under a hazy moon, invented them. How can one think of Chopin as a febrile and soft composer when such music sounds?

CHAPTER

VI

MUCH FAME, SOME FORTUNE,

LITTLE LOVE

TWO YEARS after he arrived in Paris, Chopin had become the local representative of French Romantic music. As its agreeable advocate, he was as well the man one had to, and wanted to, invite for dinner. (Liszt, equally glamorous, was here today and gone tomorrow, while Chopin stayed and played.) If there beckoned a promise of an evening during which he might sit at the piano, the hostess could count on as full a house as if Louis Philippe had scheduled an appearance. The best wine was brought from the cellar, the finest Brussels napery spread on the table. If Chopin came, Hugo or Balzac or de Vigny would not be far behind. The candles shone on those miraculous hands. There was silence. How exquisite, the privilege to be the first to hear that new Ballade, even if one did not quite understand it!

On his part, he liked to entertain, giving dinners for a few friends, planning every detail of the menu himself. He was proud of his Rue d'Antin lodging, which he now refurnished—expensively—in the current Louis Philippe mode. He had the chairs, originally covered in red, changed to white silk: "impractical but ravishing, and red hurts my eyes." The furniture was of rosewood, some pieces exhibiting first-class marqueterie. Over the fireplace stood a fine Louis XV clock, in the living room a vitrine displayed French porcelain. The grand piano by Pleyel occupied the most prominent place. A second piano, an upright, was in the bedroom, and with the door open, he could accompany a pupil. The bed stood in an alcove firmly closed off by a curtain of white tulle. An easy chair was placed before it, covered in a tapestry embroi-

[94]

dered by his mother, and next to it, a marble secretaire which held a silver vessel for burning incense. In a chest he kept a rank and file of medicines: he was the apothecary's favorite customer. The bathroom was primitive, to say the least, with a small tin tub. Throughout the apartment, curtains of clear silk and snowy muslin softened the light. Liszt noted "the presence of etchings and paintings of harmonious beauty." The dining room was comfortably intimate, the silver service antique.

He could pay for this because his income was growing steadily. While he was active as a teacher, his earnings amounted to eighteen to nineteen thousand francs annually. James Rothschild and Grzymala—who speculated heavily—gave him an occasional tip and he made money on the Paris Bourse. And as his compositions became more widely published in Europe, they augmented his earnings; altogether, however, they brought in no more than thirty thousand francs.

His expenses:

Rent for the apartment on Rue d'Antin*	1275 frs.
Valet's salary	840
Clothes	500
Food and wine for himself and guests	5000
Carriage and driver	3600
Miscellaneous: Gifts, contributions, flowers, gratuities (he tipped lavishly)	5000
	16,215 frs.

Between sixteen thousand for expenses and eighteen or nineteen thousand income, not much was left over.

His popularity did not spoil his modesty. Marie d'Agoult assured him that she had but to hear one of his Nocturnes to be cured of her migraine. De Vigny called him *"Chopinetto mio."* The famous actress Mlle. Mars wrote him tender letters. Heine kept praising him, spreading his reputation to Germany. Liszt, Kalkbrenner, Ferdinand Hiller, Clara Wieck—who Chopin said was "the only woman in Germany who knows how to play my music"—performed his compositions. He formed a cordial, though brief, friendship with Bellini, who died in 1835. Balzac wrote that he saw Chopin as an angel, Liszt as a demon, and paid Chopin tribute in his novel *Ursule Mirouët.* ("Has Chopin read what I

---

*When he moved to the Square d'Orléans, his rent was only 625 francs.

wrote about him?" Balzac asked George Sand, with an author's curiosity.)

Berlioz admired him, though he harbored some reservations about the rhythmic freedom of his playing. In turn, Berlioz's proselytizing exuberance disturbed the nonproselytizing Chopin—a difference which could be symbolized by Berlioz's hair, which flew in the cardinal directions, as against Chopin's formal tidiness. The younger helped the older man, who just then was undergoing his severest crisis. Passionately in love with Harriet Smithson, Berlioz was rejected by her. He went nearly mad with grief. Then, early in 1833, Harriet broke her leg. She was now not only immobile but poor, having lost all her money in financing an unsuccessful theatrical venture. It made no difference to her stormy suitor: he implored her to marry him, and in April he enlisted Chopin and Liszt to play at a benefit for her. The sensational event—imagine hearing Chopin and Liszt in one evening!—realized two thousand francs, a goodly sum, yet a mere seventh of what Harriet owed. Nevertheless, she still refused, whereupon Berlioz swallowed an overdose of opium in her presence. She then begged him to save himself and take an emetic. He did, but even after this tragic farce she hesitated. They were not married until October of that year. In the spring of the following year they moved to the country, Harriet being pregnant, and Berlioz, who was bored by rural surroundings, begged Chopin and Liszt to come and visit them. Berlioz spoke of this visit to his sister: "We discussed art, poetry, philosophy, music and drama—in a word, all that constitutes life."

Burning the perfumed candle at both ends, Chopin would dine with Lord Rothsay Stuart, the British ambassador; appear at a reception at Baron Nathaniel de Rothschild's; accept an invitation from the banker Auguste Léo; then be driven home through the snowy night to work on the Nocturne in G minor; and often after a fitful sleep he would be ready the next morning to receive Contessa d'Este as a pupil. The accolades he received included several carefully covert approaches by Marquis Astolph de Custine, a homosexual so well known that decades later Proust may have used him as a model for the Baron de Charlus. Himself a dabbler in literature—Balzac and Baudelaire had a good word to say about his novels—he set himself up as the assessor of all the Romantics, inviting the chosen ones to keep him company at his country villa in Saint-Gratien. To Chopin he sent invitations and gifts. Chopin remained polite and distant, though he visited Custine once or twice, in company with Hugo, Lamartine, Berlioz, and Heine.

His public appearances continued to be rare, his private appearances frequent. Sometimes he played with Liszt, sometimes with Ferdinand Hiller, and once with Moscheles, performing a two-piano piece by Liszt (lost) which caused a frenzy of enthusiasm. In the spring of 1834 Hiller invited him to the Lower Rhine Music Festival at Aachen, where he met Mendelssohn. In spite of Chopin's suspicion of the "Jews," in however garbled an image he conceived that term, he at once succumbed to Mendelssohn's charm, elegance, and enthusiasm. The two, along with Hiller, went to Düsseldorf, where Mendelssohn was music director, and later journeyed down the Rhine to Cologne, where Chopin was moved to tears by the beauty of the river landscape. He and Mendelssohn were to meet once more the following year in Leipzig, when they would again exchange ideas about music, but after that distance separated them. Yet their artistic regard continued. Years later Mendelssohn, happily married to the exquisite and gentle Cécile, sent Chopin a "fan letter":

> November 3, 1844
>
> This letter comes to you to ask a favor. Would you out of friendship write a few bars of music, sign your name at the bottom to show you wrote them for my wife (Cécile M.-B.), and send them to me? It was at Frankfurt that we last met you and I was then engaged: since that time, whenever I wish to give my wife a great pleasure I have to play to her, and her favorite works are those you have written. So there you have another reason (although I have plenty of valid ones since I have known you) for my wanting always to be well informed about what you are writing, and for my taking a greater interest in you and your works than you do perhaps yourself. That is also the reason why I hope you will grant the favor I ask. Forgive me if I thereby add to the tiresome requests with which you must be inundated.

It took Chopin almost a year to answer:

> October 8, 1845
>
> Just try hard to imagine, my dear friend, that I am writing by return post in reply to the letter which brought me your good news. Since the delay is not due to any wrong feeling on my part, I hope you will welcome these lines as if they were reaching you at the proper time. If the little sheet of music is not too dog-eared and does not arrive too late, please present it from me to Mrs. Mendelssohn. Allow me also to remind you

that, if you have worthier and more intimate friends and admirers, you have none who is more sincerely attached to you.

The "little sheet of music" has been identified: it is nothing less than the Mazurka in A-flat major (Opus 59, No. 2), which the English critic W. H. Hadow called "perhaps the most beautiful of all the Mazurkas." It was composed in 1845—so Chopin sent Mendelssohn something brand new. The manuscript is now in the Mendelssohn Collection of the Bodleian Library in Oxford. Mendelssohn saved all his souvenirs.

(2)

Of course Chopin enjoyed success. And yet he experienced the homesickness of the transplanted who knows that he is better off where he is but nevertheless casts a longing look toward where he is *not*. And like all men who dwell in the region of imagination, he craved the "normalcy" of the prosaic life. The artist who would not relinquish his task for any price yearns from time to time for a regular existence and covets the conventional. Both these pulls were strong in Chopin, who walked along the Seine and dreamed of a Poland which no longer was, or who would return at midnight to an empty room. Having been brought up in the glow of a family, he longed for a family of his own. However unconforming his artistic mind, as a man he often wanted what his stout neighbor possessed. He sometimes wished himself in his friend Titus's shoes, riding out at sunrise to look after his wheat fields and, in the evening, coming home to wife and children.

He spoke of his family rarely but thought of them often. When his father wrote him that he and his wife were going to Karlsbad, Chopin made what was for him an unusual decision: he would undertake a nonprofessional voyage; he would go there, though it was a ten-day journey, simply to see the faces of his father and mother once again. The meeting had to take place outside Russian jurisdiction; Chopin did not want to show himself within the Polish border lest he be detained. Nicolas, for his part, had no end of difficulties obtaining a passport and had to submit a petition stating he needed to undergo "a cure."

Before Chopin set out he fulfilled a promise, that of appearing at a concert for the benefit of the conductor Francois Antoine Habeneck. No man had done more to stimulate the musical life of Paris: Habeneck had introduced the public to Beethoven's symphonies in serious, well-rehearsed performances, had given Berlioz a hearing, and had played Chopin's E-minor Concerto with the composer as soloist. The orchestra he formed and trained, the Conservatoire, could compare itself with the best European orchestras, even with the London Philharmonic. Soon after his arrival in Paris in 1839, Wagner heard Habeneck conduct Beethoven's Ninth. It proved a revelation to him: now he understood the work, in which formerly he had discerned only "weird shapes."

Habeneck's benefit took place on April 26, 1835, before a huge audience. The program was huge as well: Beethoven's *Pastoral*, the Scherzo from the Ninth, and the last movement of the Fifth. Amid these symphonic Goliaths, Chopin came onstage with a new work, the Andante Spianato and Polonaise for piano and orchestra (Opus 22). This is a curiously fractured composition: the Andante is for piano alone, a quiet and consoling idyll, while the Polonaise—composed before the Andante—is chained to a rickety orchestral accompaniment and in itself is a bit on the pompous side. The work is now performed as a piece for the piano alone. At the premiere the audience jumped to its feet, shouted and bravoed, and blew kisses at the slight figure standing by the orchestra. Chopin seemed lost, sunk into himself. After that concert Habeneck used to call him Frederic van Chopin.

He couldn't wait until it was time to leave for Karlsbad. He decided to make it a surprise visit, but in typical fashion he had failed to inform himself what inn Nicolas and his wife were stopping at—and Karlsbad, the famous *Kurort*, had about thirty inns*—so he ran from one to the other, finding them at last at four o'clock in the morning. Their happiness overflowed the measure. To his sisters Louise and Isabella he wrote:

> Karlsbad, 16 August [1835]
>
> Dear Children: Here is the first letter written by Papa and myself that you have ever received. Our joy is indescribable. We never stop embracing each other—what more can we do? What a pity we can't all be together here! Bobo looks wonderful.** I can't write sensibly—it's better not to try to think of anything today—only enjoy the happiness that is

---

*Often fancifully named: The Green Melon, The Palm Tree, The Golden Rose (where the Chopins stayed), At the Three Sheep, etc.

**Bobo was Louise's first child, then aged two. Chopin was commenting on a portrait of the baby.

offered to us. That's all I can do today. I find my parents exactly the same, only a trifle older. [Five years had elapsed.] We go for walks arm in arm with darling Mamma; we talk about you all, we imitate the tantrums of my little nephews, and we tell how much we have been thinking about each other. We all eat and drink together; we exchange tender caresses and then shout at each other. I am at the summit of my happiness. I see again those same little mannerisms and habits which I grew up with, and that hand which it is so long since I kissed.

Well, now, children, let me embrace you! Forgive me—I can't collect my thoughts or write about anything but our happiness at being together at this moment. To think that what I had so long only dared hope for has today come true, and happiness, happiness, happiness is here! In my joy I smother you with kisses, you and my brothers-in-law*—my dearest friends in this world.

Nicolas and his son then went to register with the police. That was obligatory and one had to pay a "Resort Tax." The father registered "Nancy, France" under "Place of Birth and Citizenship," while the son wrote "Paris." This denial of their nationality did not fool either Metternich's or the Czar's spies: they knew that Karlsbad served as a rendezvous for revolutionary Poles and they kept track of all strangers, especially since Karlsbad was preparing then for a visit of the new Austrian emperor, Ferdinand I, on his way to a meeting of four monarchs. An underground Polish newspaper reported:

We hear from Karlsbad that our compatriots had intended to honor our gifted Chopin with a banquet by taking up a collection. About twenty people agreed, but the next day twelve withdrew, fearing that they might compromise themselves. . . . The leader of the opposition was one Kazio Walewski. (Editorial comment: This man is visiting all the resorts to find out how many Poles are there, how and with whom they are living.) General Mlokosiewicz roundly declared that he had possessions and children in Poland and he was afraid to dine with the Parisian.

If Chopin knew he was being watched, he remained unconcerned. He spent three Karlsbad weeks in complete happiness.

He would not have been Chopin had he not accepted invitations to the houses of the high Bohemian nobility, including that of Count Anton Thun-Hohenstein, whose son Fritz and two daughters, Anna and

*Louise married, in 1832, a professor of jurisprudence, Kalasanty Jedrzejewicz. Isabella married a professor of mathematics, Anton Felix Barcinski.

Josefina, were all Chopin enthusiasts, Josefina being a pupil. Count Anton invited Chopin to come to the family castle in Tetschen, and when the countess and the children heard this, excitement in Tetschen ran high and letters went back and forth daily.* "All of us are mad for his coming," the countess wrote to her husband. "Josefina is beside herself. . . . Very good that you invited Chopin's parents. Twenty times I meant to suggest it and forgot to write." "He wants to stay only three days," the count replied, "but his plans are not that firm. And if he is pleased—how can he not be, considering his adoring pupil?—he'll stay longer, I think."

From these and other hints it appears that Josefina was smitten with Chopin. But her feeling remained unrequited. Her sister Anna wrote in her diary:

> Many a beautiful hour did I spend during Chopin's visit. How he enchanted us with his magnificent, truly miraculous playing, his rich imagination! He remained five days. The first day he was quite silent, when he took leave of his parents, who returned from here to Warsaw. His grief moved us and we found it fitting to leave him in peace with his sorrow. But he made up for that the rest of the days. We could not get enough of his playing. Impossible to play those finger-breaking compositions with greater ease, more feeling, stronger forte, than he did. To hear him improvise is a true delight. He let us suggest various themes and then he improvised, perhaps a half hour, as if it were nothing. What great fame will he earn, if even now when he is so young he means so much! How celebrated the name Chopin will become, if even now all the artists esteem him so highly! And besides, Chopin is an extraordinarily decent, modest, and merry human being. He kept us in stitches with his talent for imitations. He mimicked an Englishman who spoke broken French. When he played we stood around the piano, admiring, glancing at one another, enthusiastic, transported, I would say, by his magic art.
>
> *September 26, 1835*

And the countess wrote to a friend:

> September 15, 1835
> [His parents] departed yesterday after lunch. I was most sorry for the poor mother. During the whole meal she could hardly hold back her

---

*These letters only recently came to light, when the Thun-Hohenstein archives were taken over by the Czechoslovakian state.

tears. Her son was so moved that he spent the rest of the day in his room, unable to face us. How well I understand this!

Frederic promised his parents that they would meet again, sooner or later, on neutral ground. He was never to see them again.

Before Chopin left the Thun-Hohenstein castle, he wrote in the two sisters' album a joyful little waltz which in an expanded and amended version he later published as Opus 34, No. 1, which is known as the "Tetschen Waltz." Recent research suggests that he had sketched the waltz in Karlsbad, writing it cleanly in Tetschen.

(3)

His return journey took him to Dresden. There he paid a visit to the Wodzinskis, a family he had known since his boyhood. They were exactly the sort of people Chopin was drawn to—well-to-do, of noble lineage (partly descended from the Sforzas), and hospitable. Countess Teresa Wodzinska had taken a casual interest in Chopin, the kind of interest one takes in the person living next door who has become a celebrity and whom one has known "when"; she had written him a year previously, inviting him to come to Geneva, where the Wodzinskis were awaiting the return of calmer times in Poland. Chopin had refused. Now an easy opportunity presented itself to see them again.

Chopin was always drawn to childhood acquaintances, and he was fond of the countess, in spite of her bothering him for autographs of the famous people he knew, and very fond of her three sons, who had been brought up by Nicolas in his boarding school. The eldest, Anton, soon moved to Paris and Chopin remained on friendly terms with him, though Anton turned out to be a ne'er-do-well and blithely borrowed money from Chopin which he never repaid. There was, as well, the daughter, whom Chopin had thought of as a child, and who was now nineteen years old.

Chopin may have been in love with a new charmer, Delfina Potocka —his love for Constantia had passed so long ago that he casually dismissed the news of her marriage with a cold word—but his longing for an ordered existence, his desire for a wife and children, induced him now to glance at Maria with interest.

As far as one is able to judge from her behavior and her letters, few candidates less suitable to a poetic mind could have been found. For passion she substituted flirtatiousness, for fervor a facile femininity, for real comprehension a few studied phrases. She was not beautiful, not even particularly interesting looking, though her very black hair and her very black eyes produced the illusion of a mystery which wasn't there. Her chief skill lay in flattering men while remaining noncommittal; she had already teased Julius Slowacki, a Polish poet, and the young Louis-Napoleon Bonaparte.*

Such was Chopin's strange choice. One has the impression that he talked himself into it, that at least in the beginning he was in love with the family and what it represented. Yet soon he dived deeper into an infatuation to which the freshly churned emotion caused by the parting from his family contributed, and to which the beautiful city of Dresden, already familiar to him, with its rustling trees and its whispering river, played the accompaniment. Of course he played for Maria, they walked and they talked, they went to the museum, but the relationship remained somewhat tentative, although it did not go unobserved by Maria's mother. After Chopin left, Maria wrote him a sentimental letter —but it is not much of a love letter:

> Although you like neither receiving nor writing letters I wish to take advantage of Mr. Cichowski's departure to send you news of Dresden from the time you left. I shall perhaps bore you—but at least not by my playing. On Saturday, after you left us, we all walked sadly about the drawing room where you had been with us a few minutes earlier. Our eyes were filled with tears. My father soon came home and was upset at not having been able to say good-bye. My mother kept on reminding us mournfully of some little characteristic of "her fourth son, Fryderyk," as she calls you. Felix looked quite dejected; Casimir [her brothers] tried to make his usual jokes but they didn't come off, for he was acting the comedian half-laughing and half-crying. Papa made fun of us and laughed too, but it was only to prevent himself from crying. At eleven the singing master came; the lesson went very badly for we couldn't sing. You were the sole topic of conversation. Felix repeatedly asked me to play that Waltz (the last thing you played and gave to us). They enjoyed listening as I enjoyed playing, for it brought back the brother who had just left.

---

*In a later year she married Count Josef Skarbek, a son of Chopin's godfather. The marriage was dissolved (on the ground of "impotence") and she married again and lived until 1896, her life in no way remarkable.

I took the waltz to be bound. The German bookbinder stared when he was shown just one sheet. (He didn't know, this German, *who* had written it!) No one could touch anything at dinner: we kept on looking at your usual place at table and then at "Fryderyk's corner"—the little chair is still in its place and will probably stay there as long as we are in this house.

In the evening we were taken to my aunt's so as to avoid the gloom of the first evening when you were not there. Father came along later, saying that he too could not possibly stay in the house that day. It did us good to leave a place which reminded us too keenly of what we had lost. Mamma can speak of nothing but you and Anton. . . . [A plea to take care of Anton in Paris follows.]

Adieu (quite simply). A childhood friend does not require high-flown phrases. Mamma sends you a tender embrace. My father and brothers embrace you most cordially (no, that's not enough), most—I don't quite know what to say. . . . Adieu.

Chopin continued homeward, first to Leipzig—where he met Schumann, heard Clara Wieck play, renewed his pleasant exchanges with Mendelssohn—and then to Heidelberg to visit the parents of one of his favorite pupils, Adolf Gutmann. In Heidelberg he fell ill. It was just an attack of "influenza," said the doctor, but he spat up some blood and felt so weak that he didn't want to move. Presently he recovered and returned to Paris.

During the winter he was frequently ill, and withdrew from public life so completely that a rumor flew through Paris that he had died. But when spring came—that scent-laden, solacing Parisian spring—he regained his strength. With it grew his love for Maria, and when he learned in July that the Wodzinskis planned to go to Marienbad, he decided he had to see her again. Once more he climbed into the stagecoach, once more he braved the dusty road—this time for nine days. He arrived at Marienbad's elegant hotel The White Swan on July 28, 1836. The Police Protocol registered him as *"Herr Friedrich Chopin aus Paris, Gutsbesitzer"* (landowner). Why "landowner"? Did he wish to appear more "respectable"? Or did he naïvely want to confuse the Russian agents? His health was still uncertain, as we know by coincidence: Rebecka Mendelssohn, with her husband, Professor Dirichlet, happened to be in Marienbad at that time. "He didn't show himself," wrote Rebecka, "the doctor and a Polish Countess having taken complete possession of him." Rebecka ardently wished to hear him play, she had heard so much about him from brother Felix and brother Paul, so she decided to commit what she called "a solecism" and approach him as *soeur de Monsieur Mendelssohn-Bartholdy.*

> That solecism flopped completely. Dirichlet went and said Soeur, etc., just *one* Mazurka— Impossible, wretched piano, very nervous, and how is dear Frau Hensel [Fanny, Mendelssohn's other sister]? Is Paul married? Leave me in peace. . . . Well, that's the first and last time we'll do anything like *that.*

After a month he went back to Dresden with the Wodzinskis and there he at last decided to ask Maria to marry him. It happened at what the Poles in a curious idiom call "the gray hour," meaning the time of twilight when reason reigns weakest and emotion strongest. Maria consented and they both went to her mother, who gave her provisional approval. The countess said, in effect: "I am not against it, but let us wait awhile, let Frederic watch his health, let distance test their love—and in the meantime let's keep it a secret." A letter from the countess followed Chopin to Paris:

> Dresden, September 14, 1836
>
> I cannot get over my regret at your having to leave on Saturday. On that day I was so unwell that I could not give enough attention to "the gray hour" and we did not discuss it sufficiently. Had you stayed, we could have gone into it more fully the next day. . . .
>
> Don't imagine that I should think of taking back what I said. No, but we should have carefully decided on the line to be followed. Until all is settled I shall merely ask you to say nothing: look after your health for everything depends on that. Casimir arrived on Sunday. I find him quite altered from what he was when he left. If the air in Bohemia is opium-drenched, then the air where *he* has come from [Poland] must be laden with *Digitalis.* A nice prospect for Maria! Who knows what she will be like in a year's time . . . ?
>
> I shall try to stay here another two weeks from today, and by the 15th [of October] I shall be back in Warsaw for the wedding [of her son Felix; they had received permission to return to Poland]. I shall be seeing your parents and sisters and I shall tell them you are well and cheerful, but I shan't mention "the gray hour." Nevertheless rest assured that I am on your side; we must take these precautions if my wishes are to be fulfilled. We must allow time for the feelings of both parties to be tested. Adieu. Go to bed at eleven and drink only *eau-de-gomme* [an aromatic syrup drink]. Dr. Matuszynski [his friend] will agree with me. . . . Keep

well, dear Frederic. I give you my solemn blessing like a loving mother.
T. W.

Maria is sending you some slippers by Mr. Germany. They are rather
large but, I might add, that is to allow you to wear woolen stockings. Dr.
Paris recommended it and I take it that you will obey since you gave
your promise. One last word: remember this is a testing time.

The reference to opium in Bohemia and digitalis in Poland is obscure; perhaps she was already hinting to Chopin that his love was
senseless, the Polish word for digitalis—*szalej*—being as well the imperative form of a verb which means "Go mad!" Did the countess with her
convoluted pun try to warn Chopin? She knew her daughter: "What
will she be like in a year's time?" The mother saw that the daughter was
half playacting. Maria added a postscript (written in a mixture of Polish,
French, and Italian), to the letter, which hardly reads as if it were
written by a girl in the transport of love:

> We are inconsolable over your departure; the three days which have
> passed since then have seemed like ages. Are you like us? Do you miss
> your friends a little? Yes, you do—I can answer for it and I'm sure I am
> right; at least I need to believe so. I persuade myself that YES is what you
> would say. Am I not right?
> I am sending you the slippers, which are now ready. I am upset about
> their being too big, although I took one of your Warsaw boots, made by
> Takowski, as a pattern, *carissimo maestro,* but it's just like the Germans.
> Dr. Paris consoles me for it by saying that they will suit you very well
> as you must wear nice warm woolen stockings in winter.
> Mamma had a tooth out—it has made her feel quite ill and today she
> has had to stay in bed. In two weeks we shall be off to Poland. I shall be
> so happy to see your parents. And your good sister Louise—will she
> recognize me? Adieu, *mio carissimo maestro.* Don't forget Dresden
> now, and Poland later on. Adieu, au revoir. Ah, if it could only be sooner!
>   MARIA

A few friendly but rather stiff letters were exchanged during the
winter, when the family returned to Poland. In January 1837 the countess acknowledged the receipt of a handsomely bound album of his
music, and Maria added her postscript, through which her lukewarm
mood transpires.

>   Sluzewo, January 25, 1837
> Mamma has been scolding you so I will thank you very, very warmly,
> and when we meet I shall thank you still more. You can see that I am

lazy about writing, for the fact that I am postponing my thanks until we meet frees me from the obligation to write at length now. Mamma has described our mode of life so I have nothing fresh to report except that a thaw has set in—an important piece of news, isn't it?—especially important for you to know. The quiet life we lead here suits me and that is why I like it—for the time being, of course: I wouldn't wish it to be like that always. One has to make the best of things when one has no other choice. I try to find things to do to pass the time. At the moment I'm reading Heine's *Deutschland,* which is awfully interesting. But I must stop now and give you my blessing. I hope I do not need to reassure you of the sentiments of

Your faithful Secretary
MARIA

Later one more gift arrived: Chopin arranged to have his sister Louise send Maria an album, bound in red leather, Maria's name stamped on its cover; into it Louise copied some of Chopin's music and it was long considered an original Chopin manuscript, their handwriting being similar. (The Germans destroyed it, but a photographic copy is extant.) Maria replied:

[Undated]

I can only write these few words to thank you for the pretty *cahier* you sent me. I shall not say with what joy I received it—words would not suffice. Please accept the assurance both of my sincere gratitude for it and of the lifelong attachment felt for you by all our family and particularly by your least gifted pupil and childhood friend. Adieu. Mamma sends you a tender kiss. Little Teresa never ceases to speak of her "Chopen."* Adieu. Do not forget us.

MARIA

And that was the last he heard from her. It was over. No dramatic break occurred. The relationship in which Maria's brothers and perhaps Chopin's mother had regarded her as formally affianced ended in silence, the silence of indifference.

One reads in some biographies that it was Count Wodzinski who opposed his daughter's marriage with a man who was not even a baron but merely an artist, and not one in the best of health. Maria was supposed to have obeyed the fatherly interdict. It is a very doubtful story—it was the countess who ran the family and made the decisions, the Count being no Mr. Barrett. When the Wodzinskis were in Geneva

---

*She was the baby of the family, of whom Chopin was fond.

and in Germany, their possessions in Poland were confiscated by the Russian governor. They thought they had to remain exiles. But they managed to get their estate back, and when that happened they were once again wealthy. Now a connection with the young artist no longer seemed desirable to the countess. From calling Chopin "her fourth son," she now sought a son-in-law with a title and a fortune. Money must be mated to money. And Maria? A commonplace little girl; in nothing she wrote or did can one discover a trace of the abandon a nineteen-year-old would disclose to the man she truly loved. She was no doubt flattered by the attention of a handsome celebrity and toyed with the idea of marriage, until absence, which can make the heart grow less fond, made it easy for her to skip to a new chapter.

When Chopin took leave of Maria in Dresden, or perhaps in the twilight hour, she gave him a rose. Chopin kept it, preserved with it the letters from the Wodzinskis, and tied them in a bundle which he marked "My Sorrow." It is a theatrical phrase, inconsistent with his usual autobiographical style. Does it hint at a need to assure himself that he *did* love? Did he wish to put behind him an episode into which he glided on the wings of longing and the grounding of which hurt his pride? Did the two words mean that he realized he had been mistaken in his choice? Tying a ribbon around those letters, he filed his hope away.

That the scar of that experience showed is attested by a letter that Custine wrote him in May 1837, after Maria had disappeared from his life. Custine understood that something was wrong with Chopin "spiritually" as well as physically and wrote of "griefs of the heart," though he was uncertain of the cause:

> Believe me when I tell you that, in spite of appearances to the contrary, I love you more on your own account than for myself. I will prove it, for I am not afraid to come troubling you again, and indeed it is the last time I shall try to persuade you to take my advice. You are ill: what is worse, your illness might become really serious. You have reached the limit in physical and spiritual suffering. When griefs of the heart turn into illness of the body we are lost; and that is what I wish to save you from. I am not trying to console you. I respect your feelings (moreover, I can only guess at them) but I wish them to remain feelings and not become physical sufferings. It is one's duty to live, when one possesses a fountain of life and poetry such as yours: do not waste this treasure, and don't treat Providence with contempt by making light of its most precious

gifts. Such a crime would be unforgivable, for God himself will not make good the time you deliberately waste.

To preserve your *past*—which holds such a promising future—there is only one way open to you: to let yourself be treated as a sick child. You must be persuaded that one single thing is of consequence: your health; the rest will take care of itself. I am sufficiently your friend for you to allow me to go to the heart of the matter. Is it money that is keeping you in Paris? If so, I can lend you some; you can pay me later, but you must take three months rest. If it is love that has failed you, let us see what friendship can do. Live for yourself—you will have plenty of time later on to get rich. . . .

I have said all this before; but as a friend, I feel I must repeat it. You need not answer this except by coming here on Tuesday or Wednesday of next week to Saint-Gratien where you will be as free or freer than I, since you will have none of the trivial duties of master of the house to perform. This is the last time I shall trouble you, but my insistence needs no excuse, does it?

A. DE CUSTINE

The episode sensitized Chopin to a new love. (Those who have once loved are most likely to love again.) He was ready for a fresh experience. But he never again thought of marriage.

VII

THE DELFINA MYSTERY

IN JUNE 1945, one month after World War II ended in Europe, Pauline Czernicka, a Polish musicologist, came forth with the startling news that she had found a treasure trove of letters by Chopin to Delfina Potocka, one of the famous Parisian beauties, known as a fascinating and highly gifted personality—and a pupil of Chopin. The autographs were incomplete and consisted of fifty-seven pieces of paper that were un-dated and nine that were dated. She read some of the contents over Polish radio. Excitement ran high. The novelist Jaroslaw Iwaszkiewicz, who later wrote a biography of the composer, called on her, as did Bronisław Sydow, editor of Chopin's correspondence. Naturally, both scholars demanded to see the original letters. "I no longer have the originals," she responded, "only the typescripts." Where were the origi-nals? She gave contradictory answers. She had given them to a French officer for safekeeping during the war. What was his name? She couldn't remember it. Then she said that she had sent them to Édouard Ganche, a French biographer of Chopin; Ganche testified that he had received nothing. No—the woman now changed her story again—she had given them to friends living in Bialystok. The Chopin Institute sent her there; she returned empty-handed, saying that the box containing the letters had been stolen.

At first the typescripts were accepted as copies of genuine letters, strange though some of them were. Chopin discussed musical matters in a few; others were love notes, passionate—not to say pornographic —in their sexual details. The scholars were inclined to give Mrs. Czernicka the benefit of the doubt, but when she spun one story after another, suspicion became general. Years later, Adam Harasowki accidentally discovered photocopies of a few fragments. They added to the general puzzlement, since they did seem to be in Chopin's handwriting and orthography. Then she announced that she had "found" further letters; so that in the end the total documents and fragments amounted to over one hundred; these successive "discoveries" made the matter all the more suspicious. Why would she publish some and hold back others? Could her dubious behavior be explained by the fact that she had stolen the letters and feared punishment? Did she withhold the originals because she feared that the new Communist government would confiscate them, declaring them "national property"? Nobody could offer a reasonable explanation, least of all Pauline Czernicka herself. At any rate, it soon became apparent that she was a psychopathic woman, the mother of a mentally retarded son, herself unstable, disturbed, and quite poor. Four years after coming into the international limelight, Pauline Czernicka committed suicide. The original letters were never found; the case remained unresolved.

If she forged the letters, she must have been a more skillful malefactor than her personality indicated. And what could have been her motive? The obvious motive, making money by selling them, will not serve. Even the most stupid forger must have realized that before the letters could be sold in Warsaw, let alone London, Paris, or New York, the originals would have to be shown and be subjected to minute scrutiny. Chopin letters fetch a high price.* Post–World War II, who would be gullible enough to buy a fake? There had been enough fakes around during the war to make any buyer super careful. Perhaps she was prompted merely by a mischievous desire for mystification, more probably the desire to make herself, an unimportant scholar, famous, producing sensational disclosures touching the life of a hero of her country. Or perhaps it was sheer madness, a sign of the same psychic abnormality which drove her to death.**

Delfina Potocka belonged to the "comfortable fugitives." She was Polish by birth, a daughter of the Komar family. She received a superb education—she spoke French, English, and Italian fluently—and at the

---

*Recently a good two-and-a-half-page Chopin letter of minor importance was sold for three thousand dollars.

**A. Harasowski, *The Skein of Legends Around Chopin* (Glasgow, 1967).

age of eighteen she was married to Count Mieczyslaw Potocki, the son
of a man who was considered a traitor to his country because he entered
into secret dealings with the Russian court. The Potockis were greatly
superior to the Komars in social rank. Mieczyslaw, born in their palace
of Tulczyn, a huge edifice around which the winds of the plain blew,
was handsome, gay, a libertine, and probably a sadist, possibly epileptic.
The marriage soon fell apart. Delfina returned to her family, who received her coldly—at all costs she should have avoided a scandal before
the tight-lipped society of Warsaw—and then she went to Paris, eventually to work out a separation with Mieczyslaw, who probably was glad
to get rid of her and pursue his own predilections. He settled an extremely generous allowance on her, 100,000 francs annually (which
today would have the purchasing power of $200,000). With it she was
able to live in great style as one of the glorious women of French
Romanticism—her looks, voice, musicality, and intelligence all fitted
the Romantic ideal. An expert in love's game, she counted among her
lovers the Count de Flahault, a Parisian Beau Brummel; the Duke of
Orléans, one of the sons of Louis Philippe and Dauphin of France; the
Duke of Montfort, nephew of Napoleon I; Sigismond Krasinski, one of
the important Polish poets; and, probably her last, the painter Hip-
polyte Delaroche, whose portrait of her as the Madonna is now in the
Wallace Collection in London.

Delacroix called her "the enchantress" and mentioned in his *Journal*
an evening spent with her at Chopin's home:

> March 30, 1849
>
> I have heard her sing twice before, and thought that I had never met
> with anything more perfect, especially the first time, when it was dusk,
> and the black velvet dress she was wearing, the arrangement of her hair,
> in fact everything about her . . . made me think she must be as ravish-
> ingly beautiful as her movements were graceful.

Balzac's Mme. Hanska was jealous of Delfina, and he assured her
that he cared nothing, absolutely nothing, about her. "Your scolding
. . . made me smile sadly."

The finest tributes to her were offered by Krasinski. She appeared
to him a woman

> . . . alive and strong, endowed with all the gifts that God has bestowed
> on Polish women, [but] ruined by Paris and London, by the Prince of
> Orléans and Monsieur Flahault, by a meretricious husband, and by that

most contemptible of vanities, the vanity of fashion. . . .

There remains in her a longing, lasting as a note intoned by a great singer, for a higher state, a luminous peace. Yet when the fire dies or slumbers, she becomes unbearably capricious, incapable of uttering two serious words, obsessed with the need to joke so that she may escape the boredom which gnaws at her. Then she is a pampered child or a Don Juan in petticoats, who has experienced everything and now cries, "Give me the moon—I want to find out if it tastes like good marzipan."

She was the kind of woman to whom it is easy to imagine Chopin could have been attracted. But was he? Did she respond? Were they lovers? We know no details, not even the supposed beginning of an affair, nor its end. How could they have managed to hide their intimacy in the gossip mill of Paris? Here lies the mystery.

Its solution could help us draw a more accurate portrait of Chopin. Delfina was not a woman easily won, nor was she the instigator of her affairs. Her contemporaries, such as Balzac and Krasinski, spoke of her aloofness. The latter compared her to a cold Greek statue, her eyes stern, and "only her lips seemed to promise pardon and reward to an audacious admirer." If Chopin proved to be "audacious" in wooing her, it changes the image of him as a man docile in his relationship to women, a "sexually repressed man-child" (to quote one biographer), a captive caught in a silken net. Other than those more than dubious letters, are there any indications that they may have been lovers? There are some:

Chopin first met her casually in Dresden. Ten days after his first concert in Paris he wrote to Kumelski that he was at dinner at "Madame Potocka, the pretty wife of Mieczyslaw." After that he mentioned several times being at Delfina's house. The husband had left Paris. In his early days in Paris Chopin seems to have turned to Delfina on many an evening. In turn, she visited him: he wrote to Julian Fontana (the letter is undated but can be placed in late 1832 or early 1833) inviting him to an evening at which Delfina would be present among others. It is clear that she had joined Chopin's circle.

A contemporary, Mieczyslaw Karlowicz, wrote (in *Souvenirs inédits sur F. Chopin*) that one evening when Chopin was imitating the voice and gestures of acquaintances, as he often did, she said to him: "Now it is my turn. Show me your impression of myself." Instead, he went to the piano and improvised in a "melancholy vein, demonstrating that he knew and understood her to the very core of her being, beneath the veils she assumed in front of the world."

He dedicated the F-minor Concerto, previously dedicated to his former love Constantia Gladkowska, to Delfina. It was published with this dedication in 1836. The change of dedication puzzled his father, who wrote him: "Owing, I think, to certain intrigues, the dedication was not given to the first person intended, so whom are you keeping it for? It surprises me that so far you have not had a chance to associate the fruit with its tree [i.e., dedicate the Concerto to someone who was concerned in its conception]: there must be some living obstacle in the way."

Later, in 1847, he dedicated to Delfina the D-flat-major Waltz (known popularly as the "Minute" Waltz). D flat—was this a repetition of his private erotic joke?

Chopin mentioned in a letter written to his family (April 19, 1847): "You know how I love her." This has been translated as "You know how fond of her I am." But the word Chopin uses is definitely the Polish word for "love" *(kocham)*. He was extremely reticent in speaking to his family of his relations with women. Even when writing to his intimate friends, he usually referred to "Mme. Sand," not "George" or "My love." The use of the word "love" here is exceptional.

While in England, Chopin noted in his diary (July 26, 1848): "600 francs in my father's snuffbox shaped like a lion. [They are] in a little purse, very precious to me, from Mme. Delfina Potocka." When he was dying, he took a piece of paper, wrote on it, *"Nella miseria,"* signed it, and gave it to Delfina. The quotation is of course from Dante: "There is no greater sorrow than to remember the time of happiness in misery." The words refer to Francesca da Rimini's tragic love. Two days before he died, Delfina visited him and at his request sang to him, accompanying herself, her voice choked by tears.

Delfina preserved the published copies of Chopin's compositions bearing annotations in his own hand, specially written for her use. She preserved as well Chopin's compositions written in her album. All those she turned over to Karol Mikuli, one of Chopin's students, who was preparing an edition of Chopin's works. The frequency of the annotations seems to indicate a close relationship.

In 1855, only six years after Chopin's death, one Jozef Mycielski wrote a letter to his wife, mentioning that Delfina had had many lovers, among them Chopin, Krasinski, and Delaroche. The last two are indisputable—why should the first be doubted? The writer said he had his information directly from a member of the Komar family.

The biographer Hoesick interviewed several persons who had known Chopin, among them one of his pupils, Emilia Hoffmann. She told him that when Chopin was with Delfina, "he was ready to wipe the dust off her shoes." However exaggerated Emilia's words are, their meaning is unmistakable. She could hardly have been talking of a "friendship."

In August 1837, Marie Potocka wrote to Balzac: "Do you often see my charming sister-in-law Delfina? When she was here she was awfully sad. No doubt she had suffered much! She confessed herself discouraged, disillusioned, disappointed in everything. But— Women are not sobered by life except by its passing. Like the leaves of a tree, their illusions are not swept away except by winter; summer storms will not do it." Was Delfina sad over the end of the affair, which may have terminated just then, when Chopin met George Sand?

On the other hand, there are indications which throw doubt on an intimacy. Delfina punctiliously preserved the correspondence with her poet-lover Krasinski. He wrote her an avalanche of epistles, covering almost two thousand pages! She dated, ticketed, and wrapped them neatly. Would she have treated Chopin's letters so differently? Chopin may have asked her to destroy them. A perhaps spurious letter attributed to him said: "Destroy my letters, because if someone were to get hold of them you would be compromised and I might get into no end of trouble and embarrassment."*

A need for secrecy may have existed. An attempt was made to reconcile Delfina to her husband. She joined him for a brief period, but the reconciliation did not work and Delfina returned to Paris. Very likely, financial negotiations about Delfina's allowance were going on.

Krasinski was a furiously jealous lover. His letters abound with bitter (almost psychopathic) accusations, many of them unjustified. Never, not once, does Krasinski mention Chopin as a predecessor. He knew about her other lovers. Is it likely that he was ignorant of Chopin's love?

Neither Liszt nor Marie d'Agoult, who had much to retail about George Sand, mentions the Delfina affair. Liszt wrote: "Chopin assiduously frequented Mme. Komar and her two daughters, Ludmilla de

---

*Published by Sydow in the 1947 edition of Chopin's letters but eliminated in the 1955 edition, and omitted in the Hedley collection.

Beauveau and the Countess Delfina Potocka, whose beauty, indescribable grace, and spirit made her one of the most admired queens of the salon." That is all. Was Liszt being discreet? That wasn't like him.

The only letter Delfina wrote Chopin of which we possess the full manuscript reached him three months before he died. She addressed him as "Dear M. Chopin." The letter does not read as one penned by a woman who has been his beloved. It is concerned and sympathetic, not intimate. To be sure, the letter may have been carefully written not to reveal any secrets. She knew that Chopin was very ill, perhaps too ill to read it himself. She knew—"do not write yourself"—that Chopin might give the letter to somebody—"Mme. Etienne"—to answer. A sad and wintry spirit pervades the letter. Though she meant to comfort a very ill man, her own unhappiness emerges.

> Aix-la-Chapelle, 16 [July 1849]
>
> Dear M. Chopin:
> I do not wish to trouble you with a long letter but I cannot remain in the dark regarding your health and your plans for the future. Do not write yourself, but ask Mme. Etienne [the concierge] or that kind old woman who dreams about cutlets, to inform me of the state of your strength, your chest, your choking attacks, etc., etc. You really must think seriously of Nice for the winter. Mme. Augustine Potocka, in her reply to my letter, said she will make every effort to obtain a permit for Mme. Andrzejewicz [Jedrzejewicz—his sister Louise] but that the difficulties are enormous in that unhappy country. It grieves me to think of your being left alone in your illness and depression; please send me a few lines—to Aix-la-Chapelle, poste restante. I would like to hear whether that Jew [Dr. Fraenkel] made his appearance, and whether he did you any good. Things are sad and dull here, but for me life flows on monotonously wherever I am. When I think of what I have already had to go through, it would be enough if only life would pass without worse sufferings and trials. Somehow life has not smiled on me either in this world. Every individual whom I have ever wished well has always repaid me with ingratitude or various other *tribulations.* In short, life is simply one huge discord. God protect you, dear M. Chopin. I hope to see you at the beginning of October at the latest.

These portraits of George Sand and Chopin by
Eugene Delacroix were originally a single painting, done in 1838, and cut apart sometime after
1875. Sand is standing near Chopin's right shoulder while he is playing the piano. (Sand: *Musée
d'Ordrupgaardsamlingen, Copenhagen, Den-
mark;* Chopin: *Musée du Louvre*)

Chopin. Pencil drawing
by George Sand (1841)

Solange Sand Clésinger.
(Courtesy R. Lalance)

This portrait of Chopin by Nicolas Eustache Maurin (1799–1850) is dated 1845. Maurin, member of a large family of artists, was a highly regarded French portrait painter. The picture belonged to Marie de Rozières, passed into a private collection after her death, is now in Warsaw and has not been reproduced previously.

At some time, somebody wrote on the back of the picture: "Countess Rozières (*demoiselle*), whose parents were ruined in the Revolution, was a talented pianist and teacher. Being a passionate admirer of Chopin, she hoped to take lessons from him and was saving up for this purpose; she knew that a lesson cost 50 frs. She called on the great pianist and he liked her playing, but he thought the lessons would be too expensive for her. She insisted. 'Are you patient?' he asked. 'Yes, I am very patient.' 'Then go with me to see my friend (George Sand), whose daughter is a *hellion*. If you can cope with her, I will give you a lesson for each lesson you give her.'"

She succeeded, and became a friend of the Sands. Chopin became very fond of her. He found out that she brewed excellent chocolate: he would have her prepare it and tell his valet to bring it from the "Cafe Rozières."

Chopin. Pencil drawing
by Franz Winterhalter (1847)

Chopin daguerreotype
by L. A. Bisson (ca. 1849)

Caricature of Chopin by Pauline Viardot. *(Courtesy Mme. M. Maurois)*

Caricature of Chopin and Pauline Viardot drawn by Maurice Sand. The text means: "That's how Liszt plays—not necessary for accompanying a voice." (*Courtesy Mme. M. Maurois*)

Paul Delaroche used Delfina Potocka as a model. *(The Wallace Collection, London)*

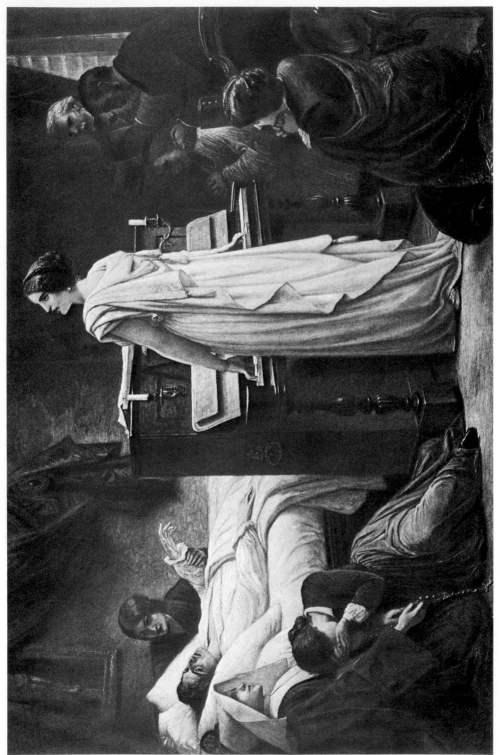

Death of Chopin. From the painting by Felix Joseph Barrias

(2)

There remains the question of the "Czernicka letters." Are they of any use? Those of which nothing but typescripts exist can be judged for authenticity only by internal evidence, such as stylistic inconsistencies with genuine Chopin letters, wrong dates, etc. The photographic fragments can and have been examined graphologically. Yet these examinations do not seem to have been undertaken quite dispassionately, and the results are contradictory. For example, evidence presented in 1961 at a conference in Nieborow, Poland, led to the conclusion that the letters were forgeries. Yet the tone of the discussions implies political pressure, the purpose of which would clearly have been to excise any warts on the face of a national idol. On the other hand, an examination undertaken in 1973 by the "Criminalistic Laboratory, University of Warsaw," offered elaborate proof that the letters were "written by Frederic Chopin without doubt."

Let us review a few of the pros and cons, as they were advanced by different scholars:

Arguments that the letters are forgeries

Counterarguments

The two or three erotic letters are extremely prurient, one speaking of "the fun we've had with your little hole." (This letter has never been published, but when the poet Wierzynski was writing his biography, published in New York in 1949 and bearing the endorsement of Arthur Rubinstein, he showed a few friends a transcript of it.) In another letter Chopin voices the rather childish theory that spending himself on a woman sucks him dry of inspiration and that his absorption in her has left unborn many a nocturne and mazurka. Again, he speaks of "your sweetest little D-flat major."

Casimir Kozniewski, a Polish scholar, writes: "A Chopin writing such letters to a beautiful woman seems closer to me, more human, more amusing and real, and in every way more attractive than a morose Chopin wearing a chastity belt." However delicate Chopin's nature may appear—and he certainly was not all that ethereal—however reticent he was most of his life, it is perfectly possible that an intense erotic attraction made him break out in frankly amorous language. We have Mozart's famous filthy letters to his cousin and to his wife, and surely no one would characterize Mozart as

When she returns, "for a whole week you won't be able to tear me away from the little D-flat major." It is said that Delfina no longer can have children: "Grass does not grow on well-trodden paths." He wants to have a child by her. Such sexual frankness is totally inconsistent with Chopin's reserved nature.

coarse. Beethoven made bathroom jokes while composing the *Missa Solemnis*. Goethe, Mark Twain, Balzac, Edith Wharton, have left testimony of their pleasure in prurience. It is naïve to believe that Chopin was above it all. Nevertheless, it seems to be difficult for the sentimental school of biography to swallow the idea that the author of the Nocturnes sometimes used language such as: "If the Preludes are in print it is a dirty trick by Probst [a publisher]. Shit on him! When I get back there will be no more walking arm-in-arm. Scoundrel Germans! Jews, crooks, swine, sharks—I leave you to finish the list." (Letter to Fontana, Marseilles, April 25, 1839) In describing people he disliked, Chopin used the word *gnoy*, meaning "manure" but standing for "shit." His father reproached him.

Phrases are used which were current only after World War I. Words are used which Chopin did not ordinarily employ.

This is debatable: Chopin's vocabulary was large. Writing to Delfina, he may well have used unusual expressions.

There is a reference to a talk with Norwid, dated 1836. Norwid was then fifteen years old and had not left Poland.

It is possible that the dating is wrong. It often is in Chopin's correspondence.

Supposedly around 1835 Chopin mentions that he is sending some books to one of his pupils, including "a good selection of . . . Krasinski." It could only have been the *Undivine Comedy*, which, however, was first published anonymously. Could Chopin have known who the author was?

The dating of the letter is only approximate, but even at that time the authorship was an open secret among the Polish colony and Chopin could well have known it.

He discusses music with Delfina and writes about Beethoven, Bach, Liszt's playing of the Mazurkas, etc. He was not in the habit of expressing his ideas on music in writing. Few of his letters contain musical commentary.

That is no proof against his doing it once with a woman whom he loved and who was a brilliant musician.

The letters state one or two prophecies—one, that Schumann would go mad. It sounds like a prophecy after the fact. Schumann's madness did not manifest itself until the early 1850s, when Chopin was dead.

Such a prophecy might have been made by anybody who read the turgid conversations of Florestan and Eusebius. Chopin's phrasing is: "Schumann's articles are idle talk and nonsense. . . . He'll go crazy, I predict, and will sign my name to it." The phrase "I predict . . ." is a Polish idiom, something like our "You can bet your bottom dollar." He used the same phrase writing about George Sand's son, Maurice.

The Hilton Report

We felt that a fresh, unbiased examination of the fragments would be useful and in 1977 we asked Mr. Ordway Hilton of New York to subject them to graphological analysis. Mr. Hilton has had long experience in examining documents in court cases, such as disputed testaments, contracts, etc. He is a member of the American Academy of Forensic Sciences and the American Society of Questioned Document Examiners. He agreed to undertake the work and spent many weeks on it, "because of the intrinsic fascination of the challenge." His full report is given in Appendix 2. The sum and substance of it is this:

1. Two of the fragments are unquestionably spurious. They have been pasted together by snipping words from authentic letters and assembling them to form a message.

2. Two other fragments seem to be authentic, though in one of these two "there is evidence . . . that outlines of letters and words have been traced with a second writing instrument." (Numbers 55 and 87b)

3. One fragment is, in Hilton's "best judgment . . . Chopin's original writing." (87a)

(Letters referred to here are given in Appendix 1, as are some other "Delfina letters.")

What can be concluded? Evidently, we have been left a mixed bag of truth and falsehood. Pauline Czernicka was unquestionably a liar, possibly a thief. That is as apparent from the direct evidence of the false letters as from the indirect evidence of her behavior. It is possible to theorize what happened. Pauline did discover certain letters or fragments, probably in the possession of Delfina's relatives,* copied or stole them. When she saw what excitement her find created, she did what other dishonest scholars have done—she began manufacturing evidence. She could not step out of the light of publicity; the hoard of Chopiniana grew outrageously. The result of her forgeries is that *all* the evidence must be regarded with suspicion. No doubt some of the fragments are genuine. But as Mr. Hilton wrote in an accompanying letter (April 5, 1977):

> In respect to the material of letter 55 and letter 15, there is very little to question that Chopin wrote these letters except that the photographic print we have fails to reveal any paper background. Since we are dealing with material that can be shown in some instances to have been assembled with scissors and paste, I am a little hesitant to give these two documents an absolute clear bill of health, but they are probably parts of actual letters written by him.

Whatever the extent of the forgery, the presence of *some* genuine material indicates that Chopin wrote Delfina certain letters, which have been lost or willfully destroyed.

That proves that a relationship between Delfina and Chopin did exist. When one adds this fact to other indications, the impression grows that this relationship was one of intimacy and love. And although one must be wary of anecdote, one cannot treat tradition lightly. The tradition here is too strong. It is significant that Hoesick, when working on his biography, wrote to the man in whose home Delfina died and to his niece to try to dig out more information about the "time when Chopin was one of the lucky predecessors of Krasinski." Half a century after Chopin's death the tradition was alive. Hoesick was investigating it: he believed that some letters existed. This was at a time when Pauline Czernicka was a baby and hardly able to commit trickery.

That "the enchantress" Delfina Potocka, with her beauty, her talent, her unhappy marriage, the sadness of her life—all her children died in

---

*Pauline Czernicka claimed that she was a relative of the Komar family.

infancy—should have had her choice of extraordinary men is easy to believe. If she chose Chopin it is a tribute to him. If Chopin chose Delfina it is a tribute to her.

Yet in absence of incontrovertible proof, the Delfina-Chopin affair must remain in the realm of conjecture. Unlike that love which possessed him in his central years—his affair with George Sand—definite documentary evidence is lacking.

VIII

CHOPIN'S DARK LADY

AUCASSIN AND NICOLETTE, Héloïse and Abélard, Tristan and Isolde, Troilus and Cressida . . . Chopin and George Sand almost belong to the pantheon of Love, the real story having long been lifted into a special mythology. We assume that it was an idyll played in a castle in Spain —a classic chronicle, in the melting mood. Yet however *kitschig* are the souvenir post cards sold in Valldemosa, the reality lacks the sentimental sweep, the tragic end, the lofty renunciation. Here truth is smaller than fiction.

In other respects the truth is more fictional than fiction. That these two opposites—the defiantly free-wheeling Sand and the fundamentally "correct" Chopin, the rebelliously demonstrative woman and the undemonstrative man who detested excessive rhetoric, that muddy torrent of a writer and that clear brook of a composer—that these two should have found satisfaction seems right out of a novel by Stendhal, possibly to be entitled *The Red and the Ivory*. Novelistic, too, are the different interpretations which it is possible to assign to the two protagonists. Much has been written about their intimacy, though more about Sand's role than Chopin's, as it is filtered through the prism of the lovers' personalities, one writer embracing the belief that Sand never really loved Chopin, having trapped him "like an insect in her web"; another, that Chopin exercised a deleterious influence on Sand, acting as "her evil genius"; another, that Sand found her only emotional fulfillment with the composer; another, that Sand, playing fast and loose, hastened Chopin's death; and so on to the extraordinary theory, voiced by Édouard Ganche *(Souffrances de Frédéric Chopin)*, that Chopin was unable to perform the sexual act. Space for such a range of opinion is provided by Chopin's taciturnity on the one hand and Sand's dissimulations on the other.

What did Chopin see when he first looked on Sand? The date and place of that meeting are uncertain. Sand, always curious about the interesting personalities of her time, had wanted to meet the celebrated composer and had asked Liszt, who at the moment was fast friends with Chopin, to bring about the occasion. It happened probably in November 1836, either at Chopin's or at Custine's house, or at the Hôtel de France, where Liszt and Marie d'Agoult, returned from Geneva shortly before, had rented an apartment which Marie at once turned into a literary-musical salon. Chopin played. Sand, dressed in a startling Turkish costume with wide purple pantaloons, her black hair bound by a red scarf, sat by the fireplace, smoking cigars one after the other, but not before asking the company whether smoking bothered them. (It bothered Chopin, but evidently he did not say so.) Present were Liszt and Marie d'Agoult, Mickiewicz, and Sainte-Beuve. George Sand sat silent, seemingly absorbed in the music, her dark stern eyes, now and then lit by the flickering of the fire, fixed on the player. Chopin's first impression was negative: this was not the kind of woman Maria or Marcellina or Delfina was. Yet she did impress him. In December he wrote to his family:

> I met a great celebrity: Madame Dudevant, known by the name of George Sand. I don't find her face sympathetic and she didn't at all please me. Something about her estranges me.

This is confirmed by a note from Hiller to Liszt:

> One day at your house you gathered all the flower of French literature. Certainly George Sand could not fail to be present. When we went home Chopin said to me: "What an unsympathetic woman! Is she really a woman? Almost, almost I doubt it."

On December 13, a little more than a month after their first meeting, Chopin invited a "couple of friends" to his house. It turned out to be a memorable evening for more than a couple of friends, the guests including Liszt and Marie, the great tenor Nourrit, the pianist Pixis, Custine, Eugène Sue, Grzymala, Heine, Dr. Matuszynski, Count Potocki and his brother. Liszt played, Chopin performed a travesty on the melodies of Meyerbeer's *Huguenots,* Nourrit sang Schubert. Chopin invited Sand, and this time she appeared as a woman, dressed in the Polish colors, white and red, which set off her pale complexion. Again she remained silent.

Not long after, Sand invited Chopin to her country house, Nohant. Chopin refused.

We have many portraits of Sand, several from the Chopin years, and they differ as widely as do her contemporaries' opinions about her. However good a likeness these portraits capture, and whatever their artistic merit, it is evident that the sitter was somebody to challenge a painter's eye. In one superb painting by Delacroix she appears as a sibyl in a trance, plump and dreamy, while in another she was portrayed listening to Chopin play, her arms crossed, her pose devotional, her profile beautiful. This portrait was originally the left half of a painting, of which the right half is the profound and tragic study of Chopin's face. Apparently Delacroix was never satisfied with the portrait of Sand and kept the picture in his studio, planning to work on it further. He never did, and after his death somebody—presumably an avaricious art dealer —cut the canvas in two, with the result that the Chopin section is now in the Louvre, the Sand in Copenhagen. What was long considered the standard portrait, Sand in a tall mannish top hat tilted at a provocative angle, has now been proved to be neither by Delacroix nor of George Sand.* Auguste Charpentier painted her in a proud pose as in a portrait by Ingres. In a drawing by the Italian artist Luigi Calamatta she looks out-and-out ugly, her expression that of an indolent young *Hausfrau.*

The writers who knew her could agree even less. De Musset considered her "the most womanly woman I have ever known"—and he knew plenty. Flaubert remarked: "One needed to know her as I knew her to realize how much of the feminine there was in this great man." Hugo referred to her as "that man who calls herself George Sand." Baudelaire: "She is stupid, she is ponderous, she is long-winded. Her moral ideas have the depth of judgment and delicacy of feeling of those of concierges and kept women." Elizabeth Barrett Browning came to kneel at her feet and to call her "the finest female genius of any country or age." (Where did that leave Jane Austen and the Brontës?) "You will

---

*Curtis Cate in his recent biography says it was painted by Couture and may be a portrait of Sand's son, Maurice, but he is doubtful of even that attribution.

be the Lord Byron of France," Chateaubriand wrote to her after reading *Lélia*. Balzac, a devoted friend, called her a *"vache à écrire,"* a
writing cow, when he was angry at her, but when they were at peace,
as during his visit to Nohant when she taught him to smoke the water-
pipe, he called her "this nightingale in her nest . . . great-hearted,
generous, devout, and *chaste.*"

The best description of her was Heine's, written in 1854:

> Her forehead is not high, her delicious chestnut brown locks reach her
> shoulders. Her eyes are somewhat languid, at least they are not brilliant,
> and their fire may have been dimmed by many tears, or may have
> consumed itself in her works, which have lighted conflagrations in all
> the world, have illumined many a dark prison cell, but also set on fire
> some temples of innocence. The author of *Lélia* has quiet, gentle eyes
> which remind one neither of Sodom nor of Gomorrah. She has neither
> the emancipated nose of an eagle nor a witty little snub nose. It is an
> ordinary straight nose. A good-natured smile usually plays around her
> lips, but it is by no means provocative. Only her somewhat protruding
> lower lip suggests sexuality. Her shoulders are beautiful, no, magnifi-
> cent. Ditto, arms and hands, small like her feet. Her breasts I leave to
> others to describe, I confess incompetence. Her body is a bit thick and
> seems too short. Only the head bears witness to her idealism and re-
> minds me of the finest examples of Greek art. In this connection one of
> our friends likened her to the Venus de Milo statue in the lower hall of
> the Louvre. Yes, George Sand is as beautiful as the Venus de Milo; she
> even excels her in some respects—for example, she is much younger.
> . . . She speaks naturally and with charm. As to her singing—not a trace!
> At best she sings with the bravura of a *grisette* who hasn't yet had her
> breakfast. . . . She possesses nothing of the bubbling *esprit* of her compa-
> triots, and nothing of their verbosity, either. Her silence, however, is not
> due to modesty or her absorption in somebody else's concern. She is
> monosyllabic because of pride, not thinking it worth while to waste her
> intellect on you, or because of self-centeredness, taking in the best of
> your thoughts to incorporate them later in one of her books. That
> George Sand is miserly in conversation, never giving, always taking—
> that Alfred de Musset pointed out to me years ago. Never does she say
> anything "smart": indeed, she is one of the least smart Frenchwomen
> I know. . . .
>
> She endowed our much beloved Frederic Chopin with a good deal
> of worldly wisdom. This great composer and pianist was long her *cava-
> liere servente*, she dismissed him before his death. To be sure, his office
> had for some time become a sinecure.
>
> *Lutezia I*

Sand was constantly surprising, constantly unpredictable. "I would rather play dominoes in a café than spend an hour of the afternoon alone—alone, what horror!" she wrote to Sainte-Beuve; yet she locked herself up for six or seven hours daily, covering twenty pages with her hasty scrawl. Nothing could interfere with the work she did—alone. Her will power and discipline combined with an inborn energy to produce her vast output, some sixty novels, 104 published works in all, not including some nineteen thousand letters. She would recover from such labor by going at dawn to the river, where she would hang her dress on a tree and, clad in her chemise, "lie on the sand with the water up to my chin, smoking a cigar and looking at the reflection of the moon in the stream around my knees." She was forty-two when she did this; at about the same age she could still walk ten kilometers, climb a mountain, or gallop off to join a lover. "My body needs movement as others need repose."

"I always ate in a hurry, thinking of other things, a long séance at the table made me sick"—but she was a superb hostess and her domestic arrangements at Nohant were ordered with military precision. At 7 A.M. the servants lit the fire in the dining room, at exactly 5 P.M. the gong sounded for dinner; the guest rooms were always warm, glasses of sugar water were provided before retiring, and in the hall there was a mailbox for the letters the guests wrote or to communicate any wish they might want to express.* She entertained constantly and generously, and indeed she was generous in all respects, even when she didn't have money, which was often. Though she earned a great deal—about a million dollars by the time she was sixty—she spent more than she earned. When her carpenter died of typhoid, she took charge of his three little children. She begged the actress Marie Dorval in an eloquent letter** to contribute her services to a charity affair she was organizing for the benefit of the Polish exiles. "When humanity struggles, suffers and bleeds, I care very little about my Muse and my lyre." She meant it, at the moment.

She loved playing elaborate jokes. Musset and she gave a dinner party to which she invited a juggler as a guest of honor, pretending he was an important British diplomat. When he was asked what he thought

---

*One night Sainte-Beuve asked for a comb. He was given his choice of thirty the next morning.
**The manuscript is in the Morgan Library.

of the problem of the "European balance of power," he spun a plate in the air to illustrate, until Musset poured a jug of water over him. When a lawyer from a neighboring village insisted on making her acquaintance, she dressed up her maid to impersonate her. Everybody had a pet name: she and her children were the Piffoels ("long-noses"), Liszt and Marie "The Fellows" (in English), Chopin "Chop" or "Chip-Chip" or "Chopinet." Yet she could sink into depressions during which she would lash out at her friends and lovers and could be maddened by two words of criticism from a provincial scribbler: "I have never acquired a raincoat to protect myself."

Other garments she had aplenty. We picture her in those mannish trousers, but in point of fact she wore them seldom, and hardly ever in middle age. She loved silks and finery and jewels, and though she scorned the Parisian modes, she paid great attention to her appearance, dressing now flamboyantly, now soberly and elegantly. Chopin himself was enlisted in choosing dresses. He did so willingly, writing to her from Paris:

> The dress you ordered is of black levantine of the finest quality. I chose it myself, as you ordered. The dressmaker has taken it away with your instructions. She considers the material very beautiful, simple but very suitable. I think you will be pleased with it.

As a mother she was half good: she adored and spoiled her son Maurice, but she could summon but scant love for her daughter, Solange—whom she dressed as a boy when she was little—and even that love weakened as Solange grew up, rebellious and difficult.

She was fanatically self-devoted both as woman and artist; therefore she could be devoted to weak men who looked up to her. It was her friends who made the mistakes, her lovers who were found wanting, her editors who did not value her sufficiently, while she was always in the right, forever in the right. When, in her autobiographical books—*Lettres d'un voyageur, Histoire de ma vie, Journal intime*—she twisted the truth, she was not lying: as she was writing she believed what she was setting down. Yet in these pages she was not above falsifying some letters in her anxiety to justify herself.

The readers of *Indiana,* the novel which scored her first great success, believed that she wanted to abolish marriage. She did not at all. She did want to abolish the double standard and to claim for women the right of free love which men claimed for themselves. She also preached universal suffrage, taxing the rich, and other utopian ideas, all rather vague and derivative. Frances Trollope, in *Paris and the Parisians*, published in 1835, the year before Sand met Chopin, wrote:

> It is impossible that she should write as she has done without possessing some of the finest qualities of human nature; but she is and has been tossed about in that whirlpool of unsettled principles, deformed taste, and exaggerated feeling, in which the distempered spirits of the day delight to bathe and disport themselves, and she has been stained and bruised therein.

It was her often self-conscious revolt against the bourgeois standard which shocked Frances Trollope and it was her explicit treatment of the erotic in *Lélia* which helped to make her the celebrated author of her time. Taine said that after reading her novels, "one could write the moral and philosophical history of the century." Her work was overrated. Heine thought her greater than Victor Hugo. Dostoevsky and Thackeray looked up to her, Henry James and later Marcel Proust read her eagerly. Nowadays she is little read, even in France. Yet her personality still fascinates.

Why did so many men of merit fall in love with her, whose beauty could not vie with that of a Marie d'Agoult, a Cristina Belgioioso, a Marie Dorval? Curtis Cate in his biography says that the number of her lovers "does not reach twenty," but others put the number higher. Of course there were those eyes, which Musset called "serpent eyes"; she did not use them for overt flirtation and that made her all the more desirable. When she wrote explicitly about the man-woman relationship, when she analyzed the play of the sexes, she or rather her work threw a glow over her own person, a blush which excited a man's imagination. Her fame was enlarged by scandal; a man was titillated. Paradoxically, she who preached equality could be submissive and compliant: she brushed the frown from her lover's face. She sat on the floor while he sat in the armchair.

Her lovers were literary material to her—Oscar Wilde said, "Like Goethe, George Sand had to live her romances before she could write them"—and even in bed some portion of her remained at the writing desk. Her abandon was an abandon of words. After her break with Musset she could write: "My body, that warm and supple body—you will no longer hover over it and give it new life as Elijah did to the dead child," but her unhappiness, while real, was as well "novelistic," her cries carefully shaped for posterity.

Because she could not give herself completely—always observing herself and analyzing—she was never satisfied completely by any of her lovers. She was to repeat throughout her life what she wrote to Dr. Pagello, the lover she took while still with Musset: "Alas! . . . I have sought perfection so ardently without finding it. Is it you, is it at last you, who will realize my dream?" She got rid of Pagello soon after.

Why was she attracted to Chopin? The outward reasons are easily perceived: he was handsome, well mannered, well dressed, a charming physical apparition. He was detached, undemonstrative, not to say aloof: that must have intrigued her. Like herself he was a celebrity— and nothing interests a celebrity so much as another celebrity. She responded emotionally to music and played the piano tolerably; she was of course quite aware of Chopin's genius. Liszt, who as a social lion was equally renowned, was firmly caged by Marie d'Agoult; in the beginning it may have amused her to capture a similar king of the artistic jungle. Yet a deeper force pushed her toward him; she felt at once that here was a man who needed a shelter she could create. He was six years younger than she, and far less experienced. Here again, as in her love for Musset, she could be mother and mistress.

She took the lead in forming the relationship. She sent him a note: *"On vous adore"* (cleverly using the impersonal form), to which Marie Dorval—with whom Sand may have had a lesbian relationship—added the personal scribble: *"Et moi aussi! et moi aussi! et moi aussi!"* It made an impression on Chopin, for he pasted the note in an album as a keepsake. Yet it was still some time before they became intimate.

Why was he drawn to Sand? Obviously, she attracted him sexually, that attraction being so strong that at first it expressed itself in dislike, then in denial, before it invaded him completely. He was as dissimilar from her as can be; great hatreds and great loves may be born from such opposites. He was first challenged, then enraptured by her mystic quality: "an abbess in a faraway land," Musset had called her. Chopin responded to the enigma; she was different from those perfect creatures who seemed to have stepped from the pages of a fashion journal, not a hair out of place. Her fame was great, greater at the time than his, but before him she appeared with folded hands. Nevertheless, as he soon felt, she, being strong, would lend him strength. She was a fellow artist and as such as revolutionary and unorthodox in words as he in notes. He felt that kinship.

In short, she was there, willing, famous, a romantic woman interestingly illuminated by the light of an irregular reputation, creative, attractive—and somebody he was free to love.

(2)

Enough of Chopin's work had by now been published—such as the Scherzo Opus 20, the Ballade Opus 23, the Twelve Etudes, Opus 25 (dedicated to Marie d'Agoult)—for him to be offered an extraordinary invitation, that is, to become "Pianist to the Imperial Russian Court." The offer was instigated by Pozzo di Borgo, the Czar's ambassador in Paris. It was characteristic of Chopin that he refused the honor, writing openly to Pozzo: "Even if I did not take part in the Revolution of 1830, my sympathies were with those who did. Therefore I consider myself an exile: it is the only title to which I am entitled."

He did accept another invitation that summer. Camille Pleyel invited Chopin to accompany him and his wife, Marie-Félicité, to London. Marie-Félicité was a nymphomaniac with whom Berlioz had at one time been in love; her husband was a good pianist, an indifferent composer, a music publisher, and a manufacturer of first-rate pianos.* He had become wealthy and he was able to make the excursion luxurious. The three went to the opera, visited Hampton Court, Richmond, Brighton, and other tourist attractions. But the skies were dark and Chopin complained to Julian Fontana—who had become friend, pupil, and the kind of general factotum that every artist likes to have around—writing of London's "gray mud":

[London, July 1837]
Huge urinals, but all the same nowhere to have a proper piss! As for the English women, the horses, the palaces, the carriages, the wealth, the splendor, the space, the trees—everything from soap to razors—it's all extraordinary, all uniform, all very proper, all well-washed BUT as black as a nobleman's ass! Let me give you a kiss—on the *face*.

It is probable that the London interval came opportunely for Chopin; it served to put a distance between himself and George Sand, in

---

*Later Camille Pleyel got a separation from his promiscuous wife and lived with an English girl, Emma Osborn, who was a great admirer of Chopin.

which he could probe his feelings toward her. It is certain that as summer passed into autumn and winter Sand was in Chopin's mind, and he in hers. Slowly they neared each other. By January she wrote to d'Agoult confessing, half seriously, half jokingly, her wish to see him again "because Sopin is very *gentil"* (in English French).

What she wanted she pursued. Sand remained in Paris in the spring of 1838, while her lover Mallefille remained at Nohant with the children. As often as she could—she was heavily involved in a lawsuit with her husband and behind in the delivery of a novel—she saw Chopin. On May 8 she had herself invited to Custine's house, where Chopin played and Duprez sang selections from Gluck's *Orfeo* before a salonful of Romantics: the Victor Hugos were there, as were Charles Nodier, Jules Janin, the novelist Sophie Gay, and Heine. A few days after, Sand managed to snare Chopin for an evening at which *she* was the hostess. To Delacroix:

> [Paris, May 12, 1838]
> My dear Lacroix: I leave tomorrow at 5 A.M. I don't want to leave without having bid you farewell and without telling you that your *Médée* is magnificent, superb, exciting. You are really quite a master dauber! To tempt you to come tonight, I'll tell you that Chopin will play for us in limited company, with his elbows on the piano, which is when he is truly sublime. Come at midnight if you don't go to bed early and if you should meet any of my acquaintants, say nothing to them, because Chopin is dreadfully afraid of *Welches* [meaning "barbarians"]. If you don't come remember me and love me a little. G.S.

By that time, May 1838, Sand and Chopin had become lovers, exchanging their first embraces, as yet uncertain of the permanence of the new relationship. Yet it soon assumed for both a deeper significance than the kind of bedroom excursion most of their friends undertook. It became serious for Sand, as she recognized the seriousness of her lover. Chopin appealed to all that was pensive and profound, all that was tender and sensitive, in her nature; while he looked up to the stellar woman and knew that she would understand him beyond all explanation which could be passed in words. She loved him—her actions prove that, even if we are inclined to discount her words—and he loved her because she offered him all of herself, for once forgetting literature. For so great a prize he needed to, and he could, overcome his horror of notoriety and scandal.

She must soon have desired a permanent and open connection with her lover. At the end of May she wrote to Albert Grzymala, their benevolent confidant, from Nohant, whereto she had returned from Paris in a hurry because of her son's illness. This letter, covering thirty-two pages, is an amazing document and has been most contradictorily judged. It was written some two weeks after Sand wrote to her stepsister: "My dear sister, pardon my silence, I am most culpable in that respect. I don't write three letters a year." (There are extant 157 letters from that year alone!) Comments on her letter range from "This letter suffices to refute forever the assertion of her enemies that she was a hypocrite" to "This woman reveals in this letter that she practiced duplicity like hygiene" to "It shows all the trump cards of her game" to "The frankness, the honesty, is so unmasked as to appear stark naked." The letter is too long an effusion to be quoted in full. What is its essence?

She seeks Grzymala's counsel about continuing and intensifying her relationship with Chopin. She has no wish to interfere, to take him away, to appear as *femme fatale:* she knows about Maria Wodzinska. But:

> This young lady whom he wants or ought, or thinks he ought, to love, is she the right one to secure his happiness or is she likely to deepen his sufferings and melancholy? I am not asking whether he loves her or whether she returns his love, or whether he loves her more than me. I have a pretty good notion, judging by my own feelings, of what must be going on inside him. What I want to know is which of the *two of us* he must forget or give up, if he is to have any peace or happiness or indeed any life at all, for his nature seems too unstable and too frail to be able to stand up to great anguish. I don't want to play the part of the evil spirit. . . . I would never have bent down to breathe the scent of a flower intended for some other altar.

Nor would Chopin have surrendered to her had he known that she was "as good as married" to a "noble creature," Mallefille, who is "like a piece of soft wax." Such were the obstacles. But:

> But I can, without forswearing myself, perform [my role] in two distinct ways: the first would be to keep as far as possible from Chopin, to avoid trying to occupy his thoughts and never to find myself alone with him; the second would be to do the opposite and come as close as possible to him without causing Mallefille any misgivings. I could slip into his

thoughts when he is at peace with the world, I could from time to time permit a chaste embrace whenever it pleased the wind of Heaven to lift us up and carry us to the skies. . . .

If his spirit, which is *excessively,* perhaps *crazily* or perhaps wisely, scrupulous, will not allow itself to love two different beings in two different ways; if the one week that I may spend with him during each season is likely to prevent his being happy at home for the rest of the year—then, yes, in that case I swear that I will do my best to make him forget me. I shall adopt the second method if you tell me one of two things: either that his domestic happiness can and must be achieved by means of a few hours of chaste passion and gentle poetry; or that happiness as a family man is out of the question for him and that marriage or any similar union would be the graveyard of this artist soul. . . .

She continues at great length in self-justification: if she does play two roles, she is yet faithful! After this equivocation she confesses that she is "disturbed and frightened at the effect this little fellow [Chopin] had on me" and that:

I no longer felt the same tenderness toward poor M. when I saw him again. It is certain that since he returned to Paris (you must have seen him) instead of impatiently awaiting his arrival and being sad when he is not there I suffer less and breathe more freely. . . .

There was yet another matter of which she had to speak to Grzymala frankly. She noticed that Chopin seemed to regard physical union with some fear and distaste. How contrary such a view was to her ideas!

He seemed to despise (in the manner of a religious prude) the coarser side of human nature and to blush for temptations he had had, and to fear to soil our love by a further ecstasy. I have always loathed this way of looking at the final embrace of love. . . .

Can there ever be love without a single kiss, and a kiss of love without sensual pleasure? *To scorn the flesh* can only have a wise and useful meaning for creatures who are nothing but *flesh;* but when two people love each other it is not the word *scorn* but *respect* that should be used when they abstain. In any case those were not his actual words. He said, I think, that "certain actions" might spoil our memories. It was foolish of him to say that, wasn't it? And can he mean it? Tell me, what wretched woman has left him with such impressions of physical love? Poor angel. They should hang all women who make vile in men's eyes that which in all creation is most holy and most worthy of respect, the divine mystery, the sublimest and most serious act of universal life. . . .

With all its casuistry, the letter is neither a tissue of hypocrisy nor a game. Though her eloquence ran away with her, though her words, words, words drown us, one certainty lies between the lines: she loved him and wanted him. What Grzymala answered we do not know, but we may guess that he told her that Maria no longer proved an obstacle. George Sand returned to Paris forthwith, asking Grzymala to keep her visit a secret from "the little one." She was going to surprise Chopin. He, in turn, appealed to Grzymala. He knew she was coming. He, too, had been troubled:

> [Paris, late June 1838]
>
> My dear friend,
> I simply must see you today—even if late at night, at twelve or one. Don't be afraid that I have some trouble in store for you. You know how I have always valued your sincerity—it is a question of giving me some advice.

And again:

> [Paris, early July 1838]
>
> My dear friend,
> You can't give me a *surprise* because I saw Marliani yesterday and he told me about her arrival. I shall be at home till five, working at my lessons (I've just finished two). God knows how things will turn out. I am not very well. I have been to your house every day to embrace you on your return. Let's have dinner together.

In the summer their love showed its true color, shedding all camouflage. Liszt knew about it, which means that Marie d'Agoult knew about it, which means that the whole Paris circle knew about it. But Mallefille did not. Sand had sent him away with Maurice on an "educational excursion": he had now come to Paris, where he had to learn that "a chapter in his life had closed": he was dismissed. He proved not as malleable as wax. His bitter jealousy was all the more embittered by his having just then published (September 9) in the *Revue et Gazette Musicale* an article praising Chopin. Beside himself with fury and embarrassment, Mallefille determined to take revenge. Two versions of this incident exist. Marie d'Agoult's:

> Poor Mallefille:—there he is, confined to his bed, suffering from ingrowing vanity, for ever *dis*abused, *dis*enchanted—and all the other *dis*'s in the world. . . .

Prompted by what devilish inspiration I do not know, he began to get suspicious, and hung about, watching the door of Chopin's apartment, where George was in the habit of going every night. The dramatic author became a character of drama. He shouted, he yelled, he was terribly fierce and all out for blood. Friend Grzymala flung himself between the illustrious rivals. Mallefille was calmed down, and now, off George has gone to bask in the sunshine of a perfect love under the myrtle trees of Palma! Confess now, that is a far better story than any novelist could invent. . . .

The other version:

Having left him for Chopin, Félicien Mallefille posted himself before the house of his fortunate rival. She emerged, he hurled himself toward her. Luckily, at this moment a huge wagon, taking up the whole street, rolls up and separates them. She flees, finds a fiacre, throws herself into it, the coachman whips the horse! What would have happened without that fiacre?

Paul Perret in Gaulois

Mallefille disappeared from her life, as did all thoughts of other women from Chopin's life. Both were fulfilled and ecstatic. George Sand gave words to her feeling, writing to Delacroix:

[September 7(?), 1838]

I am still in the state of bliss in which you found me. No cloud obscures the pure heaven, no grain of sand troubles the lake. I have begun to believe that there do exist angels in human form who visit us on earth for a time, to comfort us and to draw toward their heaven those poor, desolate, tired souls who are ready to perish below. These are follies which I would not utter to anybody except you and Grzym[ala]. You won't mock me, I know it, you who know me profoundly. You know that this love is not a thing created on purpose, nor as a last resort, not a caprice, nothing one makes believe, to fool oneself while fooling others. I have by chance wandered into a region which I find so beautiful, so enchanted, so delicious that I could never think of leaving it. I sleep under the stars, under the trees, under the flowers, without giving a thought to rain. . . .

Can we not—indeed *must* we not as much as we are able to—make our nest while the winds of summer and love blow on us? You believe it cannot last longer than a season of spring? If I consult my memory and my logic, yes, it cannot last. If I consult my heart and my poetry, it seems to me that it cannot cease. What matter? If God makes me die in the

next hour, I will not bemoan my fate. I have experienced three months
of bliss unalloyed. . . .*

They decided to spend the winter away from their accustomed
environment, wholly devoting themselves to each other, and in a climate which would be beneficial both to Chopin and to Maurice, who
was still ailing. Manuel Marliani, the Spanish consul, suggested Majorca
—sun-filled, untouristed, and inexpensive. Grzymala thought the long
journey would prove too much for Chopin—but Chopin laughingly
dismissed the caution. He was anxious to get away from the Parisian
cacklers of gossip. Would he have a piano, however? He couldn't live
without one. Camille Pleyel immediately offered to ship one of his
instruments to Palma. Chopin agreed to sell him a series of twenty-four
Preludes for two thousand francs, five hundred of which were to be paid
as an advance. Chopin needed money for traveling expenses. So did
Sand, and she took the usual course of asking her editor, Buloz, for an
advance: six thousand francs were granted.

As soon as Custine heard of the Majorca project, he wrote his friend
Sophie Gay:

October 22, 1838
The luckless fellow [Chopin] doesn't realize that that woman loves like
a vampire! She goes to Spain and he follows her. He'll never return. He
didn't have the courage to tell me that he was joining her, he talked only
of needing a good climate and rest. Rest— with such a vampire!

In October Sand started south with her two children and a maid.
At Perpignan Chopin joined them, not at all exhausted by a four-day
stage journey, looking "fresh as a rose and pink as a turnip." They
boarded the paddle-wheel steamer—a conveyance little Solange and
Maurice had never seen and which delighted them—and arrived at
Barcelona, finding rooms in a "nasty inn." The weather was beautiful,
the sky blue, the city, so similar to Paris, not at all forbidding. They
remained five days, waiting for the next boat to Majorca. This was a
freighter, *El Mallorquin,* which usually carried pigs from the island to
Spain. Now, going in the opposite direction, the boat was fairly empty,
though dirty below deck. George Sand and Chopin spent the night on

*This letter has been ignored by Chopin biographers who hold the theory that Sand
never really loved him. The letter (of which only a portion is given here) is one of Sand's
long, long epistles; she pours out her heart and it rings true.

deck, watching the stars, watching the shimmering wake, and listening to the sailor in the lookout singing some soft, sad chant to keep himself awake. At Palma they received an unpleasant surprise: they could find no quarters, no inn, not the simplest shelter, since the little city was bursting with Spanish refugees who had fled the war on the mainland. Finally the French consul was able to make available two small rooms near the harbor, in a disreputable quarter which teemed with sailors, gypsies, and prostitutes, which stank of rancid oil, and where at night they were driven to distraction by mosquitoes. George Sand spent hours every day trudging the streets to find better quarters; and after four days she did find a little house on the outskirts which at least had windowpanes and clean, though crude, camp beds. The house was surrounded by a garden, where flowers and lemon trees were still in bloom as if to deny that there was such a month as November, and beyond the garden there were the silvery olive groves on one side, the Mediterranean on the other. On November 15 Chopin sent Julian Fontana an ecstatic report: this was probably the happiest day of his life.

Palma, November 15, 1838

My dearest friend,
Here I am at Palma, among palms, cedars, cacti, olive trees, oranges, lemons, aloes, figs, pomegranates, etc.—everything that is to be found in the hothouses of the Jardin des Plantes. The sky is like turquoise, the sea like lapis lazuli, the mountains like emerald and the air as in Heaven. In the daytime, sunshine; everyone goes about in summer clothes and it's hot. At night, guitars and songs for hours on end. Enormous balconies with overhanging vines: Moorish ramparts. Everything, including the town, has an African look. In a word, life is marvelous. Love me still. Do call at Pleyel's, for the piano has not arrived yet. Which route have they dispatched it by? It won't be long before you receive the Preludes. It is settled that I shall live in a wonderful monastery on the most fabulous site in the world: sea, mountains, palm trees, a cemetery, a crusaders' church, ruins of a mosque, olive trees a thousand years old. Oh, my dear fellow, I am really beginning to live. I am close to all that is most beautiful. I am a better man. Hand the letters from my parents to Grzymala, and anything else you want to send me: he knows the safest address. Embrace Johnny [Matuszynski]. How quickly he would recover here! Tell Pleyel he will receive the manuscripts soon. Don't say much about me to my acquaintances. I will write fully later on. Tell them I'll be back at the end of the winter.

There's only one postal collection a week! I am sending this through the local French consulate. Send off my letter to my parents just as it is. Post it yourself.

The "wonderful monastery" had been discovered by them while they rapturously explored a countryside which with every step seemed greener, lusher, readier to offer more flowers and juicier fruit. On top of a rocky hill sat this abandoned building, called the Charterhouse of Valldemosa, which, as they didn't know, had long been offered for sale but had found no buyer, the local population believing that the place was cursed. Now the pianist thinking of the Preludes and the novelist thinking of her obligation to deliver the next book couldn't wait to move into it, lock, stock, and barrel. But they had no lock, stock, or barrel and Sand wore herself out, shopping for sheets and mattresses, cutlery, and plates, pots and pans. In addition, she did the cooking, the servant she had hired proving "raw, bigoted, lazy, a glutton."

The sun shone every day during their first week in Palma. It was pure bliss. The second week the weather changed to a warning they ought to have heeded, had they been less bedazzled. A storm of almost hurricane force sprang up, caught Chopin on one of his walks, soaked him, and when with difficulty he had made his way back to the house, he was racked by coughing. It turned bitter cold—"never have I suffered so much from the cold," Sand was to remember—and the wetness seeped through the walls, turning pillows and clothes into clammy lumps. Everything one touched felt moldy. There was no fireplace, no stove, and though George Sand got hold of an open brazier, it smoked so much that it worsened Chopin's cough. She appealed to her friend the French consul, who dispatched several doctors to the house. Chopin to Fontana:

Palma, December 3, 1838

The three most celebrated doctors on the island have seen me: one sniffed at what I spat, the second tapped where I spat from, and the third sounded me and listened as I spat. The first said I was dead, the second that I am dying, and the third that I'm going to die—and I feel the same as always. I can't forgive [Matuszynski] for not advising me what to do in the event of acute bronchitis, which he might have expected me to catch at any time. It was all I could do to stop them bleeding me or applying blisters and setons; but thanks to Providence I am today just as I was. However, it is all having a bad effect on the Preludes—God knows when you will receive them. In a few days I shall be living in the most beautiful surroundings in the world: sea, mountains, everything. It

is a huge, old, deserted Carthusian monastery whose monks seem to
have been cleared out by Mendisabel [the Spanish president] especially
for me. It's near Palma—impossible to imagine anything more marvelous: arcades, the most poetical cemetery—I know I shall be all right
there. There is only one thing: I have no piano. I have written directly
to Pleyel, Rue Rochechouart. Find out what's happening. . . .

P.S. Don't tell people I have been ill or they will make a fantastic story
out of it.

Before Chopin was well enough to move to the monastery, the
rumor spread that he was consumptive. The Palma landlord, frightened
beyond all sympathy lest the disease infect his family and the neighborhood (tuberculosis was considered highly contagious), told them not
only that they had to leave his house at once, but that they had to pay
for replastering and repainting the walls and replacing the beds and
bedding, which, according to Spanish law, had to be burned. Once
more the French consul came to the rescue, inviting them to stay at his
house until they were ready to load their belongings, including a rented
piano, on a mule cart and slowly trot up the mountain. Sand wrote to
Charlotte Marliani:

> Palma, December 14, 1838
> Unheard-of troubles, just to get a bedcover, or firewood, or linen, or
> what else? . . . What is beautiful is the country, the sky, the mountains,
> Maurice's good health, and Solange becoming so much *sweeter.* The
> health of our good Chopin is not all that brilliant. After having con-
> quered very well—perhaps *too well*—the great fatigue of the voyage,
> the nervous force which sustained him has abated and he has been
> extremely dejected and suffering, But now, with every day, he is gaining
> strength and I hope he'll soon be better than ever. I nurse him as if he
> were my child. He is an angel of sweetness and goodness. . . .
> Everything is very expensive and the food difficult if one can't stom-
> ach rancid oil or pork grease. I'm getting used to it but Chopin is ill every
> time we ourselves don't prepare his food. In short, our voyage here, with
> all its harmony, is a terrible fiasco. But here we are. If fate does not deal
> me a nasty blow, I think the worst is over, we will reap the fruit of our
> labors, spring will be delightful, Maurice will regain all his health, Cho-
> pin will live a life of ease. . . .
> How can one complain when one's heart is alive? . . .

Their hearts were alive—but that did not save their bodies from
further troubles.

How impractical they were! To spend the winter in a compound of stone so vast that, as Sand wrote, it could have housed a small army, located on a high plateau toward which the winds and the rains rushed with a vindictive force from the summits of snow-covered mountains; to be cut off from Palma for days, the floods having turned the road into a quagmire; to expose a man subject to colds to the drafts of a cell; to shoulder the task of housekeeper, tutor of her children, and nurse of an ailing lover—it was romantic foolishness, and they both bore an equal share in not realizing that more than oranges and mimosa were needed for existence. But no—they refused to see this paradise as what it could become: a freezing hell. And even after the truth was pressed on them, they refused to give up. Chopin to Fontana:

> December 28, 1838
>
> . . . between the cliffs and the sea a huge deserted Carthusian monastery where in a cell with doors larger than any carriage gateway in Paris you may imagine me with my hair unkempt, without white gloves, and pale as ever. The cell is shaped like a tall coffin, the enormous vaulting covered with dust, the window small. In front of the window are orange trees, palms, cypresses; opposite the window is my camp bed under a Moorish filigree rose window. Close to the bed is an old square grubby box which I can scarcely use for writing on, with a leaden candlestick (a great luxury here) and a little candle. Bach, my scrawls and someone else's old papers . . . silence . . . you can yell . . . still silence. In short, I am writing to you from a queer place. . . .
>
> Nature is kindly here but the people are rogues, for they never see foreigners and so they never know what to charge for anything. You can have oranges for nothing but they demand an enormous sum for a trouser button. However, all that is a mere grain of sand compared with the poetry which everything here exhales and the coloring of this most marvelous scenery still untainted by the eye of man. Few are those who have ever disturbed the eagles which daily soar over our heads.

George Sand to Charlotte Marliani on the same day:

> We live . . . in a spot truly sublime which I hardly have time to admire, so much am I occupied with my children, their lessons, and my work. Our poor Chopin is quite feeble and suffering. The rains here are such as one cannot imagine, frightening deluges, with the air so wet and heavy one cannot drag oneself about. . . . I am all rheumatism. . . . My little Chop is overburdened and coughs a lot. For his sake I await impatiently the return of the beneficent season, which won't be long, luckily. Finally his piano arrived, but it is still in the claws of the Customs, which demand 600 frs. for an import permission and show themselves intracta-

ble. Ah! How little did Marliani know Spain when he told me not to worry about the Customs. On the contrary, they are execrable. To know Spain one must go there every morning: what one saw there yesterday one does not see today and won't see tomorrow. God knows. I assure you I had no idea of such human disorganization. It is a depressing spectacle. Luckily, as I said, I have no time to think. With Maurice I am deep in Thucydides and company, with Solange in the impersonal form and the agreement of participles. . . .

Yet both she and Chopin were still deeply enamored of the chartreuse, "its silence, its abandonment. . . . I find myself unworthy of dwelling in a place made to order for a Byron."

After fifteen days of negotiation, they liberated the Pleyel piano, using the subterfuge of transporting it through a side opening in the city wall rather than through the official portal of the city and paying four hundred francs. That ludicrous evasion, along with the substantial payment, satisfied the customs officer. George and Maurice went down to Palma to make the final arrangement. The morning was clear and bright. In the afternoon the rain clouds suddenly drew together and heaped such a cloudburst on the two travelers that the driver of their cart refused to go on, leaving them to grope their way up the mountain on foot, in darkness, and over terrain of washed-out paths, often sinking into the water up to their knees. When three hours later they finally stumbled into the monastery, there was Chopin, sitting in front of the rented piano, distraught, desperate, playing one of his recently finished Preludes:

> When he saw us enter the room he jumped up with a great cry, and, in a strange tone, and with a wild look in his eyes, said—"Ah! I was so sure that you were dead! . . ." When he had recovered his spirits, and saw how we were, he made himself quite ill by imagining all the dangers we had faced. He later confessed to me that, while he had sat there waiting for us, he had seen everything happening as in a dream, and then, finding it impossible to distinguish dream from reality, had grown quiet, and as though numbed, while he played the piano, so sure was he that he, too, was dead. He had a vision of himself drowned in a lake. Heavy, icy, drops of water, he said, were falling rhythmically upon his heart, and when I made him listen to the raindrops which were, in fact, dripping with measured regularity upon the roof, he denied that they were what he had heard.

> *Histoire de ma vie*

Whether that Prelude is the one in D-flat major (No. 15), popularly known as the "Raindrop" Prelude, is a moot question. It is certain only that, in spite of fear, loneliness, and bouts with ill health, Chopin kept on composing, the Scherzo in C-sharp minor (Opus 39) and the tragic Polonaise in C minor (Opus 40) belonging to the Majorca period. He completed the Twenty-Four Preludes (Opus 28), those amazing pieces, some fleeting, some introspective, some gay, some tragic. Though they are not all of equal quality, they contain ideas of startling originality which have nourished most subsequent piano music.

The problem of living became more complicated from day to day. The monastery housed a guardian, a fat sacristan who not only refused any help but had to be fed. A "housekeeper," Maria Antonia, cooked food which they found inedible, and then stole the pieces of chicken, the cutlets, or the pale fish which Sand managed to obtain. Maria Antonia was assisted by Catalina, who could not be admitted to their quarters since she spread lice, and a retarded little girl they called Nina (the dwarf), who was equally adept at thieving. All three had voracious appetites. The boy who brought the milk Chopin needed drank half of it on the way and watered the rest. The farmers sold them tomatoes or potatoes at five times the normal price. Sand bought a goat and a sheep, which had to be watched lest Catalina secretly milk them. Everything was pilfered, and there were days when they had no bread to eat because it was waterlogged.

One night a half-mad old man who had been a monastery servant appeared out of nowhere. He tapped his way through the empty corridors and knocked at the doors with a shepherd's crook, intoning in a drunken voice, "Nicolas, Nicolas," presumably the name of a monk who had befriended him long ago. But Chopin heard the cry in the night as his father's name. The porter tried to stop the intruder, but he found his way in night after night until he disappeared as suddenly as he had come. Was it all a trick the inimical locals were playing on the foreigners?

Sand herself made things more difficult by refusing to adapt her ways to village customs. Not once would she attend Sunday Mass, or appear at their saint's day festivals, or speak a friendly word to "those monkeys," or make a secret of her cigar smoking. . . . What were they doing here, in the heart of the winter, the villagers wanted to know. Surely they were emissaries of the devil. Neither Sand nor Chopin spoke Spanish and both refused to learn it, rendering their ostracism sharper. Sand summed it up by indulging in sweeping generality: "One may state as an axiom that there where Nature is beautiful and generous, men are mean and miserly."

Why did they not pack up and flee? Undoubtedly from one day to the next they were hoping for the coming of that radiant spring which would turn their abode into Arcadia. Probably they did not want to admit defeat, even to themselves. So they stayed on—and remarkably, in spite of their trials, in spite of Chopin's illness, in spite of his disposition, which longed for the city and the salon, no harm came to their love. They were cooped up, thrown upon each other, deprived of visitors and admirers—even the longed-for letters from their Parisian friends arrived seldom and irregularly—but at no time did they weary of each other, at no time did they quarrel or blame each other. The idyll was rain-soaked, but it remained an idyll still.

Their sojourn in Majorca has become so famous that visitors to Valldemosa are given the impression that they lived there for years. Their stay lasted less than fourteen weeks. They arrived in Palma on November 8, 1838, and left on February 13, 1839. Sand described their return:

Barcelona, February 15, 1839

[To Charlotte Marliani]
We knew ten people who possessed wagons, horses, mules. None of them was "able" to lend them to us. We were forced to hire a rickety cart without springs, with the result that Chopin had a terrible hemorrhage by the time we arrived in Palma. And why such lack of help? Because Chopin coughs. Whoever coughs in Spain is declared consumptive. Whoever is consumptive is pestiferous, leprous, mangy. There aren't enough sticks, stones, or *gendarmes* to chase him and because consumption is catching one ought to beat the sick person to death, as one drowned the insane 200 years ago. What I am telling you is the literal truth. We were pariahs in Majorca because of that cough and because we would not attend Mass. They threw stones at my children and they called us heathens. One would need ten volumes to give an idea of the baseness, the bad faith, the egoism, the foolishness, the spitefulness of this stupid race, thieving and bigoted.

Marseilles, March 9, 1839

[To François Rollinat, her lawyer] We embarked on the only steamer available, one which serves to transport pigs to Barcelona. [The *Mallorquin*, the same boat on which they had traveled to Majorca.] It was the only means to quit this cursed land. We had for company 100 pigs, whose

continuous wailings and horrible stink prevented any repose or breatha-
ble air for the ill man. He arrived in Barcelona spitting a basinful of
blood and dragging himself like a specter. There, luckily, our fortunes
improved. The French consul and the commander of the French mari-
time station welcomed us with a hospitality and a graciousness unknown
in Spain. We were put on a French brig,* where the doctor at once set
to work and managed within 24 hours to stop the bleeding.

After their stay on the brig, the French consul sent his carriage to
take them to the Hotel of Four Nations, where they remained for a
week. They then took a French steamer, the *Phénicien,* to Marseilles.
The boat seemed to them a veritable luxury hotel; the captain was a
music enthusiast and tried to make the voyage as comfortable as he
could for Chopin. When they got to Marseilles, Chopin at once placed
himself under the care of a competent physician, Dr. François Cauvière, who prescribed a month of complete rest. Sand could write to
Charlotte: "At last, we are in France," and then proceed with one of her
usual letters (ten pages) to discuss future plans, to rejoice that Chopin
"no longer spits blood, sleeps well, coughs little," and to impart the
news that she had dismissed her maid Amélie as soon as they arrived
in Marseilles: "A bad creature who plotted with the tradespeople and
innkeepers to rob me . . . and yet I loved her."

(3)

While Chopin recovered—and he did recover in a very short time—he
and Sand kept very much to themselves. They closed their doors to the
celebrity hounds—"the riffraff of literature and the riffraff of music," as
Sand put it—and though they found Marseilles a crassly commercial
city, concerned only with "a sugar loaf, a box of soap, or a bunch of
candles," they were content to hear the sound of French once more, to
receive mail regularly, and to have nobody insist on burning Chopin's
bed linen.** Their stay in Marseilles was a tranquil routine, Chopin

---

*George Sand, afraid that Chopin was going to die, wrote a note to the captain of the
French brig anchored near the *Mallorquin* and threw the note with a tip overboard to
a man in a bark. She asked to be rescued. The man delivered the note and the captain
of the French boat, who knew who Sand and Chopin were, acted immediately.

**In fairness it should be stated that there did exist a strict Spanish law demanding
the "removal by fire of all personal articles handled by tubercular patients." Chopin and
Sand were unaware of this law—or chose to ignore it.

playing, composing, and obeying Dr. Cauvière's orders—"I drink no coffee or wine, only milk. I dress warmly and look like a girl," he wrote to Fontana—while Sand, in a room of her own, stitched up the plot of a new novel. They lived in the Hotel Beauvau, where five years previously Sand had stayed with Musset. Did the recollection mean anything to her? At present she was body and soul dedicated to her new lover, whom she described to Charlotte: "His goodness, tenderness and patience sometimes make me anxious. I believe he is too fine, exquisite and perfect a nature to live for long in our gross and heavy terrestial existence." Similarly, Chopin wrote about her to Grzymala:

> Marseilles, March, 12, 1839
>
> I had to look on while she, continually harassed, nursed me (the less said about those doctors the better), made my bed, tidied my room, prepared hot drinks. She deprived herself of everything for me, while all the time she was receiving no letters and the children needed her constant attention in these unusual circumstances. Add to this the fact that she was writing her books. [The rest of the letter is lost.]

And again: "You would love her still more if you knew her as I do today."

Only two events impinged on his convalescence. They were saddened to learn that an artist they admired, the tenor Adolphe Nourrit, "who may well have been the greatest singing actor among all the dramatic tenors of opera history,"* had jumped to his death from the window of his lodging. He had been a man of wide interests, knowledgeable in art, a good poet (the words to the famous aria "Rachel, quand du seigneur" in *La Juive* are his), and he introduced some of Schubert's songs in France, translating them himself. Both Chopin and Liszt valued him highly. A funeral service was held in Marseilles's church of Notre-Dame-du-Mont and Chopin played Schubert's "Die Sterne" on a wheezy organ. The autograph hunters were out in force, sure George Sand would be there: she was, but she hid in the organ loft and they couldn't find her. Chopin slipped out with her immediately after playing.

And from Paris came news which disturbed Chopin for some days. To Grzymala:

---

*Henry Pleasants in *The Great Singers*.

Marseilles, April 12, 1839

Marliani writes that there is a rumor that my mother is anxious about me and is coming to Paris. Although I don't believe it, I am writing today to reassure my parents—please be kind enough to have my letter taken to the post office. That will be my third letter from Marseilles. If you hear any more about this, send me a line. It would take something quite out of the ordinary to make my mother leave my father. Father is poorly and needs her more than anyone. I just could not imagine such a separation.

Four days later:

The news about my mother puzzles me. It is certain that somebody must have frightened her with some tale, for her to consider such a voyage. Unless some Polish blockhead has fabricated the whole story. . . .

It was not that Chopin would not have been happy to see his mother. He was as yet reluctant, however, to disclose to his family his living with the "notorious" woman. Chopin had kept his sojourn in Majorca a secret from his parents: when he wrote to them he sent his letter to Grzymala or Fontana in Paris, asking them to post it. He did so again while he was in Marseilles. He didn't want to worry his conservative family; it was a long time before he admitted the liaison to them. In their eyes, what could come of it? Wasn't she married, though separated from her husband? Wasn't she inconstant in her affections? Wasn't she older than Frederic?

Chopin and George Sand moved to Nohant in the summer of that year, after making a two-week excursion to Genoa. (She had been there, too, with Musset.) It was then easier for Chopin, a man twenty-nine years old, to tell his family about the connection, though he still seems to have been vague about it. For a while he pretended he was merely a houseguest. His father wrote: "We are glad you are being well cared for, but we should very much like to know the details of this intimate friendship."

Nohant, the estate George Sand had inherited, is situated in the province of Berry in middle France, in a valley which Sand called "The Black Valley" and described as:

A parceling out of fields, meadows, copses and communal paths, offering a variety of forms and nuances, within a harmony of somber green relieved by a tint of blue; a jumble of luxuriant closures, thatched huts hidden under orchards; curtains of poplars . . .

The house itself (now a museum) is foursquare, surrounded by a park and protected by a stone wall, outside which stands the plainest of country churches. (George Sand is buried in its churchyard.) It has many small rooms, the largest being a kitchen with an array of copper utensils, a rude table, and a stove huge enough to cook for an assembly of artistic appetites. That and the dining room, the table still set as if for dinner, are on the ground floor, the living rooms and bedrooms upstairs. Sand's studio and the room assigned to Chopin were separated by a tiny gallery. The rooms are filled with mementos of living, her son's paintings, portraits of herself, bibelots, gifts, vases, medals, clocks, books, sculptures, porcelain, chessboards, placed helter-skelter on varied pieces of furniture, none of it first rate. In short, they are characteristic of nineteenth-century France, where every corner was a collector's corner. At the back of the house is a theater, really two theaters, one called "grand" (it is as grand as a pocket handkerchief), where the guests performed, often in playlets written by Sand—funny pieces such as "The Inn of the String Bean" or "The Recalcitrant Cadaver"—while the other served as a marionette theater. This was Maurice's special project, and contained almost two hundred superb puppets, whose costumes George Sand sewed. Chopin often played the accompaniment to the puppet plays. Guests came and guests went: Liszt and Marie, Balzac, Pierre Leroux, her very good friend the brilliant lawyer Emmanuel Arago; later—and often—Flaubert, Gautier, Turgenev, Delacroix.

Such, then, was the place which George Sand occupied part of every year since she had come to it as a girl of sixteen and written (in English) the poetic message "at the setting of the sun" on the window of her room. (The penciled lines can still be seen.) To it Chopin now moved with eagerness. That Sand wanted him to remain, that she hoped to make their union lasting, is indicated by a letter she wrote to Camille Pleyel:*

[Marseilles] April 9, 1839

Monsieur: I plan to be in Berry the first of May with Chopin and I would like to give him an agreeable surprise by placing one of your pianos in his room.

---

*This letter, not published in the *Correspondance*, was owned by Sacha Guitry and was kindly given to us by Georges Lubin.

Would you be so kind as to send one? I do not know if it is your practice to rent out pianos by the month and ship them to the provinces, but may I tell you that nobody in my house plays music; it will be Chopin alone who will place his hands on the instrument. I know a carter who is reliable and I'll send him to you around the 15th or 20th of this month; he'll deliver the piano back when Chopin leaves for Paris. It is understood that should any accident happen to the piano I will be responsible.

Please have it packed at your place at my expense. Above all I desire that the piano be a first-class one, because for some time now Chopin has been playing on pianinos and he longs for an instrument more appropriate to his new strength. I know you'll be delighted to hear that his recovery is almost complete. Please, keep my little *surprise* secret. With very best regards.

GEORGE SAND

P.S. The address for the piano:
Madame Sand, Nohant at Châteauroux (Indre).
The distance is 70 leagues, a voyage of 7 days.

It was probably on this piano, and certainly in Nohant, that Chopin created his finest works during the next years. In that first glorious summer of 1839, he completed what was for him a cornucopia of compositions: using the 1837 Funeral March in B-flat minor, he now composed in the same key a sonata which is surely one of the great achievements of piano music, in spite of the bathos which bad playing has smeared over the third movement. The next year he began what very possibly is the masterpiece of his masterpieces, the Fantaisie in F minor (Opus 49), the very essence of romantic music, a bold concept, structurally perfect, not a bar too long or too short. The exultant Ballade in A-flat major, composed in the same year, the mighty Polonaise in F-sharp minor (Opus 44), three Mazurkas, three Etudes—the evidence becomes strong that his love for Sand, the peace of Nohant, his improved health, all proved beneficent to him. Indeed, it is substantially correct to say that Chopin's best music dates from the Sand years.

Chopin experienced a summer happiness in Nohant. The landscape reminded him of Polish woods and fields. He gave Solange piano instruction, patiently showing her hand position and scales. A little coffee-colored dog was always underfoot; Chopin had found it on the street and brought it to the house. Though "the little fellow did his business on the carpet and made us a gift of fleas," Chopin loved it and "Mops" loved Chopin, but was "ferociously jealous of Solange." Gradually Chopin became the family man around the house, integrated into its life, accepting the fatherless children. Solange inherited a beautiful watch and chain; Maurice envied the gift and felt hurt. At once Chopin ordered an expensive watch from Leroy et Fils, one of Paris's leading jewelers, and had it engraved with Maurice's name and the date. Nevertheless Chopin felt closer to the little girl, headstrong, self-willed, often "in a fury" (as her mother said), but pretty and graceful.

But even when they were attuned to each other, their loves unclouded, their loyalties unshaken, their admiration for each other as fresh as the air of Berry—a condition which lasted for several years—Sand and Chopin could not deny their natures. Underneath love lay an incongruity of temperament and character. Chopin's climate was not the country, nor could the informal life content him. He preferred Chardin's "Bouquet de Chantilly" to the perfume of the "somber green" fields. And he missed his Parisian friends. Sand recognized this soon enough. She begged Grzymala to come to Nohant. As early as June 1839 she wrote to Charlotte Marliani:

> Come, then, to see me, dear friend, because I cannot come to you. Urge that old Grzym; his coming is necessary to complete the cure of the *little one.* . . .

And, in a P.S. to a letter from Chopin to Grzymala on July 8, she added:

> Well, then! Fickle husband [Sand called him her husband as a joke], we await you in vain. You mock our impatience and cradle us in vain hopes. Really, you must come, dear friend. We need you. Our little one is always *quam-quam.* I believe he needs a little less of the calm, solitude, and regularity of existence which life in Nohant offers. Who knows? Perhaps a trip to Paris. I am prepared for any sacrifice rather than see him consumed by melancholy. Who can define the distinction between physical illness and mental depression? He won't confess to me that he is bored. But I think I can guess. . . .

Underneath, Chopin wrote: "She won't let me read what she wrote to you. That's a shame!!!"

After Chopin's death, George Sand attempted an analysis which, though of course self-justifying and couched in the language of the romancer, is not unjust to him:

He was responsive to the sweetness of affection and the smiles of destiny at one moment, only to be hurled into misery for days—no, for weeks, by somebody unimportant who showed himself inconsiderate, or by the tiny annoyances of daily life. Strange—but a real pain did not shatter him as much as a small one. . . . The force of his feelings stood in no relation to their cause. He endured the precarious state of his health heroically during crises, and tormented himself miserably during the most insignificant alternations. . . . Gentle, witty, fascinating in company, Chopin, ill, could be despairing in intimacy. No soul was more noble, more delicate, more dedicated, more faithful, no spirit more brilliant when gay, no intelligence more serious or more comprehensive of all that lay within his ken, but—alas!—no character was more unstable, no imagination blacker or more errant, no susceptibility more prone to irritation, no heart more exigent and impossible to satisfy. Nothing of this was his fault: it was the disease. His spirit was rubbed raw: the crease of a rose petal, the shadow of a fly, made him suffer. . . .

Histoire de ma vie

And what had Chopin felt about Sand? How odd he must have thought her eternal scribbling, dashed off without correction, he who was so punctilious a craftsman. He must have been often put off by her positiveness; she who knew all the answers to all the social questions. How he must have been puzzled by her melodramatic costumes, the Arab burnoose one day and a conservative black robe the next, a peasant's apron the next. He must have cringed when, as Elizabeth Barrett Browning reported, a Greek stranger enclosed her in his arms, while an "excessively vulgar" actor threw himself at her feet. He was undoubtedly offended when at a dinner Sand challenged his friend Grzymala to put his hand up her leg and describe her knee—everybody had drunk too much champagne—a little scene which Marie d'Agoult reported in a letter to Liszt (February 6, 1840). Chopin wasn't there, but he was sure to have heard about it.

In the first years her tenderness toward him knew no bounds; she was unaffectedly devoted. She called him "That being whom I have adopted and who has become another Maurice to me." She said that she now had three children, of whom the grownup did not require the least of her care. When she went on a brief journey in the summer of 1840 she sent home combination letters to Chopin, Maurice, and Solange, addressing all three as "Dear children," telling them that she was bored stiff with the dinners, the speeches, the platitudinous conversations, that she was "beginning to understand why Chop did not want to give concerts," and closing one letter with "Good night, Chip-Chip, good night Solange, good night Bouli [Maurice] . . . love your old lady as she loves you." Chopin answered with a gay long letter, written in double-talk Italian: *"Gli fanciulli si portano admirabilimamentissimamente."*

Yet he did not always feel comfortable with her. She overprotected her "little one," because it was in her nature to do so: she was a composite of a hetaera, a blue stocking, and a Florence Nightingale. He let himself be protected and possessed, because it accorded with *his* nature as a stranger who wished to "belong," a troubled being beset by prejudices, suspicion, and, eventually, jealousy.

All the same, it is evident that Chopin found his haven in Nohant. On a gloomy November day in 1843 he wrote to George Sand from Paris urging her to come and "to bring us [himself and her son Maurice] your lovely Nohant weather." He added: "Be assured that we are both well, that illness is far away and that the future holds nothing but happiness." The future—he saw it in no way except with George Sand. Nor did she think of separation from him. And that, considering her history, was extraordinary.

From 1839 to 1846—that is, from Chopin's twenty-ninth to his thirty-sixth year—his life followed a pattern: winters in Paris, summers in Nohant (with the exception of 1840, when he and Sand spent the entire year in Paris). An occasional concert did not interfere with his main tasks, composing and teaching. By the end of that period he had arrived at Opus 62, the last two Nocturnes to be published during his lifetime.

CHAPTER

IX

FRIENDS AND ENEMIES

GOOD-BYE TO TREES and fields in the autumn of 1839. Chopin and Sand had to return to Paris, he to his pupils, she to supervise the rehearsals of her new play, *Cosima*. At first they took individual lodgings, but they hated being separated from each other if only by a few city streets, and soon they took up life together in Rue Pigalle.* Chopin's love proved stronger than his conventional scruples; the move signified an open declaration of their relationship; he even received his pupils in their home.

Two years later they moved once more, to a complex of buildings, enclosed by gardens, at 3 Square d'Orléans. In that square Chopin's apartment was on the ground floor, to the left of a courtyard in which shubbery was planted (No. 9); Sand's apartment was on the right, one floor up (No. 5). There she had provided an extra room for Chopin's use, so that he didn't even have to step across the courtyard to be with her. Their friends the Marlianis lived in the center of the building, and often they all ate their meals together in Charlotte's dining room. In addition, Chopin leased a studio at 5 Rue Tronchet, where he gave his lessons

---

*George Sand in her *Histoire de ma vie* gives a very different reason for their moving together: "He coughed in an alarming manner and I was constrained either to be his nurse or to spend time continuously going there and back." Therefore she "offered" him part of her own apartment. Sand was romancing. Chopin was not ill in the winter of 1839–40 and the apartment was paid for by both of them.

(and where he felt he could not hang a reproduction of the Giorgione nude: "it might offend his pupils.")

The Square d'Orléans resembled a pleasant rustic island among the stones of Paris, serving as home to several artists; the air was full of music: the pianists Kalkbrenner, Marmontel, Alkan, and Zimmermann (Gounod's father-in-law) lived in the Square, as did Maria Taglioni the dancer, Dantan the sculptor, Ortigues the writer.

Chopin attempted once more to conquer his hatred of public performance. He was invited to the court at Saint-Cloud to play for Louis Philippe and the Queen. Moscheles was in town, so the two played together, though it must have been difficult for them to become inspired, the King's face being as expressive as a drop of oil, while the Queen knitted.*Chopin received a big porcelain vase as compensation —a fee would have been more welcome. Though the concert—and refreshments—lasted till almost midnight, Chopin had himself driven back to Paris to spend the night with Sand. She had not been invited to Saint-Cloud. After his appearance before the royal couple, he was urged again and again to give a concert. It took him more than a year to decide—and then he was half tricked into it. George Sand wrote to the singer Pauline Viardot:

April 18 [1841]

The big, the very big, news is that Chip-Chip is going to give a grrrrrand concert. His friends pushed him so hard that he let himself be persuaded, hoping all the time that it would be difficult enough to arrange for him to be able to cancel it. But things went faster than he dreamt. No sooner had his fatal "yes" escaped than everything fell into place as by a miracle. Three quarters of the available seats were sold even before there was an official announcement. Well, he shook himself as if awakening from a dream. No more amusing sight could be imagined than the meticulous and irresolute Chip-Chip forced not to change his mind. He was hoping that you would appear and sing, accompanied by him. When I received your letter and that hope vanished, he wanted to cancel the concert. It was no longer possible, he was too deeply committed. . . . The Chopinesque nightmare will take place in the Salle Pleyel on the 26th. He does not want any [printed] programs, he does not want a large audience, he does not want any talk about it. So many things alarm him

---

*Moscheles's report of the occasion, however, is enthusiastic. "Chopin and I reveled like brothers in the triumph achieved."

that I proposed to him that he should play without lights, without an audience, and on a mute keyboard. . . .

The concert did take place and was extravagantly praised by all the critics, not one voice dissenting. "Everyone," one report said, "went away full of sweet joy and profound meditation." The price of the tickets had been set at fifteen and twenty francs, prices only members of high society could afford. Pleyel distributed a few complimentary seats in the first row to Chopin's friends, so that he could see them smile and nod. Sand, Delacroix, Heine, Liszt, Mickiewicz, Legouvé were present. Chopin earned about six thousand francs from ticket sales; nevertheless it took almost another year before he appeared once more at the Salle Pleyel (February 21, 1842), at which concert Pauline Viardot sang and his friend Auguste Franchomme, the cellist, played. To the entreaties which were heaped on George Sand, in the belief that *she* could persuade him to play more frequently, she had to answer: "He hasn't played for eight years; perhaps he won't play again for another eight years." She was nearly right.

As soon as the first clement days warmed Paris, Chopin told his valet to pack his trunk with his impeccable clothes, his fine linen, his battery of medicines, and a quantity of notepaper. This paraphernalia then lumbered to Nohant. There he could compose, there he found family life when he wanted family life and solitude when he wanted solitude. Sand's friends respected his need for privacy. Some of them—they increased in number and variety as both her fame and his increased— became *his* friends.

The new acquaintance he treasured most was Pauline Viardot. Daughter of the famous Spanish singer Manuel Garcia, sister of the intense María Malibran, whom Delacroix painted and who "passed over the stage like a meteor," only to die at the age of twenty-eight, Pauline was equally extraordinary, both as an artist and as a woman. She studied composition with Antonín Reicha, piano with Liszt, and played so well that Ferdinand Hiller thought of engaging her as head of the piano department at the Cologne Conservatory. In 1841, when she visited Sand and Chopin in Nohant, she was only nineteen years old and at the beginning of her long and great career. She was one of the most intelligent singers who ever lived, and was accepted as an intellectual equal by Sand, Musset, Rossini, Gustave Doré, Gounod, Berlioz. Meyerbeer admired Pauline so much that he wrote the role of Fidès in *Le Prophète* for her, and later Brahms composed the *Alto Rhapsody* for her. She was not at all pretty, yet she had such charm that men adored her. Musset proposed to her, having written two paeans of praise in the *Revue des Deux Mondes*, and though she was flattered, she looked at his red-rimmed eyes, heeded George Sand's warning, and refused him. Now she was newly married to Louis Viardot, twenty-one years older than she, a critic and a Spanish scholar, who had given up the directorship of the Théâtre Italien to devote himself to Pauline's career. Their relationship turned out to be satisfactory. Later she became—and remained for forty years—Turgenev's great love. That love suffuses his play *A Month in the Country*. It was characteristic of Pauline that she took into her home Turgenev's illegitimate child, born of a casual liaison with the daughter of his mother's seamstress. Pauline was one of the most enchanting women of the Romantic Age.

As a young married woman she earned Chopin's friendship and Sand's wholehearted affection. Chopin accompanied her singing; she turned some of his Mazurkas into songs; and she served George Sand as model for the heroine of what is possibly Sand's best novel, *Consuelo*.* The statesman Charles Duvernet recalled in his *Mémoires* that once at Nohant, when Chopin played and Viardot sang, "I was so moved that without being aware of it, two tears trickled down my face. George Sand took me by the hand to Mme. Viardot, saying to her: 'Look, Pauline, I bring you these while they are still hot.'"

Their music making was not always quite so lachrymose. They studied Bach, eighteenth-century songs, and most earnestly *Don Giovanni*, beloved by both of them. And while Chopin played and Pauline sang, Delacroix painted in a studio Sand had fitted out for him, young Maurice tried his hand at sketching, Louis Viardot corrected his translation of Cervantes, and their hostess worked on *Consuelo*.

Two summers later, when Pauline was going to Vienna for an operatic engagement, she and her husband left their baby daughter in the care of Sand and Chopin. The foster parents could not have been hap-

---

*While she was finishing *Consuelo*, Sand wrote to Delacroix (May 28, 1842), inviting him to Nohant: "I have good tea and delicious cream for your breakfasts. I can read to you a portion of *Consuelo*, of which I think you know only the beginning. Up to now it is entertaining. Chopin has composed two adorable Mazurkas worth more than forty novels; they'll be remembered long after the entire literature of this century." Like Cyrano, she said these things lightly enough herself about herself, but she allowed none else to utter them.

pier. "Your little girl has brought forth four fine teeth this week," Sand wrote to Pauline. "If she continues she'll eat you alive. She dances, laughs, chatters, speaks Polish with Chopin, Berrichon with Françoise [the maid], Sanskrit with Pistolet [the dog], pees everywhere, eats, sleeps, and makes us happy." Chopin "spends his life kissing her hands." She flirted with him "in a way which melts all the Chopins in the world." He adored little Louise as he loved her mother. After Pauline returned from her triumphs in Vienna and Berlin, young Maurice Sand fell in love with her, worshiping at her feet with an adolescent adoration which lasted for some time.

Chopin was lucky in his friendship with the physician who took care of him in Nohant. This was Dr. Gustave Papet, who lived close by and who had been a friend of George Sand's since her childhood—Sand had a way of keeping on good terms with her friends, if not with her lovers. Papet was wealthy and practiced medicine "to help suffering human-ity." Whenever Chopin felt ill, Papet was willing to mount his horse, trot over, and comfort him. Papet gave it out that Chopin did not have tuberculosis, but merely an inflammation of the larynx. He understood Chopin's nature, "that organization which remained a mystery to all the others; he alone could reassure and reanimate him," Sand wrote to Delacroix. Nothing about the treatment of tuberculosis was known; Papet treated Chopin psychologically, calming his "overexcited nerves" and "too sensitive disposition." From Paris Chopin wrote (No-vember 1839) to Papet: "Dear, dear doctor, thanks to you here I am on my legs, and if you want me to jump, I'll try to fall on your neck [in gratitude]."

(2)

Chopin's best friend in France was Eugène Delacroix, a man protean not only in his genius but in the breadth and profundity of his intellec-tual interests. Racine and Goethe, Shakespeare and Molière, Montaigne and Rousseau, were his companions. He knew most of Mozart's works by heart. His *Journal* is the document of a gracious mind, one of the most delightful records of thoughts, life, and love affairs written by a nonliterary pen. Like Chopin, Delacroix was elegant in bearing and despised excesses of speech or behavior. Like Chopin, he was a bit of a hypochondriac. Like Chopin, he was a bit of a snob. Like him he was an enclosed nature, soft-spoken, elaborately courteous, and noncom-mittal—it was said that he could give twenty different intonations to the words *mon cher monsieur*—but unlike Chopin, he loved solitude, and withdrew to his house in the Place Furstenberg more and more as he grew older, though when he walked out he submitted to the adoring group of students who immediately surrounded him. Like Chopin, he had his enemies, who accused him of painting with a "drunken broom"; but like Chopin's subtly shaped compositions, even when superficially they appear improvisatory, Delacroix's "turbulent forms in all their complexity are as carefully patterned as David's stylized ones." Like Chopin, he was an "innovator with a deep sense of tradition" and like him he was a Romantic artist who denied being a Romantic. "They enrolled me willy-nilly in the romantic coterie," wrote Delacroix after *Massacre at Chios* had created a sensation, "so making me responsible for their folly." Yet in his self-portrait of 1830 he looks like the Byronic hero.

Music was a necessity to him: the frequent mentions of music in the *Journal,* his tragic painting of Paganini, his sketches of singers, his portrait and drawing of Chopin, remain as evidence. Chopin was sup-posed not to have understood Delacroix's work, was indeed supposed to have disliked it. The evidence, repeated by all biographers, rests on a passage in George Sand's *Impressions et souvenirs* (1873):

> Going to the salon, we [Sand, Delacroix, and Chopin] were discussing Ingres's *Stratonice.* Chopin does not like it, he finds the figures man-nered and emotionless, though he does admire the refinement of the painting. . . . He says he really doesn't know what to make of it and, in truth, doesn't know what to say.
>
> Chopin and Delacroix love each other, one may say, tenderly. Their characters are similar and they share the same affinities of heart and spirit. But where art is concerned, Delacroix understands Chopin and Chopin doesn't at all understand Delacroix. He esteems, values, respects the man: he detests the painter. Delacroix, more versatile, appreciates music, knows and understands it; he loves Chopin's music and knows it by heart. Chopin accepts this homage and is touched by it, yet when he looks at a painting by his friend he suffers and cannot say a word. He is a musician, nothing but a musician. His mind can only express itself in music. He has spirit, refinement, cleverness, but he understands nothing of painting and sculpture. Michelangelo frightens him, Rubens makes

him shudder, everything which seems to him eccentric scandalizes. He is tightly enclosed in the conventional. Strange anomaly! . . .

In weighing this evidence, we need to remember, first, that Sand wrote it many, many years after the breakup with Chopin, bitterness over which lingered in her memory; second, that she was at the time greatly impressed by Delacroix's posthumous fame. Sand may have had a brief affair with Delacroix, but she could not dominate him. Their love relationship, if there was one, ended calmly, leaving behind mutual esteem. She may well have wished to praise the painter above the composer. At any rate, Chopin never expressed himself negatively about Delacroix's work; we have but a few words, written to Sand's daughter: "Delacroix has done a little Christ which is much admired." And in a letter to his friend the cellist Franchomme, Chopin called Delacroix "the most admirable artist possible." Such is the only direct evidence.

A friendship as firm as that of the two men could scarcely have been one-sided, one man "detesting" the other's work. No artist, however broad-minded, could have endured it. Nor was the subject passed over in silence between them. "We talked for two and a half hours," Chopin wrote to George Sand, "about music, painting, and above all about you." Let us note: music *and* painting.

Delacroix's opinion of Chopin is clear. Here are some jottings from the *Journal:*

> After I had finished my dinner I went to call on Mme. Sand. It was snowing a blizzard and I had to wade through slush to get to the Rue St. Lazare. That good-natured fellow Chopin played for us. What an enchanting talent!
>
> *March 12, 1847*

> To the Chambre des Députés in the morning. Then to Chopin, for a session at three o'clock. He was divine. They played his trio for him with Fauchon [*sic*], etc.: he then played it himself, and in a masterly manner.
>
> *July 1, 1847*

> Went to see Chopin in the evening, I stayed with him until ten o'clock. The dear fellow! We talked of Mme. Sand, of her strange life and extraordinary mixture of virtues and vices. All this was in reference to her *Mémoires.* Chopin says that she will never be able to write them. She has forgotten the past; she has great outbursts of feeling and then forgets very quickly. For instance, she wept for her old friend Pierret, and then never thought of him again. I was saying to Chopin that I foresaw for

her an unhappy old age, but he does not think so. She never appears to
feel guilty about the things for which her friends reproach her. Her
health is extremely good, and may well continue to be so. Only one thing
would affect her deeply, the death of Maurice [her son] or his going
wholly to the bad.

As for Chopin, his suffering prevents his taking an interest in anything, least of all his work. I said that what with age and the unrest of
the present day, it would not be long before I, too, began to lose my
enthusiasm. He said he thought that I had strength enough to resist:
"You will have the enjoyment of your talent," he said, "in a kind of
serenity that is a rare privilege, and no less valuable than the feverish
search after fame."

January 29, 1849

Went with Chopin for his drive at about half-past three. I was glad to
be of service to him although I was feeling tired. The Champs Élysées,
l'Arc de l'Étoile, the bottle of quinquina wine, being stopped at the
city gate, etc. We talked of music and it seemed to cheer him. I asked
him to explain what it is that gives the impression of logic in music. He
made me understand the meaning of harmony and counterpoint; how
in music, the fugue corresponds to pure logic, and that to be well
versed in the fugue is to understand the elements of all reason and
development in music. I thought how happy I should have been to
study these things, the despair of commonplace musicians. It gave me
some idea of the pleasure which true philosophers find in science. The
fact of the matter is that true science is not what we usually mean by
that word—not, that is to say, a part of knowledge quite separate from
art. No, science, as regarded and demonstrated by a man like Chopin,
is art itself, but on the other hand, art is not what the vulgar believe it
to be, a vague inspiration coming from nowhere, moving at random,
and portraying merely the picturesque, eternal side of things. It is
pure reason, embellished by genius, but following a set course and
bound by higher laws. . . .

April 7, 1849

To see Chopin in the evening; I found him in a state of collapse, scarcely
breathing. After a time, my being there seemed to do him good. He said
that boredom was the worst evil he had to suffer, and I asked him
whether before he fell ill he had not known the unbearable sense of
emptiness that I sometimes feel. He said he could always find some
occupation or other, and that having something to do, however trivial,
filled in the time and dispersed the vapors. Real grief is something quite
different.

April 14, 1849

Is it conceivable that a man of Delacroix's stature could have grappled to his soul a friend unable to follow his flight of thought and insensitive to that which lifted him to enthusiasm? Would these discussions of two and a half hours' duration have taken place with a companion who was "nothing but a musician"? Chopin may not have responded fully to the more daring of Delacroix's works, but to be wholly blind to them, to "detest" his friend's art . . . ? We must doubt George Sand's pronouncement, doubt it very much, though it has been unquestioningly accepted. Not only the *Journal* but Delacroix's letters give evidence that the friendship was a balanced admiration and that Delacroix learned from Chopin—and vice versa.

To Sand in Nohant:

> May 30, 1842
>
> Tell my dear Chopin that the parties I like are to stroll with him in the garden discussing music or in the evening to stretch in an easy chair and listen while God descends through his divine fingers. . . .

From Nohant to a friend, Fr. Villot:

> June 14, 1842
>
> I have endless discussions with Chopin, whom I love, and who is a man of rare distinction. He is the truest artist I know. There are few such, whom one can admire and esteem. . . .

To Sand in Nohant:

> June 1842
>
> Take care of Chopin. Perhaps he is working now that I no longer interrupt him. I know that several times he neglected his work to keep me company.

And so it continued until after Chopin's death, when Delacroix went to Champrosay and wrote that he was so moved by the tragedy that he "sought refuge here, as quickly as I could, in spite of the bad season." Twelve years later, in 1861, Delacroix wrote to Grzymala remembering "the seraph we have lost and who must at this moment be charming the celestial spheres."

(3)

Another firm friend of Chopin's was Heinrich Heine, a man very different from Delacroix. The poet had joined the French Romantics. Protesting against political oppression in Germany and calling himself "a son of the French Revolution," he came to Paris, became famous, and never left the city. He wrote some of the most exquisitely mellifluous poetry of the German language, poetry which sounds like music even when it is spoken and has invited innumerable composers to turn it into lieder—"Du bist wie eine Blume" has been set to music by some 160 composers, "Die Lorelei" by Schubert, Schumann, and others. At the same time he was a wintry satirist, a Pietro Aretino of the Romantic Movement. His aphorisms were rushed to the Faubourg St. Germain, there to cause delicious nose tickles. Of Musset, who in his youth was a debauched drunkard, he wrote: "Ah—there's a man with a promising future behind him," and of Hugo's play *Les Burgraves,* that it was "Sauerkraut set to verse." With all his admiration for Liszt, he called him "the Pied Piper of Hamelin, the modern Attila, who appears as God's scourge of Érard pianos; they begin to tremble at the very news of his coming and they wince, bleed, and whimper under his hands, so that the Society for the Prevention of Cruelty to Animals ought to look into the matter." Yet for Chopin this caviler and carper had nothing but praise, valuing him as man and musician. He called him "the Raphael of the piano" and wrote:

> With Chopin I forget the pianist. I forget the "master," and I plunge into the gentle depth of his music, into the doleful delights of his creations, as delicate as they are profound. Chopin is the poet of music, an artist of genius whom one may name in the rank of Mozart, Beethoven, Rossini, and Berlioz.
>
> *Lutezia I*

The two remained friends until Chopin's death; by that time Heine was a pitiful wreck, suffering from syphilis of the spine, which condemned him to a "mattress grave."

Though Chopin made some new friends in the George Sand years, two old ones passed from his life. Julian Fontana emigrated to America at the end of 1841, having been unable to make much of an impression on Parisian audiences. He was exactly the same age as Chopin and both had studied with Elsner. He was a gentle man who loved Chopin and joyfully did errands for him, from proofreading a Mazurka to finding a lost hot-water bottle, renewing a subscription for the humorous periodical *Charivari,* hiring a valet, choosing the wallpaper, shopping for "a little ivory hand for scratching one's head," copying a Prelude, or looking in a special shop for special scented soap. Very possibly it was this subservience which determined Fontana to seek a field where he would not be known merely as "Chopin's friend." George Sand was glad to see him go: she disliked him. Chopin missed him at first and presently forgot his existence. Fontana remained in America for eight years; after Chopin's death he returned to Paris, where he edited Chopin's posthumous works; he killed himself at the age of fifty-nine.

Fontana's place was taken by Adolf Gutmann, a man with big hands of whom Lenz said that Chopin "tried to carve a toothpick out of this log." Gutmann remained one of the faithful.

Jan Matuszynski had been Chopin's friend, "made of the same stuff as I," since boyhood days. Chopin rejoiced when, after graduating from medical school, Jan came to Paris, and was proud when his fellow emigrant became a successful physician. They lived together for a time, until Jan married. But the physician was cut down by tuberculosis and died after horrible suffering on April 20, 1842. Chopin, sitting by his bedside and watching him vomit blood, was given a preview of his own fate. When it was over Chopin went to pieces: he shut himself up, would talk to no one and see no one except Sand. She comforted him as best she could and, as she wrote to Pauline, hoped that "Nohant will cure him as quickly as possible." For weeks nightmares invaded his sleep; he screamed that Jan's skeleton had appeared at the foot of the bed, spitting blood at him from an empty mouth. Now the number 20 (the day Jan died) assumed the ominousness of the number 13. It was a long time before he rid himself of the phantom.

(4)

If Chopin was capable of love and friendship, if he could be faithful to a George Sand, earn the loyalty of a Delacroix, open his talent to a Pauline Viardot, open his purse for sentimental reasons to an Anton Wodzinski, be understanding of so buffeted a child as Solange, he yet could be peremptory in conceiving sudden dislikes. Some bitter al-

monds stuck in the honey of his nature. His first disagreement with
George Sand was due to his antipathy to some of her friends, Pierre
Leroux for one, Sand's "sublime philosopher." Leroux believed, like
Rousseau and Condorcet, in man's essential goodness, which was to be
restored by what he called universal "solidarity." He denied religion:
there was no heaven, no hell; the purifying process must take place on
earth, through education and the sharing of wealth. No landowner is to
live off the wealth created by those who till the land. Sainte-Beuve said
of him: "Leroux writes on philosophy like a water buffalo floundering
in a marsh."

George Sand was not a professed atheist—"We have no atheists
here; God is not considered worthy of the trouble of denying him,"
Heine wrote—but she hated the ceremonies of religion and she in-
structed the director of the boarding school to which Solange had been
sent not to subject the girl to "the hypocrisy of genuflections and signs
of the cross nor to the idol worship with which the holy figure of Christ
is dishonored." Nor was her daughter to attend Mass. Chopin, who was
not particularly religious either, believed in its traditional observance
and was shocked by iconoclasm. As to this business of universal sharing
which Leroux expounded in his major work, *De l'humanité,* Chopin
pointed out that Sand, whatever her philosophic beliefs, regularly collected the rents from her Nohant tenants. But the "sublime philosopher" so impressed Sand that she was willing to contribute money to
the development of a printing machine on which Leroux had been
working for years and which would revolutionize the industry, while
Chopin, advised by an engineer friend of his, dryly pointed out that the
invention had no merit. Soon after, she became disenchanted with
Leroux and his continuous appeals for money. Then she agreed with
Chopin that Leroux was what Victor Hugo called him, a "sharposo-
pher."

More petty than this and yet more disturbing was Chopin's sudden
irritation with a rather silly but harmless enough woman, Marie de
Rozières. She had been a pupil of his, and around 1840, when she was
thirty-five years old, he had recommended her to George Sand as a
piano teacher for Solange. Subsequently she had come to Nohant and
Sand had grown fond of her. Then Chopin learned that Marie had
become the mistress of Anton Wodzinski. He was livid with fury. To
Fontana he wrote:

Nohant [August 24, 1841]

. . . she enjoys showing off her intimacy with him and poking her nose into other people's business. She exaggerates and makes a mountain out of a molehill—not for the first time either. Between ourselves, she is an intolerable old sow who by some strange chance has dug her way under my fence and grubs with her snout looking for truffles among the roses. She is a creature to keep well away from, for whatever she touches brings forth unheard-of indiscretions. In fact, a regular old maid. We old bachelors are far better.

[Nohant, September 12, 1841]

I introduced this slut to Mme. Sand as a piano teacher for her daughter. She has wormed her way in, and by pretending to be a victim of her love and to be fully informed of my past, thanks to members of the Polish colony whom she has met on various occasions, she has forced her way into Mme. Sand's confidence—and you wouldn't believe how cunningly, with what perfect skill she has managed to exploit my relations with Anton. You can imagine how pleasant it is for me especially as Anton (you must have noticed) loves her no more than he might love anyone who sticks like a leech and costs him nothing. With all his good nature Anton has no strong feelings and is easily taken in, particularly by such a cunning schemer who, as you may imagine, is full of desire for him. She covers herself by using his name, and proceeds from there to drag me in (not that it matters) and, what is worse, Mme. Sand. She seems to think that because I have been intimate with Anton since childhood, so [A whole sentence is here crossed out.]

Marie was of course neither an "old sow" nor a "slut," but a not very bright woman in her thirties, head over heels in love with a devil-may-care wastrel, eight years younger than she, who soon enough left her and returned to Poland, called back, or pretending to be called back, by his mother. It broke Marie's heart.

Chopin, himself a guest at Nohant, forbade her the house. George Sand to Marie de Rozières:

Nohant, July 11, 1841

Now let me tell you one of our secrets. A certain person here is irritated against you for reasons which I do not know. This attitude does not make sense and resembles a disease. . . . The same thing happens every time I speak up against his judgment and opinion on behalf of any individual; and the more I care for that person and the warmer my support, the greater is his mortification. If I had not for the last three years been a witness of these unbalanced veerings from sudden attraction to active dislike I should be baffled, but I am unfortunately too used to them not to realize that they are real. . . . I tried to cheer him by assuring him that Wz. [Anton Wodzinski] would not come here. He jumped to the ceiling, saying that if I was so sure it was apparently because I had told Wodzinski the whole truth. To which I replied Yes—and I thought he would go crazy. He wanted to leave the house, saying that I was making him look like a ridiculous, jealous lunatic, that I was causing trouble between him and his best friends, that my gossiping with you was the cause of it all, etc. Up to then I had talked smilingly, but perceiving that he was really terribly upset, that the pill was too strong, I retracted and told him that I was just setting a trap for him to punish him, but that in reality neither you nor Wz. knew anything. He believed me and calmed down at once, but all day long he changed color. . . .

What *was* the cause of Chopin's behavior which, as Sand wrote, made him spend "the whole day without saying a word to a soul"? True, Marie was a tattletale. True, he may have thought that her influence on Solange was not beneficent. (Solange did not need Marie to be spoiled.) Then, too, he had promised Anton's mother to watch over Anton, and now this rather ridiculous connection of Anton with a nobody of a woman had come about, and Chopin may have wondered what the Wodzinskis would make of it and whether they would blame him for exercising insufficient surveillance over their son. Yet we may guess that the root of his anger can be traced to his own unhappy experience with Maria Wodzinska. Anton would tell the details of that wooing to Mlle. de Rozières. It was a chapter—it may have been freshly painful just then, when he heard of Maria's marriage—that Chopin wished to remain closed. He hoped that "My Sorrow" would have dipped below the horizon of memory, and now it threatened to sail into sight again, to furnish a topic of gossip between two irresponsible people. So he vented his "unjustifiable prejudice" (Sand's words) on the Rozières woman, whom, anyway, he did not like and for whom George had expressed too loud an enthusiasm.

Curiously enough, after Anton disappeared from the scene, Chopin forgave Marie de Rozières. He wrote her a charming note from London (June 1848), telling her what he was doing, and asked her for various small favors.

(5)

Another Marie was responsible, at least overtly, for the break of the Chopin-Liszt friendship.

Marie d'Agoult, whom George Sand described in the good early days as "straight as a candle, white as a holy wafer," and whose bewitching blond beauty tempted more than one writer to burst into ecstasies, was deeply in love with Liszt and yet saw him clearly. She saw the greatness of his interpretative talent, she knew his struggle to become a composer of more than bravura pieces and pyrotechnical transcriptions; but she perceived as well the mummer in him, his oscillation between the wish to abstract himself from the world and the need to hear the ohs and ahs in the green room. Marie attempted to lead Liszt toward a less flamboyant life, to concentrate his talent on composition, and to smooth the rough edges of a man who, intellectually more curious than Chopin, stood far behind him in refinement of thought. Liszt listened to her as long as he was in love with her. Marie, Liszt, and George Sand were good friends even before Chopin joined them. They traveled together, discussed current ideas, and gossiped together about the artistic world. The relationship was not without tension: Marie harbored the suspicion that George was attracted to Liszt. It might once have been so, though George denied it: "Liszt? I'd rather eat spinach."

Later, George in her turn felt that Marie was only too willing to detract from Chopin's merit in favor of her lover's. And didn't she seek to rival George as an author, writing under the pseudonym Daniel Stern? Predictably, George thought very little of Daniel Stern.

Yet, when in the summer of 1837 Liszt and Marie left Nohant to set up house in Italy, they parted lovingly. All was amiable. Half a year later, George gave Balzac an analysis of Liszt and Marie which Balzac fashioned into a *roman à clef, Béatrix.* In it Sand appears as a noble, unselfish being, while Marie-Béatrix is a woman who hides intellectual shallowness behind the art of making herself desirable to men. As to Liszt, who has become the Italian singer Conti:

> He carries you up to heaven by a song which seems to be some mysterious fluid, flowing with love; he gives you a glance of ecstasy; but he keeps an eye on your admiration; he is asking himself: "Am I really a god to

these people?" And in the same moment he is perhaps saying to himself, "I have eaten too much macaroni. . . ."

One may imagine the effect the publication of *Béatrix* in 1839 had on Marie. Yet before that she had more than matched George in bitchiness. From Florence she wrote to Charlotte Marliani:

[November 20(?), 1838]

This trip to the Balearics amuses me. I'm sorry it didn't happen a year earlier, when G. was having herself bled. I always said: *In your place I'd rather have Chopin.* How many stabs of the lancet would have been spared her! Then she wouldn't have written the *Lettres à Marcie*, then she wouldn't have taken Bocage [a prominent actor, who had been Sand's lover for a brief time, prior to Chopin], and some good people think that would have been all the better. Will the Balearic establishment last long? Knowing them both as I do, they will be at daggers drawn after a month. . . . Their temperaments are *antipodean,* but never mind, it's all too pretty for words, and you wouldn't believe how I rejoice for them both. . . . Really, I'm sorry not to be able to gossip about it all with you. I assure you it couldn't be funnier. . . .

Again, in January 1839 Marie wrote the unkindest cut of all, that George's talent had become feeble, that the time of "emotion so magnificently revealed in *Lélia* and *Lettres d'un voyageur* had passed," that none of her lovers past or present now could help her.

Marliani was an officious goose: she felt she had to warn George against her so-called friend. She showed her Marie's letters, making her promise not to reveal that she knew about them. The result was a silent earthquake. All George could do was to refuse to have anything further to do with Marie.

Later, some sort of reconciliation took place between the two women. But it was a patch-up; George never really forgave Marie.

Chopin remained aloof from the distaff war, yet it gave him an excuse to freeze an already cooling friendship. The evidence suggests not only that Chopin envied Liszt's strong constitution and his ability to dominate the crowd, but that Liszt envied Chopin's creativity.

The rift was known and gave rise to one of those famous anecdotes which are dragged through biography after biography. The story went that once, in Nohant, Liszt played a piece by Chopin, embellishing it with his own inventions. Chopin said, "I beg you, dear friend, if you do me the honor to play one of my works, play it as it is written. Only

Chopin has the right to change Chopin." "Well, then," answered Liszt, "*you* play it." "Willingly," responded Chopin. At this moment a gust of wind blew out the candles. Chopin did not want them relighted and played in the dark. Liszt listened and exclaimed at the end, "You are right—the works of a genius are sacred. To touch them is profanation. You are a poet, I am a charlatan." Five days later, again in the dark, Liszt played, pretending he was Chopin. And Chopin himself said, with a smile, "I thought it was I who played." The story is almost certainly made of whole cloth: Liszt and Chopin were never in Nohant at the same time. Liszt's last visit took place in 1837, Chopin's first in 1839.

There is no need of dubious anecdotes lit by candlelight to show that almost from the beginning, "ambivalent" was the word to describe the Chopin-Liszt relationship. Mutual admiration was there—and mutual difference. Liszt declared he would have given four years of his life to have composed Chopin's Etude in E minor (Opus 10), though he also called the Polonaise Fantaisie (Opus 61) a product of deranged nerves. Chopin dedicated the Opus 10 to Liszt and had nothing but admiration for Liszt as a pianist, writing to Ferdinand Hiller:

> June 20, 1833
> I am writing without knowing what my pen is scribbling, because at this moment Liszt is playing my Etudes and putting honest thoughts out of my head: I should like to rob him of the way he plays my own studies. . . .

Chopin did not live long enough to be able to properly evaluate Liszt as a composer. The greater Liszt, the Liszt of Weimar, the Liszt of the symphonic poem (the first, *Ce qu'on entend sur la montagne,* performed in 1850), the Liszt of the Transcendental Etudes, emerged only after Chopin's death.

Liszt, who nicknamed Chopin "Mazurka," wholeheartedly loved Chopin's playing, a style as different from his own as sunset from noon. Whenever Liszt could, he went to hear Chopin, he applauded for all to see, he studied his works. They valued each other's executant ideas. Chopin wrote of *rubato:* "Imagine a moving tree with its branches swayed by the wind. The trunk moves in steady time, the leaves move in inflections." Liszt: "Do you see those trees? The wind plays in the leaves, life unfolds and develops beneath them, but the tree remains the same—that is Chopin's *rubato.*" Evidently they had discussed the matter.

Yet their personalities stood at opposite poles. That dazzle which emanated from Liszt, that compulsion to play Don Juan, his casting himself as the spokesman of intellectual movements, of which he was only a sciolist, brandishing a sword of honor which some crowned head or other had awarded him, a sword richly filigreed but without a cutting edge, his espousing (or pretending to) Saint-Simonism or the Catholic revival, his tampering with other men's compositions to make them more difficult to play, his constantly showing that he could play better than any other pianist (which he could)—all this was retrograde to Chopin's reserve. Chopin was not amused when Liszt signed a hotel register: *"Coming from:* Doubt. *Going to:* Truth. *Place of Birth:* Parnassus. *Occupation:* Musician-philosopher. Chopin would have been the last man to claim that he came from Parnassus and was seeking Truth.

To Julian Fontana Chopin wrote:

September 12, 1841
One of these days he'll be a member of parliament or perhaps even the King of Abyssinia or the Congo—but as regards the themes from his compositions, well, they will remain buried in the newspapers together with those two volumes of German poetry [written in Liszt's honor].

Liszt had his own way of retaliating; he wrote to Marie:

Limerick, Ireland, 14 January 1841
The Sand-Chopins are ridiculous. I am saving up a nice evening for them, but I don't agree that we should force them to an explanation. In such cases it is better to smile and deliver a more subtle blow. Don't worry, I shall look after that. . . .

The "more subtle blow" was delivered in April of that year, on the occasion of Chopin's concert at the Salle Pleyel. Liszt asked the critic of the *Gazette Musicale,* Ernest Legouvé, to let him write the review. According to Legouvé's autobiography, Chopin, on hearing this, said with a smile: "He [Liszt] will grant me a little kingdom within his empire." The review (probably written by Marie d'Agoult but signed by Liszt) is fulsomely laudatory, but contains tiny bubbles of venom. It speaks of Chopin "addressing himself to a society rather than to the public" and giving the impression of an "elegiac poet" with a "pale face."

Chopin's first biographers claimed that a rift in the friendship became pronounced when Liszt used Chopin's rooms for an assignation with Marie Félicité Pleyel during Chopin's absence. It is not a likely story, Chopin hardly being that much of a prude. If the Pleyel incident did occur, the most probable date would have been 1834, and Chopin and Liszt remained friends for quite some time after that.

The cooling off was not due to one incident, nor to the female feud (though it aggravated the situation), but to a succession of chills, the most obvious being Liszt's tampering with Chopin's notes and Chopin's envy of the energy which permitted Liszt to undertake concerts all over the European map, teach in Geneva, climb an Alpine glacier, and enjoy himself on the Italian lakes. Chopin possessed his own form of energy, a fey form. Though he was a hypochondriac, he couldn't resist hearing the chimes at midnight. But he couldn't do what Liszt could, travel and perform, perform and travel.

Liszt, who was not so vain as to be free of the artist's self-doubts, longed for Chopin's inventive vitality, which he displayed in the marvelous years with Sand. How did Liszt feel when he received a remarkably frank letter from Ernest Legouvé?

[1840?]

Schoelcher [French musicologist who wrote a life of Handel] tells me that one of my articles about Chopin, in which I preferred him to you, struck you as unpleasant. Since I expressed a purely personal musical opinion, I will not attribute to vanity the resentment you voiced to Schoelcher. Isn't your displeasure rather due to the sentiment of a friend who feels himself attacked, as it were, by another friend? If so, I sympathize with that feeling so strongly that I feel obliged to explain and justify myself. . . . In art, it seems to me, complete unity must be accorded first place. I hold that Chopin is complete—as executant musician and as composer his qualities are harmonious and of equal value. . . . You, on the other hand, and I tell you so with all frankness, you have arrived only halfway to your goal . . . the pianist has arrived, the composer waits in the wings. . . . I believe with all the sincerity I can muster that on the day that the intimate Liszt will usher forth, the day when his exceptional executant capacity will be matched by creative work (that day perhaps is not far off), on that day you will not only be called the first pianist of Europe, that day you will be known by quite another name!

Liszt continued to chase a virtuoso's triumphs, his itinerary from 1840 to 1844 including Hungary, Germany, England, Scotland, Belgium,

France, and Russia, until he came to anchor at Weimar. Chopin continued to stay away from the public* and during the same period published the Sonata in B-flat minor, the Ballade in F major (Opus 38), the
Two Polonaises (Opus 40), the great Polonaise in F-sharp minor (Opus
44), the Ballade in A-flat major (Opus 47), the Fantaisie in F minor (Opus
49), and so on to Opus 54, the Scherzo in E major. During these years
Chopin and Liszt saw each other less and less frequently and when they
did they were all too polite. After Chopin's death Liszt wrote to his
sister Louise: he wanted to "pen a few pages to honor the memory
. . . of one of the most noble glories of our art." He referred to "my long
friendship with your brother." It was but half true, as was the biography
Liszt published** only three years after Chopin's death, which Eleanor
Perényi, Liszt's recent and admirable biographer, characterized as
"abominable" and "a grave disservice." Sainte-Beuve read the manuscript. He said: "It needs to be completely rewritten."

---

*Actually he did not play in public between 1842 and 1848.
**It was probably written not by Liszt but by Carolyne Wittgenstein.

X

THE DUSK OF LOVE

IN A RELATIONSHIP such as that of Chopin and Sand, time acts either to move the two figures closer together—or else to enlarge the distance between them. What time does not and cannot do is leave the measure unchanged, the span constant. Constancy is a prerogative, rare indeed, of two people who have arrived at understanding—or of two people who have abdicated emotion. Though in the first years the two shared the joys of physical love and though their minds were for some years attuned, Sand could not—not profoundly—understand the nature of the genius who ever so slowly shaped emotion into sound, nor could Chopin quite fathom a talent which swallowed all experiences and then poured them quickly onto paper without a backward glance. Both these endowed beings lived their lives at high emotional tension, yet here, too, a difference prevailed: Sand's heart beat, as it were, democratically, with the wish to save the world, while Chopin, with all his worldliness, found his true existence in an imagined region, and was not concerned with improving humanity. As the years passed, the differences in their natures came to the surface and tended to separate them. With the distance increasing, the bright light which had encircled them began to fade and be diffused. Yet nothing decisive happened—until it did happen.

It would be simplistic to say that Sand "fell out of love with him," though the sexual ingredient of love did play a leading role in Sand's feeling. She was not a nymphomaniac, compulsively taking off her clothes and seeking a night's physical pleasure from one lover on Monday, to hitch up with another on Wednesday. Each affair seemed to be the end of the world. Whether its duration was long, as with Jules Sandeau or Michel de Bourges, or short as with Mérimée or Bocage, the feeling was intense and, in her own opinion, lofty. Each time it was to be the one enduring liaison. Yet her sexual transports cooled off as rapidly as they mounted, she became weary of the same bedfellow, her body as restless as her imagination.

By 1842, when Sand was thirty-eight and Chopin thirty-two, she had been with him for four years. That was a long time, as her time of loving went. Yet inevitably her passion passed, although his did not. Tenderness, which from the first had been an ingredient of their relationship, was to endure for some years beyond. We do not know exactly when physical relations ceased or what reasons Sand gave for putting him off. She said later that continued sexual relations "would have killed him." She consulted "his best doctor in our part of the country, who was as well one of his friends," Dr. Papet, who advised her "to loosen the bond between [them] until it ceased to be one altogether." No evidence exists that Dr. Papet made such an unscientific recommendation or that anybody else did. If abstinence began about 1843, which is the most likely date, it was groundless, Chopin's health being good at that time.

Sand, as so often, gave herself a justifying reason for what she wanted to do. She still "loved" him, but she no longer desired him. Although the attacks of his disease and his coughing during the night might have detracted from his desirability as a lover, her cooling off was more a symptom of her own instability. Even when he was well—and that was often—he no longer appeared to her as the mesmerizing partner. Yet she did not want to lose her *"petit Chopin."*

The termination of their sexual relations exacerbated Chopin's nerves. He could not accept the fact that her desire had paled, and he became tense, now breaking out in a loud quarrel over a trifle light as air, then withdrawing behind a show of distant courtesy. Between times they would be considerate and devoted. Solange, now fifteen, aware, and almost dry behind the ears, called him "No-sex Chopin." He called her "the little coquette" and began to be attracted to the pretty girl. Marie d'Agoult reported to Liszt: "I think it won't be long before the Chopin household breaks up. Some of our friends say he is morbidly jealous." It was *Schadenfreude,* but there was truth in it.

Jealous he was. In his code a woman "belonged" to a man. Too many shadows obscured the life of his beloved. What was she thinking? And

of whom? Was she secretly seeing another man? Did not her history,
some of which he knew, denote her inconstancy? He made scenes. He
scowled.

George Sand to Pierre Bocage, with whom she had had a brief affair:

> [Nohant, Summer 1843]
> . . . As for the jealousy of a certain young man [Chopin] over a certain
> old woman, it is calming down—it had to, for lack of sustenance. But I
> cannot say this malady is completely cured or that one does not need
> to spare it by concealing the most innocent things. The old woman had
> made the mistake of supposing that sincerity and honesty of purpose
> were the best remedies. I have advised her to say nothing of the letter
> from a certain old fellow [Bocage] for whom she can easily preserve in
> silence an eternal and loyal friendship.

There was no cause for jealousy . . . then. Sand did not have an affair
until 1845, when she became involved with the philosopher Louis
Blanc, who was a year younger than Chopin. Chopin remained ignorant
of that interlude.*

Louis Blanc, blond and handsome, fulfilled George's physical need,
but he was not and could not be a substitute for Chopin. Sand remained
deeply attached to him. If she lost her first fine rapture, if she was
offended by his sickly moods, he on his part was often disaffected by her
houseful of transients, by her mercurial enthusiasms, and by her in-
creasingly radical attitudes. He tired as well of her lap-dog endear-
ments, of her patronizing, of her being the sibyl to the postulant. Even
at the worst moments, however, he had not the strength to break away.

As in a marriage, which in effect it was, habit, concern, companion-
ship, affection, the gentler facets of both of them, remained. Because
of her work Sand lingered on in Nohant through the autumn of 1843,
while Chopin went to Paris. She wrote to Charlotte Marliani:

> [1843]
> Here comes my little Chopin. I entrust him to you, so take care of him
> in spite of himself. His daily routine goes to pieces when I am not there.
> He has a manservant who is all right but is stupid. I am not worried about
> his dinners because he will be invited right and left, and besides at that
> hour of the day it will be just as well if he has to bestir himself. But in

---

*The affair, a brief one, remained unknown until recently, when Georges Lubin
discovered a love letter from Sand to Blanc, dated February 1845.

the morning, in the rush of his lessons, I am afraid he will forget to swallow a cup of chocolate or clear broth. When I am there I pour it down his throat. . . .

Chopin is quite well now: all he needs is to eat and sleep like a normal person. I am obliged to stay here another two weeks . . . but I rely on you to let me know if Chopin should be in the slightest degree unwell, for I would abandon everything to go and look after him.

In May of the following year, Chopin received the news that his father, seventy-three years old, had died in Warsaw of a disease of the lungs (not tuberculosis). In his last hours he scribbled a message, written when he could no longer speak, which biographers for years have erroneously attributed to Chopin. The message was: "As this cough may choke me, I adjure you to have my body opened, so that I shall not be buried alive." It has now been proved beyond doubt that the handwriting is Nicolas's—but of course the anecdote will not disappear.

Chopin moaned and wept, his grief so terrible as almost to deprive him of sanity. He would see nobody except George Sand. She acted at once. She wrote a consoling letter to Chopin's mother—it was the first time she had communicated with her:

Paris, May 29, 1844

Dear Madame:

I do not think I can offer any other consolation to the excellent mother of my dear Fryderyk than to assure her of her admirable son's courage and resignation. You will realize how deep is his grief and how his spirit is overwhelmed; but thank God he is not ill, and in a few hours we shall be leaving for the country, where he will rest after this terrible crisis.

He thinks only of you, his sisters and all his family, whom he so warmly cherishes, and whose sorrow distresses and occupies his mind as much as does his own grief. For your part at least, please do not worry about the outward circumstances of his life. I cannot hope to remove his deep, lasting and well-justified sorrow, but I can at least care for his health and surround him with as much affection and watchfulness as you yourself could show. This loving duty is one which I have been happy to take upon myself, and I promise that I shall never fail in it, and I hope that you, Madame, have confidence in my attachment to him.

I will not say that your bereavement affects me as much as it would have done had I known the admirable man whom you mourn. My sympathy, sincere as it is, cannot lessen that terrible blow; but I know that by telling you that I will devote my life to his son, whom I regard as one of my own, I shall in some measure calm your fears in that respect.

It is for this reason that I have taken the liberty of writing to express my attachment to you as the adored mother of my dearest friend.

Justyna answered with equal tenderness:

> Warsaw, June 13, 1844
> ... And so Fryderyk's mother thanks you sincerely and entrusts her dear boy to your maternal care. Be his guardian angel as you have been an angel of consolation to me, and accept our respectful gratitude which you may be sure equals your invaluable devotion and care.

Presently Chopin's favorite sister, Louise, and her husband, Kalasanty Jedrzejewicz, decided that they would make the long and expensive journey from Warsaw to Paris to visit and comfort their brother. Sand wrote them an affectionate welcoming letter: "I bless the resolve you have made. . . . Come, then, and believe me when I say I already love you as a sister." Chopin was in a fever of anticipation—and he was as eager to see his sister's husband as he was to see Louise.

Sand immediately offered them her Paris apartment. Then, having seen Paris, they must come to Nohant. They must! It was the most cordial of invitations. Chopin wrote to Mlle. de Rozières, whom previously he had so strongly berated, to ask her to assist his relatives until he himself arrived in the city. Marie was more than willing to accept the task. As soon as he could get a seat in the stagecoach, crowded in the mid-July travel season, Chopin hastened to Paris to embrace the sister he hadn't seen for fourteen years. They kissed and wept, they wept and kissed. Then he began to show the city of his choice, with invitations to attend the Opéra, to see Rachel act, to watch a display of fireworks from a window seat at the Tuileries, to meander through the Louvre, to ride in the Bois. It proved too much for Chopin; he left Louise and her husband in Paris and fled back to Nohant. They followed at the beginning of August. George Sand was hospitality itself, and the garden and the fields welcomed them with the warmth of summer. George and Louise liked each other, Chopin's sister sympathizing with Sand's work and political views. Louise harbored no prejudices against her brother's liaison; on the contrary, she approved, and dispersed his fears. "It is a notable conversion," wrote Sand, and claimed that Louise was "worth a hundred times more than he." To which Chopin agreed. Sand even liked Kalasanty and called him "That rascal of a husband." Harmony reigned. When, after three weeks, Louise and her husband left, everybody was heartbroken.

All in all, it was still a good year. Chopin put the finishing touches on the Berceuse Opus 57, an enchanting lyric invention, a distillation of a mood which, simple enough in its melody, again opened up new dimensions of keyboard potential. He composed the Sonata in B minor (Opus 58), one of his greatest works, in spite of a banal stretch in the Largo movement. As to its bold last movement—it stands comparison with Beethoven.

(2)

The weather changed.

The summer of 1845 was beset with rain, the piano went out of tune, and Chopin could not solve certain compositional problems to his satisfaction. He began the Barcarolle Opus 60, but did not finish it until the following year. Similarly, the composition of the last of his major works, the Polonaise Fantaisie (Opus 61), had a two-year genesis. It was not that Chopin's creative pulse had become enfeebled; rather, it beat irregularly because he began to feel that the harmony of Nohant had undergone a change. A shadow passed through their rooms. When he appeared at dinner, he was silent, picked at the food, and looked like a schoolboy who has failed his exam. What was cause and what effect, he could not say, nor could George. To herself—and to him—she still professed that her feelings were the same. At the end of November, when Chopin had returned to Paris, she wrote urging him not to overtire himself and closed with: "Love me, my dear angel, my dear joy. I love you."

But the dear angel's mood continued uncertain. Louise's visit had reawakened in him a longing for his family, and he—for whom writing a letter was a chore—now wrote several long, chatty reports to Warsaw, describing his activities, what was going on in Paris, informing them that the "new electric telegraph between Baltimore and Washington is giving wonderful results," that at Bonn they were selling "so much old furniture, old desks and bookcases 'belonging to Beethoven' that the poor composer of the Pastoral Symphony must have had a vast furniture business." It reminded him of the concierge in Paris who kept on selling "Voltaire's walking stick." Victor Hugo, he wrote, was running away with his young mistress, Juliette Drouet, "in spite of Mme. Hugo, his children and his poems on family morality." For the benefit of Louise's husband, he included in one letter some rather feeble French jokes and puns. He mentioned with resigned humor that he had to get rid of his valet, Jan, because the fellow was always at loggerheads with Suzanne, George Sand's personal maid, and "the children don't like him either." He hated dismissing the old man—with whom he could speak Polish— but he did it "for the sake of peace."

Some time before, George Sand had taken into her home a distant relation, young Augustine Brault, whose mother was little more than a prostitute and whose father was a tailor's assistant. Sand had from time to time helped the family with money and in 1845, foreseeing nothing but a hopeless future for the pretty and intelligent Augustine, she decided virtually to adopt her. She could not legally do so, but she did refer to Augustine as "her fourth child." Augustine was a slim, dark-eyed brunette, a contrast to the juicy, blond Solange. The girl loved George with an open affection surpassing mere gratitude and contrasting with Solange's standoffish behavior. George made the mistake of setting up Augustine as an example to her own daughter. The result was to be expected: after a period of easy friendship between the two girls, replete with giggles and secrets, Solange began to hate Augustine.

Maurice could hardly treat the attractive Augustine as a sister. He was twenty-two, in need of love, just recovering from his infatuation with Pauline Viardot. He began to make advances to the girl. The rumor of the situation reached Augustine's father, who, acting like Eliza Doolittle's father, accused George Sand of having lured his virginal daughter to Nohant to provide Maurice with a handy mistress. Chopin, considering himself part of the family, confronted Maurice: if Maurice had slept with the girl he ought to "make honorable amends." Maurice, in full consciousness of his young manhood, first denied having had anything to do with Augustine, then told Chopin that it was none of his business, that he, Maurice, was now the head of the family and the master of Nohant, and, his anger begetting anger, implied that neither he nor his sister wanted Chopin to stay around any longer.

Curiously, Chopin took Maurice's outburst with equanimity. He shrugged his shoulders. Why pay attention to a young man's bad temper? But Maurice's behavior made Sand unhappy and she tried to keep the peace, asking Chopin not to criticize her idolized son—"since then he has been reasonable and you know how kind, considerate, and wonderful he can be when he is not angry"—and attempting to smoothe the tension between Solange and Augustine.

At the beginning of the summer of 1846 every sign indicated that Sand expected Chopin to stay on at Nohant. She was considering installing a form of central heating, largely for his benefit. And a machine for making ice cream, which Chopin loved, had been procured. Yet as the summer went on Sand distanced herself from her lover more and more. That summer was as hot as the previous one had been cool, and it produced summer lightning within the house. Sand had always welcomed Chopin's friends as her guests in Nohant; now she refused to entertain the Polish composer Josef Nowakowski, an old friend of Chopin's, who had come to visit France. The bedrooms were occupied; there was not only Augustine to be taken care of, but a young art student, Eugène Lambert, whom Maurice had met in Delacroix's studio. Maurice had invited him and George had said yes. Quite understandable, but Chopin, now touchy, interpreted it as a slight.

In July Grzymala came to visit. He brought along Countess Laura Czosnowska, whom Chopin had insisted on inviting, because she was a friend of his family. Sand did not like her—and objected to her little dog, Lily—nor did Augustine, and as Chopin wrote in another long letter home, "so of course neither did the son. They made jokes and passed from jokes to coarseness." Yet it was equally true that Chopin treated some of Sand's friends with silent disapproval.

Sand tried to find refuge from these intramural stresses in her own way, with pen and paper. She was working on a new novel. She had changed her working habits, rising at 6 A.M. and writing much of the day, so that in the evening all she could or wanted to do was to go to bed—alone. The new novel was *Lucrezia Floriani*, the story of a famous actress who has known the homage of the world, has experienced love in many forms and with many lovers, and has now retired to her Italian villa, believing that she has freed her heart of entanglements forever and desiring only one benison, peace. By chance a prince, Karol de Roswald, "delicate in body and spirit" and as handsome as Chopin, arrives at the villa. He is ill, she nurses him and soon falls in love with him. The first months of this love give her undiluted joy and she is certain that at last she has found her true affinity, but soon she realizes that it is an illusion—noble-minded though Karol is, he torments himself and her with reminders of her past life. He turns suspicious, querulous, intransigent—and most of all jealous: "One day Karol was jealous of the Curé who had come to collect money. Another day he was jealous of a beggar whom he mistook for a wooer in disguise. . . . Karol was even jealous of the children. What am I saying—even? He was that above all." In the end Lucrezia dies, sad and embittered.

Though Sand denied it strenuously, *Lucrezia Floriani* contained an obvious portrait of Chopin as she then saw him. It was a *roman à clef,* the key being in plain view. It infuriated Heine:

> October 12, 1850
>
> George Sand, that bitch, never bothered about me since I took ill. That emancipator, or rather "emanci-mater," of womanhood, maligned my poor friend Chopin in an abominable novel, divinely written. . . . [Letter to Heinrich Laube]

The writer Hortense Allart to Sainte-Beuve:

> May 16, 1847
>
> I am indignant about *Lucrezia.* . . . Sand . . . shows us a Chopin in most ignoble details, undressed as it were, and with a coldness which nothing can justify. . . .

Some of the details are almost ridiculously biographical: Lucrezia is six years older than Karol; Karol comes "from a German background, but is Slavic, his name Polish"; Lucrezia, "when she ceased loving, did not betray her lovers but cut the cord cleanly"; Lucrezia's children loved Karol, "except Celio" (the son); shortly before meeting Lucrezia he had lost his betrothed, and so on.

Yet the novel was not written for a vengeful purpose, but because Sand felt the need to describe and define the dusk of her love. It may have been her attempt to exorcise her dark depression by fastening it between the covers of a book. Lucrezia did not want to separate from Karol. It is certain that when Sand wrote *Lucrezia Floriani* she had not decided to cut the tie.

In August Delacroix came to Nohant. Sand read the novel to him, Chopin, and the rest of the company one evening. It must have been a long evening. Delacroix was dumfounded at this embarrassing strip-tease. Acutely uncomfortable, he kept looking at Chopin as Sand revealed stroke after stroke of the portrait. What was he thinking? What was he feeling? Chopin sat there apparently unconcerned. Delacroix later described the incident to a friend, Caroline Jaubert:

> I was in agonies all the time the reading was going on, but I don't know what astonished me more, the executioner or the victim. Madame Sand appeared to be completely at her ease, while Chopin expressed the

warmest admiration of the story. At midnight, we left together. Chopin
wanted to accompany me, and I took the opportunity to find out, if I
could, what he really felt. Was he playing a part for my benefit? No, the
truth was that he just had not understood.

Souvenirs, lettres et correspondance

Did he really not understand? Unlikely. Did he not recognize himself? Impossible. Did he not want to give himself away? Did he bury his
hurt beneath politeness, to fester unnoticed? Probably.

Whatever Chopin's reaction, there was no thought in his mind—nor
in hers—that the summer of 1846 would be his last in Nohant. He
returned to Paris in November; from time to time during the winter he
wrote to Sand telling her what he was doing. For New Year's he sent
her "my usual gift of sweets, *stracchino,* and cold cream from Mme.
Bonnechose."

(3)

That autumn Solange announced that she had a suitor. She was going
on eighteen and wanted to get married "only so as to be called Madame," according to her mother. The suitor was a landowner of Berry,
a young and personable aristocrat named Fernand de Preaulx, whom
Chopin liked. He came of a good family, his political sentiments, such
as they were, were royalist, he was gentle and not too intellectual.
Surprisingly, George Sand liked him too, and this consensus made them
content when they all met in Paris in early February 1847. The marriage
was planned for April.

Then it was all off. Solange decided she didn't like her Fernand. She
had probably chosen him in the first place to prove to Augustine that
she could attract an eligible young man; then on closer acquaintance
she became bored with him, he was too submissive to suit her hoydenish
temperament, she taunted him and finally dismissed him. Fernand,
grief-stricken, returned to his family, who made no secret of their relief
in no longer having to accept the offspring of the wicked George Sand.

Almost immediately a new suitor appeared, as different from Fernand as whiskey from cream. Auguste Clésinger was black-bearded,
cocky, as swaggering as d'Artagnan, and sure, at thirty-three, of his
immortality as a sculptor. George and Solange accepted his invitation
to visit his studio, where George admired a faun he had sculpted. The

next morning a messenger brought the faun to the Square d'Orléans. Clésinger now insisted that he had to perpetuate George's and Solange's likenesses in "eternal marble," and he sculpted Solange as a young Diana, shoulders bare, hair flying in the wind.

George was rather taken with this exuberant young man and flattered by the huge bouquets of flowers which arrived daily. Solange on her part was bewitched. She saw him more and more frequently. Now George, like any conventional mother, made inquiries about the new suitor. The reports were bad: Delacroix, as well as her wise friend Emmanuel Arago, the lawyer, were of one mind: Clésinger was an unstable and untrustworthy drunkard, who paid neither new nor old debts, who had had to flee from his creditors in Italy, and who beat his mistresses, one of whom was even then pregnant. The loudest warning was Chopin's. He had made his own inquiries about Clésinger and what he found troubled him. But Sand would not heed these voices, and it is even probable that Chopin's outspoken opposition served only to swing her to approval of the marriage. She managed to assuage her doubts by collecting favorable opinions from two artists, but she nonetheless thought it temporarily prudent to put a distance between Clésinger and her daughter by taking her to Nohant. At once Clésinger followed them. He demanded a yes or no and he demanded it at once. George was quite impressed by his impetuous fervor, never suspecting that he thought he was wooing the daughter of a rich author. "He will get his way," Sand wrote to her son, "because his mind is set on it. He gets what he wants by sheer persistence. I am amazed, I am even rather pleased by the spectacle of such strength of will." She consented. Solange was ecstatic.

George thought that Clésinger could tame "the lioness," the girl she was unable to control, and having come to her decision, she treated Clésinger and Solange generously, settling a considerable dowry on them. But she postponed telling Chopin of her decision as long as she dared. Perhaps she felt a trifle jealous of his love for Solange. "Not a word to Chopin," she ordered Maurice. "It is none of his business, and when once the Rubicon is crossed, *ifs* and *buts* will do nothing but harm." (April 16, 1847)

The Rubicon was crossed in a way which threw Nohant into panic, with Chopin in Paris knowing nothing. Solange, having gone to bed with Clésinger, missed her period and thought she was pregnant. She plunged into an icy river—and then told her mother all. George de-

cided that the wedding had to take place as soon as possible as privately
as possible. It was scheduled for May 19.

Not until the beginning of May did she notify Chopin. On the eighth
she wrote to Mlle. de Rozières:

> I am very frightened. Is it true then that Chopin has been *very* ill?
> Princess Czartoryska wrote and told me yesterday that he is out of
> danger; but how is it that you don't write? I am ill with anxiety and I
> feel quite giddy as I write. . . . Tell Chopin what you think best about
> us. However, I dare not write for fear of upsetting him too much; I fear
> that he will hate the idea of Solange's marriage, and that every time I
> mention it he will suffer an unpleasant shock. But I could not keep it
> from him, and I had to act as I have done. I cannot make Chopin the
> head of my family and its counselor—my children would not accept such
> a situation and my personal dignity would be lost. Good night, darling.
> Do write.

Four days after, she wrote Grzymala one of her serpentine letters,
an extraordinary mixture of truth and falsehoods:

> Nohant, May 12, 1847
> I shall be in Paris for a few days at the end of the month, and if Chopin
> can be moved I will bring him back here I tell you, my friend, I am as
> satisfied as it is possible to be with my daughter's marriage, since she is
> in raptures of love and joy, and Clésinger seems to deserve her, to love
> her passionately and to be able to give her the life she wants. . . .
>
> I think that Chopin, standing apart from all this, must have suffered
> from not knowing the persons and factors involved, and from not being
> able to advise. But his advice in the real business of life cannot possibly
> be considered. He has never looked straight at realities, never under-
> stood human nature on any point; his soul is pure poetry and music, and
> he cannot tolerate anything that is different from himself. Moreover, his
> interference in family affairs would mean for me the loss of all dignity
> and love, both toward and from my children. Talk to him and try to
> make him understand in a general sort of way that he must refrain from
> concerning himself with them. If I tell him that Clésinger (whom he
> does not like) deserves our affection, he will only hate him the more and
> will turn Solange against himself. It is all very difficult and delicate, and
> I see no means of calming and restoring a sick mind which is exasperated
> by the very efforts that one makes to cure it. For a long time now the
> disease which gnaws at the body and soul of this poor creature has been
> the death of me, and I see him fading away without ever having been
> able to do him any good, since it is his anxious, jealous and touching

affection for me which is the main cause of his misery. For the past seven years I have lived like a virgin with him and other men. [Indeed! What about Louis Blanc?] I have grown old before my time, but even so it cost me no effort or sacrifice, for I was so weary of passions and hopeless disillusionments. If ever a woman on this earth should have inspired him with boundless confidence I was that woman—and he has never understood it. . . . He complains that I have killed him by refusing my consent [to have sexual relations with him], while I was absolutely certain that I should kill him if I acted otherwise. . . . In that connection I have achieved miracles of patience such as I should not have thought myself capable of—I who was no saint like the Princess. It has become a martyrdom to me.

And much more in the same vein.

Perhaps the driving reason for her long lamentation can be stated in one sentence: She wanted none of Chopin's advice because she wanted to divorce herself spiritually from him—and she repudiated his concern over Solange all the more because she herself harbored doubts about Clésinger.

Chopin's reaction, hidden behind conventional congratulatory notes to George and Solange, can be gleaned from a letter to his family:

> Paris, June 8 [1847]
>
> Regarding Solange's marriage—it took place in the country during my illness—I can honestly say I am not vexed that it did, for I don't know what sort of face I could have put on. The young man comes from the devil knows what family. He was introduced to them here, and no one dreamt that it would end like this, not until just before they left for the country. From the outset I did not like hearing the mother praise him to the skies. Nor did I like seeing them go nearly every day to pose for their busts at his studio, or every other day receive flowers and various other gifts—puppy dogs, etc. (That is why I wrote in my last letter that you would certainly be hearing more of him.) The mother is a dear, but she has not a pennyworth of practical common sense—she invited him to Nohant: he was only waiting to be asked. He went, and he is so smart that they had no time to look round before it was all over.

Not a single one of George's Berry friends was present at the wedding, and she, having injured her ankle, had to be carried into the Nohant chapel. But at least it was over, and as she wrote, "We can breathe freely."

But she could not. Augustine had for some time been courted by

Théodore Rousseau, one of France's fine landscape painters. She responded to his attentions and George could not have been more delighted. George announced that she would give Augustine a dowry of a hundred thousand francs. "Impossible . . . unheard of . . . disgusting," was Solange's answer to her mother's offer of a gift to the girl she hated. She had no intention of letting so large a part of the maternal capital go to "a stranger," and she went to work. With Clésinger's help and a few well-penned anonymous letters, Rousseau was scared off. Solange, her hate spurting at full force, deliberately blackened Augustine's name with Maurice, claiming Augustine was a slut, telling him that she had gone to Clésinger's bedroom and he could have had her right then and there had he wanted to. Solange, cold, cynical, remorseless, invented these slanders, embittered as she was by the truth she had learned about her husband—that he was little more than a pretentious swindler, a prating peacock, who had run up a bill of four thousand francs with his tailor; who, after swearing that his debts amounted to no more than two thousand francs, admitted a few weeks after the wedding that he owed twelve thousand, and who lolled the day through doing little work but plenty of drinking. All the same, Solange stuck to him, defended him the more truculently the more she knew him to be worthless. In June she went with him to Nohant.

(4)

There the cast of the drama assembled: George Sand, Maurice, Solange, Clésinger, Augustine, Maurice's friend Eugène Lambert, and the journalist Victor Borie, the last two, innocent guests. But one of the actors was missing: Chopin, thanks to his instinct for stepping around a dirty puddle, remained in Paris, having made up his mind not to return to Nohant.

Before the young married couple arrived, the other members of the household met and promised not to mock Solange's grand airs, nor to question Clésinger's humbuggery. Let us try to have harmony! George freshly decorated her grandmother's room for the newlyweds and filled it with flowers.

Almost as soon as Solange unpacked, she began to show her contempt for the Nohant routine, arriving at meals just as the others were finishing, ordering the servants around, and first inviting, then peremptorily commanding Augustine to take a ride with her. When George reproved her, Clésinger got on his high horse and insisted in stentorian tones that "his wife was to be paid due respect." George answered: If you do not wish to accommodate yourself to our ways, you and Solange had better leave. "Then we will," replied the furious Clésinger.

But they didn't. They remained and the bickering continued, Solange retiring to her room "very ill" (she was not) and demanding that her mother stop Augustine from playing "her" piano (it was not hers). When George replied, "Stop plaguing me," the couple started not only to pack their own belongings but to strip the room George had prepared for them of the bedcovers, candlesticks, hangings, and knick-knacks, as well as the faun Clésinger had given to his mother-in-law and another statue, for which George had paid. Clésinger, cursing the servants for being too slow in packing the crates, took a hammer himself and pounded the nails down. At this moment the curé turned up at the house; having heard that there was trouble at Nohant, he came over to see if he could help to restore peace. Victor Borie took him for a walk in the garden. Solange, spoiling for trouble, now announced to her husband that young Lambert had insulted her. She could not vent her anger on Augustine, shut up in her room, so she let it out on Lambert, who had taken Augustine's part. Clésinger sought him out, first threatened, then lunged at him with all his strength. But Lambert, though half the size of Clésinger, ducked adroitly and gave his assailant a kick in the stomach. Clésinger bellowed and Maurice and George came hurrying in. George slapped Clésinger in the face and Maurice tried to wrest the hammer from his hand. Clésinger swore he was going to kill both of them, turned sharply on George, and punched her in the chest. Maurice rushed upstairs to get his pistols, screaming he was going to shoot Clésinger. A manservant, hearing the commotion, burst into the room and pinned Clésinger against the wall. The curé and Victor Borie followed; one disarmed Maurice, the other helped the servant hold Clésinger. George Sand wept. Solange turned to her husband and said, "You have hit my mother and put yourself in the wrong. Go back to your room."

Back to their room they went and they stayed there until the next morning. Then they left, without a word, without a good-bye. They put up at an inn in nearby La Chartre. Solange immediately wrote to Chopin, giving her own version of what had happened, and asked him to send her his carriage to transport herself and her husband to Paris. She insinuated that her mother threw her out because George wanted the freedom to be the undisturbed mistress of Victor Borie and perhaps of Eugène Lambert as well, and that Maurice was content with the situation, being able to carry on his affair with Augustine. As to herself: "I left Nohant after my mother had made the most atrocious scenes. Please wait for me before you leave Paris." Before she left La Chartre she had told her tale to the inhabitants of the village; some three hundred of them stood around and smirked as she and Clésinger mounted the carriage Chopin had duly sent.

George interpreted Chopin's dispatching of his carriage as proof that he sympathized with Solange. Her lover had betrayed her for the sake of her daughter. This was not to be borne! She lay ill for several days, blinded by headaches. Then she took the measure as natural to her as breathing: she poured out her grief in letters which recounted in detail the sordid scene at Nohant. She wrote to Emmanuel Arago, to Marie Rozières, to Delacroix, and of course to Chopin. She asked Marie to take the keys to her apartment as soon as Chopin had departed, so that Solange could not use it. That girl was never to be allowed to sleep under her roof again.

Chopin did not answer her letter, and not hearing from him, she began to worry. On July 25 she wrote Marie again: "Chopin troubles me. If I don't hear anything reassuring by tomorrow, I think I'll go [to Paris . . . if only] to convince myself that Chopin loves her much more than he does me . . . and takes her part." The next day she did hear from Chopin—a letter like a slap in the face by a clammy hand. He was not coming:

Paris, July 24 [1847]

I am not called upon to discuss M. Clésinger with you. The very name of M. Clésinger did not become familiar to me until you gave him your daughter.

As for her—I cannot remain indifferent to her. You will remember that I used to intercede with you for both your children, without preference. I did this whenever I had the chance, being certain that it is your destiny to love them *always*—for those are the only affections which are not subject to change. Ill fortune may cast a shadow over them, but cannot alter their nature.

This misfortune must be very powerful today if it can forbid your heart to listen to any mention of your daughter, at the beginning of her real life as a woman, at the very moment when her physical condition calls more than ever for a mother's care. When faced with such grave realities involving your most sacred affections, I must pass over in silence that which concerns me personally. Time will do its work. I shall wait —*still the same as ever.* My regards to Maurice.

Yours most devotedly,

CH.

She answered (it is one of the few extant letters to him):

Nohant, Wednesday [July 28, 1847]

I had called for post horses yesterday and I was going to set off in a cab, in this awful weather and very ill myself. I intended to spend a single day in Paris in order to have news of you. Your silence had made me so anxious about your health that I was prepared to go so far. In the meanwhile you were taking your own time to reflect, and your reply is very calm.

Very well, my friend, follow now the dictates of your heart and assume that it is the voice of your conscience. I understand perfectly. As for my daughter, her illness gives no more cause for anxiety than last year. Neither my zeal, my attentions, my orders nor even my prayers have ever been able to persuade her to behave otherwise than as a person who *enjoys* making herself ill.

It would ill become her to say that she needs her mother's love—a mother whom she hates and slanders, whose most innocent actions and whose home she blackens by the most frightful calumnies. You choose to listen to it all and maybe believe what she says. I do not propose to engage in such a combat. I shrink from it in horror. I prefer to see you pass over to the enemy rather than defend myself from a foe bred of my flesh and reared on my milk.

Look after her then, since it is she to whom you think you must devote yourself. I shall not hold it against you, but you will understand that I am going to maintain my right to play the part of the outraged mother, and henceforth nothing will induce me to allow the authority and dignity of my role to be slighted. I have had enough of being a dupe and a victim. I forgive you, and from now on I shall not utter one word of reproach, for you have made a sincere confession. It surprises me somewhat, but if, having made it, you feel freer and easier in your mind, I shall not suffer from this strange volte-face.

Adieu, my friend. May you soon recover from all your ills. I think you will (I have my reasons for thinking so); and I shall thank God for this bizarre denouement after nine years of exclusive friendship. Let me hear now and then how you are. There is no point in ever discussing the other matters.

This letter had been preceded by another in which Sand had taken Chopin to task for making his carriage available to Solange. We do not have the text, but we can conjecture that Sand demanded that Chopin break with Solange. Chopin showed the letter to Delacroix, who noted in his *Journal* on July 20:

> This was the day I left for Champrosay, where I have been for over a fortnight. It was on this day, or the day before, that I received Mme. Sand's letter telling me of her quarrel with her daughter.
>
> Chopin arrived just as I was lunching after having been to the Louvre, where I received a commission for a copy of the "Corps de Garde." He told me of a letter he'd received, but since I've been back in Paris he has read me almost the whole of it. I must admit that it is an atrocious letter. Bitter passions and long-suppressed impatience are plainly discernible, with a contrast that would be almost funny if the whole affair were not so sad; from time to time she plays the woman's part and bursts into tirades which might have been taken straight from a novel, or a sermon on philosophy.

Thus did it end, in a fusillade of rant and rancor. The two letters quoted here were the last messages they exchanged.

What were Chopin's motives in severing this long relationship? His immediate motives are easy to list: he felt that Solange had been unjustly treated, he had a horror of becoming involved in a family quarrel, and—most important—his nervous sensibility had been rocked by a liaison which for a long time had been a liaison in name only. When, later in the year, Solange made a brief return to Nohant to talk to her mother about money matters (Clésinger was drinking his way through most of the dowry), she was received coldly and she told Chopin that it was clear to her that her mother had wanted to get rid *both* of her and of Chopin to make free with Victor Borie. In Paris, Chopin swallowed Solange's lies, as is apparent from an unusually confiding letter he wrote to his family at Christmas:

> December 26, 1847–January 6, 1848
> Sol[ange] is with her father in Gascony. She saw her mother as she was on her way there. She went to Nohant with the Duvernets but her mother received her coldly and told her that if she separates from her husband she can go back to Nohant. She saw her bridal chamber turned into a theater, her boudoir into an actors' wardrobe room, and she writes to me that her mother spoke of nothing but money matters. Her brother played with a dog and all he found to say to her was: "Would you like

something to eat?" She saw no sign of the cousin or the other guests. In short, her two visits were completely wasted—I say "two," because the next day, before leaving, she went back to Nohant and was received even more coldly. However, her mother has told her to write to her, and I suppose she has done so. Her mother is now more furious with her son-in-law than with her daughter, whereas in her famous letter to me she wrote that her son-in-law was not a bad fellow, and that it was her daughter who made him like that. One might imagine she wanted to get rid of both her daughter and myself at one stroke because we were in the way. She will keep up correspondence with her daughter, and thus her maternal heart, which simply cannot do without news of its child, will be soothed and her conscience will be stifled. She will imagine she is being just and fair, and will proclaim me an enemy merely because I took the side of her son-in-law. She can't stand him, simply because he has married her daughter—a marriage which I did my best to prevent. She is a strange creature notwithstanding all her intelligence! She was seized by a kind of madness: she is making a mess of her own life and of her daughter's. Her son too will come to a bad end—I prophesy it and will sign my name to the prophecy. To excuse her behavior she tried to find some blame to lay on those who wish her well, who believed in her, who have never done her a low-down trick, but whom she cannot bear to see near her, for they are the mirror of her conscience. That is why she has not written me another word, why she will not come to Paris for the winter, and why she never mentioned me to her daughter. I have no regrets for having helped her to bear the eight most crucial years of her life, when her daughter was growing up and her son was tied to his mother. I do not regret all that I put up with; but what does hurt me is to see the daughter, that carefully sheltered young plant, preserved by her mother's hand from so many blasts, only to be crushed with an imprudence and frivolousness that might be forgiven in a woman of twenty but not in one of forty. One need not fully record all that has been said and done. Mme. Sand can have nothing but good memories of me in her heart, if ever she looks back on the past. In the meantime she is going through the most fantastic paroxysm of maternalism, play-ing the part of a far better and more just mother than she actually is— it is a fever for which there is no cure in cases where the imagination is so dominant and the victim is let loose on shifting and uncertain ground. . . .

The letter is almost a word for word repetition of what Solange had told him. It also reveals his love for Solange, of which he was perhaps but half aware.

But the word "love" here must be rightly understood. It was not love in the sense of a desire for union and sexual fulfillment; neither was it a paternal love. It was something of both, love in an indeterminate region, the topography of which shifted as the years rolled by. When he first knew her she was a child of ten and he a man of twenty-eight, old enough to be her father. When he parted from Nohant, he was thirty-seven and she nineteen, a very grown-up nineteen. The father figure melted into the admirer, who was charmed by her romping ways, her mirthful and jaunty enthusiasm, but also by her physical beauty, the long, unruly, and glittering hair, the full, soft figure, because of which her mother called her teasingly "my dumpling." Association, family affection, and sexual attraction were mixed in his feeling for her. He never spoke of it, but we can deduce the truth from his dislike of Augustine, his taking Solange's part in the brother-and-sister spats, his patience with her caprices. His letters of 1844 and 1845 mention her often:

> Solange is feeling poorly today. She is in my room and asks me to greet you cordially.

> Yesterday I was interrupted by Solange, who made me play four-hands with her.

> I return from an excursion with Solange. She carried me off in a carriage in company of Jacques. Jacques is an enormous dog.

> Where Solange is concerned, my heart aches.

> I have eternal regrets about Solange.

It was no coincidence that the day after Chopin was notified of Solange's marriage, he had a violent attack of asthma. It was rather a symptom and George knew it. "I fear," she wrote to Mlle. de Rozières, "that Solange's marriage displeases him greatly. Every time I talk to him about it he has a terrible coughing fit."

What were Solange's feelings toward Chopin? Did she love him? Was she capable of loving anybody? There we must guess. It is certain that she was aware of Chopin's love and that she set out to charm him, at first instinctively, then purposefully. She used him. She was and remained a coquette. He continued to write to her and to help her when he could. She continued to ask for his help. Her marriage proved to be a disaster, and she took a number of aristocratic lovers, from some of whom she accepted sizable sums of money. But this was long after Chopin's death.

As soon as George Sand realized that the end had come, she once again sat down at her desk. She wrote to Emmanuel Arago the longest letter of her entire life. Not only did she review every moment of that terrible scene in Nohant, but she cried out against her child, against her fate, against Chopin's "perfidy." Certain passages of this extraordinary letter seem like tranquilizers, meant to subdue her suffering over a break to which she herself had lent a hand and which she herself had, perhaps subconsciously, desired.

Begun July 18, finished July 26 [1847]
. . . Chopin, who was going to come here, all of a sudden does not come. He hardly writes, he won't write soon again. Chopin, who is in a much better condition than one would guess from his style and writing, who has gained in energy, brightness and resistance, Chopin completely changed, completely transformed toward me, no longer languishing from that eternal love which, his friends say, I am incapable of sharing, Chopin declares that I am a bad mother, that Sol[ange] is in the right and that he will not abandon her.

For him who by habit has pretended that grand, exclusive, imperishable passion . . . for him to make so brusque an about-face, isn't it a sign that he has changed one passion for another? . . . For two years I have told myself, and now I see clearly, that his pretended love for me is in reality hatred.

That is the only good that has come out of it for me. The result will be good for him, too. Cajoled, toadied to, allured by contact with Sol and her calumnies, he'll emerge happier, less ill, I predict, than he would be in a strife with me, undertaken by him to make me join in his ugly prejudices and live in an unsocial solitude. What a relief for me! A chain broken! I have always fought against his narrow and despotic spirit, but I have always been enchained by pity and by the fear of causing his death. For nine years I, myself full of life, have been bound to a cadaver. . . .

The future [will be better] after this period of suffering, mortal boredom, and often profound indignation, because nothing was as outrageous as his absurd jealousy. Yet I felt each gesture of resistance, each manifestation of high spirit to be the throwing of a rock at his poor existence. . . .

These are only a few excerpts from the diatribe. "Heaven has no rage like love to hatred turned,/Nor hell a fury . . . "

Arago answered her fully;* he tried to comfort her and counseled her to remain adamant toward Solange. Then, he said: ". . . one day she will repent and you can forgive her. But to forgive her now would be a grave fault." As to Chopin:

I call that a revelation, yet I am not at all surprised. I have long observed and perfectly understood the hold Solange exercised over his nervous nature. I became especially aware of it once when Solange tried to play her little games on me—which I cut short.

For several years he has been fascinated by her and he tolerated in her, gladly, whims he would have found exasperating in anybody else. I saw—saw clearly—that he harbored a profound sentiment for her which at first resembled paternal affection and which then transformed itself without his really being conscious of it, as she grew into a young girl and a young woman. What I observed here, my friend, is not unique: it has happened in analogous situations.

What is there to do? Nothing. What is there to say? It is a calamity, more of a calamity for him than for you. The chain weighed heavy? Well, you are freed of it. As to them—I dare not predict, yet I am certain that their future is black. . . .

Yet neither Chopin nor Sand could banish the other from memory. In November Sand asked Marie de Rozières to have Chopin return the Pleyel piano from Nohant:

Nohant, November 22, 1847

I don't want Chopin to treat me to a piano. I don't want to be under obligation to those who hate me. The confidences Chopin has made to his friends (which, like all confidences, were betrayed) prove where I now stand with him.

Chopin to Louise:

Paris, February 10, 1848

. . . Meanwhile the mother is writing a very fine serial story in *Les Débats*. She plays the actress at Nohant in her daughter's bridal chamber; she tries to forget and deadens her feelings as best she can.

She will not wake up until her heart begins to hurt—that heart which is at present dominated by the head. I have said my "Amen" to it all. May God be with her if she does not know how to distinguish

---

*This letter seems to have been overlooked by both the Sand and the Chopin biographers. Its full text has not been published. (Collection Georges Lubin)

genuine affection from flattery. Of course it may be only I who think the other people flatterers, and perhaps her real happiness lies where I cannot see it. For a long time her friends and neighbors have been unable to make out what was going on there during these last three months, but they may have already got accustomed to it. Besides, no one will ever be able to follow such a mind in its capricious twists and turns. Eight years of some kind of order in her life was too much. By God's grace they were the years when her children were growing up; and if it had not been for me they would have gone to their father ages ago and would not have stayed with her. Maurice will clear off to his father at the first good opportunity. But perhaps these are the conditions necessary for her existence, for her talent as a writer, for her happiness. I hope you will not worry over all this—it happened a long time ago. Time is a great healer—but I have not got over it yet. That is why I have not written to you—as soon as I begin a letter I burn it.

"I have not got over it yet"—that is apparent from his words. Sand to Pauline Viardot:

Nohant, June 10, 1848
Do you ever see Chopin? Tell me about his health. I am unable to repay his furor and hate by an equal measure of furor and hate. I think of him often as a sick child, embittered and lost.

Pauline tried several times to calm them. She failed. Sand to Maurice:

Nohant, February 12, 1848
If you have any things to give back to Chopin, leave them with the concierge—it will be better not to write anything. If you happen to meet him, say "How do you do?" as if nothing were wrong. "You are well? Splendid, so much the better." That is all, and go your way. Unless of course he avoids you—in that case, do the same. If he asks about me, tell him I have been ill as the result of my worries. Don't mince words, and speak quite sharply, so as not to encourage him to speak of Solange. If he should speak of her (but I don't think he will) you can say it is not for you to go into explanations with him.

In that same month the Revolution of 1848 burst forth. Chopin, though confined to his rooms, was well aware of its impact and implication; he knew how seriously it would affect the world and he felt that the kind of artistic life to which he was used had ended. In that inauspicious month Solange gave birth to a daughter—and Chopin hurried to send her a word of encouragement:

Paris, Friday, March 3 [1848]

I cannot help writing at once to say how delighted I am to know that you are a mother and are well. As you may imagine, the arrival of your little girl brought me greater joy than the arrival of the Republic. Thank God your sufferings are over. A new world is beginning for you. Be happy and take care of yourself. I really needed your good news. I was in bed during the disturbances—an awful attack of neuralgia all last week. Paris is quiet, with the quiet of fear. Everyone has rallied to the cause of order. Everyone has joined the National Guard. The shops are open—no customers. Foreigners, passports in hand, are waiting for the damage to the railways to be repaired. Clubs are beginning to be formed. But I should never stop if I tried to tell you what is going on here. Thanks again for your kind letter.

Yours devotedly,
CH.

Just fancy! Mallefille is Governor of Versailles! That Louis Blanc should be at the Luxembourg as president of the Labor Commission (employment being the real burning question of the moment)—that is quite natural.

Chopin and Sand saw each other only once again. Their accounts of the meeting tally. Chopin had been visiting Charlotte Marliani; as he was leaving he ran into George accompanied by Lambert in the vestibule. Chopin bowed and asked, "Have you had news from Solange lately?"

"A week ago," Sand replied.

"No news yesterday or the day before?"

"No."

"Then permit me to tell you that you have become a grandmother. Solange has a baby girl and I am very glad to be the first to give you the news."

Chopin then tipped his hat, and accompanied by an acquaintance nicknamed the Abyssinian, he walked downstairs. Then he remembered that he had said nothing to Sand about her daughter's condition. So he asked the Abyssinian to go upstairs again, saying that he was too feeble to reclimb the stairs—perhaps this was a pretext to avoid seeing Sand a second time—and to tell George that Solange and the baby were well. Later he wrote to Solange:

March 5 [1848]

I was waiting below for the Abyssinian when your mother came down with him and showed great interest in asking me about your health. I replied that you *yourself* had written me a penciled note the day after your child was born. I said you had suffered a great deal but the sight of your baby girl had made you forget it all. She asked whether your husband was with you, and I replied that the address on your letter seemed to be in his handwriting. She asked how I was—I said I was well, and then I called for the concierge to open the door. I raised my hat and walked back home to the Square d'Orléans, accompanied by the Abyssinian.

(6)

Arago was right. It was more of a calamity for Chopin than for Sand; she recovered, though it could be argued that the quality of her work fell off after 1848. His creativity was virtually over: he composed only two Mazurkas (Opus 67, No. 2, and Opus 68, No. 4) in 1849, the latter being, according to Fontana, "the last inspiration Chopin put on paper . . . he was already too ill to try it at the piano." The fullness of music of the Sand years, beginning with a Waltz in 1838 (Opus 34, No. 3) and ending with a Waltz (Opus 64, No. 3) in 1847, was exhausted. His spirit retrogressed as his disease progressed. Certainly his worsening physical condition was partly responsible for the absence of fresh inspiration. Yet not altogether. We know the connection between talent and physical decline, between afflatus and disease—see *The Magic Mountain*—especially in tuberculosis. His alienation from Sand was tantamount to an alienation from his own creative capacity. As he could not forget, as he could not forgive, he became uncentered, infirm of purpose; the strength of music within him slackened. That enfeeblement hastened his disease, as in turn his disease coughed his genius away. He carried memory with him to his rooms in Paris, and he left, so to speak, his genius in Nohant. He was the kind of man Proust describes who "thinks with regret of the sort of life which the early stages of their love seemed to promise, which the sequel has rendered impossible, making of that love a thing exquisitely painful, which will render a final parting, according to circumstances, either inevitable or impossible."

Sand, less profound, was less hurt. There are indications that she might have sought a reconciliation. She did keep asking after his health.

In December 1848 Pauline Viardot, pitying them both, reported to Sand:

> You ask news about Chopin. Here it is: his health is slowly declining, with passable days during which he can ride out in his carriage and other days during which he spits blood and has fits of coughing which choke him. He no longer goes out at night. However, he can still give lessons and on his good days he can be gay. That is the exact truth. Anyway, I haven't seen him for some time. He called on me three times without finding me. He talks of you with the greatest respect. I persist in affirming that he has *never* spoken of you in any other way.

Pauline was trying to be tactful; Chopin now spoke of Sand in terms of anything *but* the "greatest respect." Many years later Pauline told the composer Julius Rietz that the break between Chopin and Sand was not due to any sudden cause: "No, read *Lucrezia Floriani*, in my opinion a literary and psychological masterpiece, and at the same time a cruel action, and you will see, as if you had witnessed it yourself, what, little by little, invisibly, fatally, brought about the end of a liaison which was poor Chopin's life, and a slow death for Madame Sand. It's a sad story. I think that in all those love affairs there was no *friendship*—that is a passion which cannot diminish, it is the most beautiful of all."

The love story has no villain and no hero. It is idle to try to apportion the blame for the final separation. Given their psychological make-up, knowing Sand's purblind egocentricity and Chopin's prideful sensibility, the disbandment was inevitable, and it is remarkable that the relationship lasted as long as it did. If the end was dark, much light preceded it.

CHAPTER

XI

THE FOGS OF ENGLAND

LIKE MANY a troubled man, Chopin side-stepped his true task by busying himself with satellite activities. He made them seem necessary, though their real function was to still that voice within the creator which says "Create!" He edited previously composed music for publication, he continued to accept pupils as far as his health permitted, he went to the country, he undertook a major journey. Motion substituted for the patient shaping of a phrase.

He gave his first public concert in six years on February 16, 1848, in the Salle Pleyel. It was hardly "public," since the tickets were priced very high, the demand for them exceeding the supply three- or fourfold, and Chopin himself scanned the list of people who he thought ought to be admitted. He wrote his family:

> February 11, 1848
> The Court has ordered forty tickets and the papers had merely to mention that I might give a concert for people to start writing to my publisher from Brest and Nantes to reserve seats. This eager rush surprises me and I must begin practicing today, if only for conscience's sake, for I feel that I play worse than ever. . . .

Those in the know were quite convinced that he was at death's door and were all the more surprised to see a pale but erect man stepping from the wings, dressed in the height of fashion, walking with certain step to the piano bench, glancing casually at the bank of flowers which surrounded the piano, and beginning a long and arduous program

[198]

which included a Mozart Trio, some of his own major works, and, with the cellist August Franchomme, the Cello Sonata, composed two years previously. At the end there was general jubilation and Chopin, willy-nilly, had to repeat the "Minute" Waltz. Afterward he nearly fainted in the artists' room.

Four days later the *Revue et Gazette Musicale* noted: "It is easier to report the welcome he received and the ecstasy he created than to describe, analyze or reveal the mysteries of an execution which can be compared to nothing else on earth."

Six days after the concert the torch of revolution was hurled into Louis Philippe's throne room. The flammable material of discontent had long been accumulating, but as usual few had noticed it and fewer still had attempted to clear it away. The prime minister, François Guizot, had long been opposed to universal suffrage, and national policies were determined by no more than 250,000 voters, who could prove that they had a reasonable income, leaving some 35 million disenfranchised. Such prejudice galled not only the Romantics, heirs to the ideals of the Revolution of 1789, but the sentimental mourners of Napoleonic glory, as well as the hard-headed peasants. The average laborer earned less than two francs a day; the peasant struggled on a near starvation diet after two disastrous harvests in 1845 and 1846.

On February 22, 1848, workmen, students, and the unemployed of Paris assembled to march on the Chamber of Deputies and the Tuileries, shouting for a change—or vengeance by violence. The Place de la Concorde was a solid mass of discord, until the National Guard, which had earlier shot into the crowd, joined the revolutionaries. Two days later Louis Philippe abdicated, the republic was proclaimed from the balcony of the Hôtel de Ville, with the arch-Romantic poet Lamartine as its provisional head. It was the wrong place for a poet.

As the 1848 revolution spread over Europe, it split into sharp and ugly factions in France itself. Those noble speeches, the great sacrifices, the efforts to create employment artificially, the fulsome new laws, the barricades and the dead—all seemed in vain. Taxes rose 45 percent in March, commerce came to a standstill, fear crept into the houses. In June terrible blood baths took place in the streets of Paris; the workers' rising was crushed by a military dictatorship, and ten thousand lost their lives. The revolution which had begun in February ended in December with the election of wily Louis Napoleon.

Who cared about art in those dreadful months? The Romantics lost their nerve. They had become middle-aged. Hugo was offered a ministry by Lamartine but refused. Sainte-Beuve went to Switzerland. Musset lost his post as a librarian. Characteristically, middle-aged George Sand was one of the few who remained unafraid. She organized her Berrichon people, she wrote pamphlets, she made speeches, she rushed up to Paris to see how she could help—that was how she and Chopin met accidentally. "My heart and head are on fire," she wrote. "I am alive, I am active, I am only twenty years old." But it was not long before she had to speak of the "disillusioning republic."

Berlioz fled to London. Returning to Paris in July, he wrote:

> What a sight! What hideous ruins! . . . the fallen trees, the crumbling houses, the squares, the streets, the quays, seem still quivering with the murderous struggle! . . . Fancy thinking of Art at such a period of wild folly and bloody orgies! . . . All the theaters are closed, all the artists are ruined; all the teachers are idle . . . poor pianists play sonatas in the squares; historical painters sweep the streets; architects are mixing mortar on the public works. . . . The Assembly has just voted fairly considerable sums toward the opening of the theaters, and in addition has granted some slight relief to the more unfortunate among the artists. But how inadequate to meet the wants especially of musicians! Some of the first violins at the Opéra only had thirty-six pounds a year, and were hard put to it to live even by giving lessons as well.
>
> *Mémoires*

(2)

Jane Stirling had first met Chopin after his return from Majorca. She was instantly attracted to him, and as instantly she conceived a dislike for George Sand. She thought that the Sand affair would be of but brief duration. Chopin, she said, became enamored four or five times during an evening but by morning he would forget all about it.

She had been Chopin's pupil for some seven years, which suggests that she was more than a social dilettante; had she not taken her studies seriously, Chopin would have lost patience with her. The fact that four years after she first entered his studio he dedicated two compositions to her, the Nocturnes Opus 55, is a further indication of the teacher's approval.

Jane came from a wealthy and prominent Scottish family. Her father, James Stirling, who had made his money in the West Indies and then became a banker in Edinburgh, owned an estate named Kippendavie, a name which conjures up a glen in a mist. Jane was born in 1804, and was of exactly the same age as George Sand. She was the "problem" child of the family: she studied music, she stayed in Paris for long periods, she befriended artists, she never married, though with her tall figure, her coquettish ringlets, her complexion which seemed to have been watered by Scottish rains, and her green eyes, she was good-looking enough. She displayed her unconventionality like a school diploma; at bottom she was a rather conventional soul. Robert Louis Stevenson's definition could have been applied to her: "Enthusiasm about art is become a function of the average female being, which she performs with precision and a sort of haunting sprightliness." Undoubtedly in love with Chopin—who gave her no encouragement—she sought to bind him to her, if only in friendship, and she had long tried to persuade him to perform in England and Scotland. When Louis Philippe stepped down, when the shouts of revolution crisscrossed Paris, when it looked as if the French aristocracy was to be, if not led away in a tumbril, at least demoted into poverty, Chopin decided to accept his pupil's invitation. Like Kalkbrenner, Thalberg, Pixis, and other artists, he sought safety across the Channel, and he arrived in England in April.

Jane and her elder widowed sister, Catherine,* did everything they could to make him comfortable in London: they saw that the chocolate he drank was on hand, that the fire was lit in his room on Cavendish Square; and they had even provided writing paper with his monogram. Presently he moved to a flat he liked better, at 48 Dover Street, spacious and airy—and expensive—large enough to accommodate the three pianos sent to him (obviously for advertising purposes): a Pleyel, an Érard, and a Broadwood. He was wined and dined all too strenuously, and he let himself be piloted to this mansion and that reception, not having the strength to say no. As always, he was much concerned with the weather. Was it going to rain? Would a fog descend? That year for the first time, the English newspapers received weather reports by

---

*In 1811 Catherine had married James Erskine, making a connection with another noted Scottish family. Her husband died five years later and Catherine remained a widow. Her temperament was more prosaic than Jane's, but she went along with Jane's enthusiasm for Chopin, largely to please her sister.

telegraph and Chopin deciphered these, believing that the weather determined the state of his health.

But in other respects he was cut off from news, not being able to speak English or to read it easily. What was happening in Paris? "I hope our district was spared [in the riots] and that our friends at least are not victims." He was worried about Solange, who was living near the danger zone. He was homesick for Paris. And while he sojourned in a strange country, his thoughts turned to his first home, to Poland. It had been a long time since he had given serious thought to his birthplace. "Things are bad at home. I am terribly concerned," he now wrote, and he kept inquiring about the progress of the Polish revolutionary movement. A dilatory letter writer, he became an industrious correspondent, writing to Grzymala, Gutmann, Solange, Franchomme, his family—and Marie de Rozières, whom he now called "a good sort." Tucked into these letters are seemingly casual inquiries after George Sand, expressed so as to assure himself he had been in the right all along. In one letter to Grzymala he wrote that George would undoubtedly forgive Clésinger because she was "once on far too intimate a footing with him not to forgive him," but then "what was to become of Augustine?" whom Chopin had so disliked and whom he now called "that doll of a girl." In another letter he wrote: "I know that Mme. Sand has written to Mme. V[iardot] and has inquired most *sympathetically* about me!!! How she must be playing the part of the honest and upright mother over there!"

London's musical and literary life was yeasty. The year before, Emily Brontë had published *Wuthering Heights* and Tennyson *The Princess.* In the year Chopin was there, the last installments of Thackeray's *Vanity Fair* and Dickens's *Dombey and Son* appeared. Chopin met Dickens, Lady Byron—"I can see why Byron was bored by her"— Samuel Rogers, George Hogarth, Walter Scott, though all these meetings had to remain casual, to the regret of Thomas Carlyle, who wrote that he hoped the two of them "shall get some language to speak in by and by." Carlyle thought Chopin "an excellent, gentle, much-suffering human soul, as I can at once see without language." The two Stirling sisters fluttered around him like hummingbirds; but he could not rouse himself from his melancholy. The "haunting sprightliness" of Jane irritated him (she irritated Carlyle as well), the covered sky bored him, the cold, so unlike the Parisian spring, made him forget that it was May, and the moist air, combined with the smoke of the factories, aggravated his cough. Or so he thought. What really underlay his discontent with outward circumstances was an inner emptiness.

He could not, or would not, live in London in a style other than that he had enjoyed in Paris. He hired a carriage. He employed a valet, an Italian who was good for nothing except stealing, and he quickly got rid of him. Then he hired a French valet, the "good Daniel," who remained with him till his death. He had his hair dressed every day. All this, along with the landlord's raising his rent, cost money—"living here is very expensive"—and he set about earning some. But no large public concert—not that, anything but that: rather, if he must, "a musical matinee for a limited audience in some private house." In the meantime, he began to give lessons to five pupils at a guinea a lesson. To Grzymala:

> London, July 8–17 [1848]
>
> They are awful liars here: as soon as they don't want anything they clear off to the country. One of my lady-pupils has already left for the country, leaving nine lessons unpaid. Others, who are down for two lessons a week, usually miss a week, thus pretending to have more lessons than they really do. It does not surprise me, for they try to do too much—to do a little bit of everything. One lady came here from Liverpool to have lessons for a single week! I gave her five lessons—they don't play on Sundays—and sent her away happy! Lady Peel, for example, would like me to give lessons to her daughter, who is very talented, but since she already had a music master who gave two lessons a week at half a guinea a time, she asked me to give only one lesson a week so that her purse should not suffer. And simply to be able to say that she has lessons from me. She will probably leave after two weeks.

He felt "more dead than alive." To Grzymala:

> London, June 2 [1848]
>
> If I could run around for whole days from one end of London to the other; if only I had not been spitting blood these last few days; if I were younger and if I were not, as I am, up to the neck in social obligations —then I might start life all over again. . . . My good Scottish ladies show me great friendship here. I always dine with them when I am not invited out. But they are used to roaming around and being shaken up in a carriage while rushing all over London with visiting cards. They would like me to visit all their acquaintances although I am more dead than alive. When I have been jolted up and down in a carriage for three or

four hours I feel as though I had traveled from Paris to Boulogne. And the distances here!

. . . I am always introduced, but I have no idea to whom, and I am quite lost in London. What with twenty years in Poland and seventeen in Paris, it's not surprising that I am getting on slowly here, particularly as I don't speak the language. They don't chatter while I am playing and they apparently all speak well of my music, but my little colleagues are usually treated with such scant respect that I appear to be a kind of amateur, and I shall soon be regarded as a kind of *nobleman,* for I have clean shoes and I don't carry around visiting cards inscribed: "Private lessons given. Evening engagements accepted."

Old Mme. Rothschild asked me how much I *cost* (*"Combien coûtez vous?"*), as some lady who had heard me was making inquiries. Since Sutherland gave me twenty guineas, the fee fixed for me by Broadwood, on whose piano I play, I answered, "Twenty guineas." She, so obviously trying to be kind and helpful, replied that of course I play very beautifully, but she advised me to take less, as one had to show greater "moderayshon" this season.

I gather from this that they are not so open-handed and money is tight everywhere. To please the middle class you need something sensational, some technical display which is out of my sphere. The upper classes who travel abroad are proud, but educated and fair—when they deign to take notice of anything. But their attention is frittered away so much on a thousand different trifles, they are so hemmed in by tiresome conventions, that it's all the same to them whether the music is good or bad, for they are compelled to listen to it from morning till night. There is music at every flower show, music at every dinner, every sale is accompanied by music. The street singers, Czechs and my pianist colleagues are as numerous as dogs—and all mixed up together. I am writing all this as if you didn't know London!

The concert at the Duchess of Sutherland's to which he referred in this letter was the first of his London appearances and took place on May 15. That he was asked to play testifies to the reputation which had preceded him; it was a gala affair and no artist of less than bright fame would have been invited, the guests of honor being Queen Victoria and Prince Albert. On that day a daughter of the Duke and Duchess of Sutherland had been christened in the private chapel of Buckingham Palace. The Duchess was Mistress of the Robes to Victoria, and the Queen had accepted the invitation to the evening's celebration. Three illustrious singers—Tamburini, Lablache, and Mario—performed; it must have cost the duke a pretty penny. Chopin described the soiree three months later in a letter to his family; evidently its excitement had not worn off:

[August 10–19, 1848]

. . . In addition to the Prince of Prussia (who was about to leave) and the royal family, there were only such people as old Wellington, and others like him—although it is difficult to be *like him.* The Duchess presented me to the Queen. Her Majesty was gracious and spoke with me twice. Prince Albert moved closer to the piano. Everyone said that these are rare favors. Among the Italians who sang that evening were Mario, Lablache and Tamburini—no women. I should like to describe to you the Duchess's palace, but it is beyond me. All those who know say that the Queen of England herself has not such a residence. All the royal palaces and castles are ancient and splendid, but have not the taste and elegance of Stafford House (as the Duke of Sutherland's palace is called) which is situated near St. James's Palace, just like the Blacha [a small Warsaw palace near the royal castle]. For example, the staircases are famous for their magnificent effect: they do not lead either from the vestibule or from an anteroom, but arise in the middle of the apartments as in some huge salon—with splendid paintings, statues, galleries, carpets, all most beautifully laid out and with the most wonderful effects of perspective. And you should have seen the Queen standing on the stairs in the most dazzling light, covered with all her diamonds and orders—and the noblemen, wearing the Garter, descending the stairs with the greatest elegance, conversing in groups, halting on the various landings, from every point of which there is something fresh to be admired. It really makes one sorry that some Paolo Veronese could not have seen something like it—he would have left us one more masterpiece.

Chopin's playing does not seem to have made an impression on Queen Victoria. She noted in her Journal:*

May 16

At 8 we dined at Stafford House, We, ladies, all in white. The good Duke & Duchess received us at the door. I sat between the Duke & Albert. . . . After dinner came the Pce of Prussia, some relations and connections of the Sutherlands & a few of the Ministers & Diplomats. There was some pretty music, good Lablache, Mario & Tamburini singing & some pianists playing. The rooms looked quite beautiful.

---

*We are indebted to R. Mackworth-Young, Librarian, Windsor Castle, for this information.

Perhaps there is an explanation for Victoria's indifference: only some six months had elapsed since Mendelssohn's death and she and Albert had loved Mendelssohn personally and adored his music. She was in no mood to listen to a new pianist-composer. Chopin himself said, "You have to play Mendelssohn if you wish to score a great success."

After that concert Chopin thought he would be asked to play at Buckingham Palace. He was wrong—and the fault may have been his. He had earlier been invited to play at one of the Queen's Concerts with the Royal Philharmonic Society. It was a coveted honor, but Chopin had refused:

> Their orchestra, like their roast beef or turtle soup, is strong and efficient, but that is all. What I have said is not really a valid excuse: there is only one impossible circumstance—they never have more than one rehearsal, since everyone's time is so valuable just now, and that rehearsal is a public one.

He didn't want to rehearse in public (tickets for this rehearsal were given gratis), when he could not correct or repeat passages. Undoubtedly his other reason was the usual one: "to avoid all big public concerts." He did make four other appearances in private homes, the first at Lady Gainsborough's, the second at Marquis Douglas's, the third at the house of Mrs. John Sartoris, who before her marriage to the rich industrialist was Adelaide Kemble, sister of the famous actress Fanny Kemble and herself a singer. At that concert Giovanni Mario, the tenor whom London worshiped, sang three selections. Jenny Lind, with whom Chopin had become acquainted and who had spent a long evening singing Swedish songs for him, was present, much to Chopin's joy. The final concert, on July 7 at the residence of Lord Falmouth,* No. 2 St. James's Square, beginning at half-past three, enlisted the collaboration of Pauline Viardot. Her presence inspired him. "He came into the room bent double and with a distressing cough. He looked like a revived corpse," wrote one who was at Lord Falmouth's, "but when he sat down to the instrument he played with extraordinary strength and animation." At each of these concerts the audience numbered between one and two hundred, tickets were a guinea, and Chopin realized 360

---

*Chopin described Lord Falmouth as "a great lover of music and a great lord; nonetheless one would be tempted to give him alms were one to meet him in the street. . . . He has a multitude of servants, all better dressed than he."

guineas—a considerable sum. Nevertheless, he was worried: "I may have only 200 guineas left after deducting the cost of my lodgings and carriages." The season was over, the exodus from London had begun, and the Stirling sisters urged him to come to Scotland with them. His mood had not improved: "I can feel neither grief nor joy. . . . I am just waiting for it all to end quickly."

(3)

Calder House, Lord Torpichen's residence, twelve miles north of Edinburgh, seemed, though near the city, remote enough to serve one of the Waverley Novels. Chopin described it in a letter to his family:

> [August 10–19, 1848]
> Lord Torpichen is an old, seventy-year-old Scot, and brother-in-law to Mrs. Erskine and Miss Stirling, my kind Scots ladies. . . . I could not refuse their invitation to come here, especially as there is nothing for me to do in London and I need a rest, and as Lord Torpichen gave me a cordial invitation. The place is called Calder House (they pronounce it Kolderhaus). It is an old manor house surrounded by a vast park with hundred-year-old trees. One sees nothing but lawns, trees, mountains and sky. The walls are eight feet thick; galleries everywhere and dark corridors with countless old portraits of ancestors, of all different colors and with various costumes—some in kilts, some in armor, and ladies in farthingales—everything to feed the imagination. The room I occupy has the most splendid view imaginable—although this part of Scotland is not the *most* beautiful.

And he wrote Camille Pleyel:

> August 15, 1848
> It is an old manor where John Knox, the Scottish reformer, celebrated communion for the first time. There are walls eight feet thick—endless corridors, full of ancestral portraits, each one blacker and more Scottish-looking than the next. Nothing is lacking—there is even a certain "red-cap" phantom which shows itself. After all that has happened on the Continent I suppose the ghost is busy changing his headgear, so as not to be mistaken for one of your French evil spirits—he has not been seen for some time. If only *your* red-caps could change their way of thinking!

How did Chopin manage that long journey from London to Edinburgh, weak as he was and ignorant of the language? It was Henry

Broadwood who helped him, showing himself "my best and truest friend." Chopin told his family the story:

[August 10–19, 1848]

One morning he came to see me—I was worn out and told him I had slept badly. In the evening when I came back from the Duchess of Somerset's what do I find but a new spring mattress and pillows on my bed! After a lot of questioning, my good Daniel (the name of my present servant) told me that Mr. Broadwood had sent them and had asked him to say nothing. And now, when I left London ten days ago, I found on the platform for Edinburgh a gentleman who introduced himself from Broadwood and gave me two tickets instead of one for seats in my compartment—the second one for the seat opposite, so that no one might be in my way. Besides that he arranged for a certain Mr. Wood (an acquaintance of Broadwood's) to be in the same carriage. He knew me (having seen me in 1836 at the Lipinskis' in Frankfurt!). He has music shops in Edinburgh and Glasgow. Broadwood was also kind enough to have my Daniel (who is better behaved than many gentlemen and better looking than many Englishmen) seated in the same compart- ment, and so I covered the 407 English miles from London to Edinburgh via Birmingham and Carlisle in twelve hours by *express train* (that is, a train with very few stops).

In spite of the generosity and hospitality shown him, in spite of the comfort of the house and the beauty of nature, Chopin could not emerge from his depression. The letter to his family continues:

How kind my Scots ladies are to me here! I no sooner have time to wish for something than it is ready to hand—they even bring me the Paris newspapers every day. I have quiet, peace and comfort—but I shall have to be leaving in a week. The lord has invited me for the whole of next summer: I would not mind staying here all my life, but what would be the use? . . . Some evenings I play Scotch songs to the old lord—the good man hums the tunes to me and expresses his feelings in French as best he can. Although everyone in high society speaks French, the general conversation is usually in English and then I regret that I can't follow it; but I have neither the time nor the desire to learn the language. Anyhow, I understand everyday conversation; I don't allow myself to be cheated and I should not starve to death, but that is not enough. . . .

On August 28 I am expected at Manchester, where I am to play at a concert at which Italians from London will sing—Alboni and others. I am getting sixty pounds for it, which is not to be turned down; so I have accepted and in a week's time I shall be traveling there, just over 200 English miles—eight hours by train. In Manchester some kind friends are awaiting me, wealthy manufacturers who have Neukomm staying with them. (He was Haydn's best pupil and used to be court conductor to the Emperor of Brazil—you must have heard his name.) . . . After the concert I am to return to the Glasgow district to visit Lord Torpichen's sister-in-law, then on to Lady Murray's and back to Stirling (Keir House). They want me to play at Edinburgh in the first days of October. If it means making some money, and if I have the strength, I shall certainly do it, for I don't know how I am going to manage this winter. I have my regular apartment in Paris but I don't know how things will turn out there. Many people would like to keep me in London for the winter, in spite of the climate. I would rather do something else, but I don't know what. I shall wait until October to see how things stand with my health and purse; and so another hundred guineas in my pocket won't come amiss. If only London were not so black and the people not so heavy and dull, and if only there were no sooty smell or fogs, I might already have learnt English. But these English are so different from the French, whom I have become attached to just as if they were my own people. They consider everything in terms of money; they love art only because it is a *luxury*. They are good kind souls, but so eccentric that I quite understand that if I stayed here I myself could become petrified or turned into a machine. If only I were younger I might let myself become a machine: I would give concerts all over the place and play the most tasteless trash (anything to make money!). But it's difficult for me to begin now to turn myself into a machine.

Nobody who knew Chopin could have believed for one minute that he would ever have been capable of playing trash or doing "anything to make money." But such thoughts are indigenous to a sick man. He wrote to Grzymala, having arrived in Glasgow:

September 9, 1848

I am unwell, depressed, and the people weary me with their excessive attentions. I can neither breathe nor work. I feel alone, alone, alone, although I am surrounded by people. [Seven lines blacked out.] . . . If I were in a cheerful mood, I would describe one of these Scotswomen, said to be the thirteenth cousin of Mary Stuart (*sic!* her husband, whose name is different from his wife's, told me so in all seriousness!). They are all cousins here, male and female, belonging to great families with great names which no one on the Continent has ever heard of. The whole conversation is conducted on genealogical lines: it's just like the Gospel —such a one begat so-and-so, and he begat another, who begat still another—and so on for two pages, up to Jesus Christ.

As to the English, now that he was a good Frenchman, he observed in a later letter that

> every comment ends with the words: "Leik water," meaning that the music flows like water. I have never yet played to an Englishwoman without her saying: "Leik WATER!!" They all look at their hands and play wrong notes most soulfully. What a queer lot! God preserve them!

His despair was even more directly expressed in a letter written from Calder House to Julian Fontana, who was stopping off in London.

> August 18, 1848
>
> If I felt better I would travel to London tomorrow in order to give you a last embrace. Perhaps we shall not meet face to face so soon. We are a couple of old *cembalos* on which time and circumstances have played out their miserable trills. Yes, old *cembalos,* even if you protest against being associated with me in such a way. That means no disparagement of your beauty or respectability: the sound board is perfect, only the strings have snapped and a few pegs have jumped out. But the real trouble is this: we are the creation of some famous maker, in his way a kind of Stradivarius, who is no longer there to mend us. In clumsy hands we cannot give forth new sounds and we stifle within ourselves those things which no one will ever draw from us, and all for lack of a repairer. . . . All that is left to me is a long nose and a fourth finger out of practice.

All the same, he had let himself be persuaded—as he wrote to his family—to play publicly in Manchester, a bourgeois town where the women must have exclaimed "Leik water!" The pianist George A. Osborne, a pupil of Kalkbrenner, who knew Chopin well, remembered that Chopin begged him to leave the hall while he played: "You who have heard me in Paris remain with those impressions. Your presence will be painful not only to you but to me." But Osborne remained:

> Notwithstanding this appeal, I was present, unknown to him, in a remote corner of the room, where I helped to cheer and applaud him. I heard him then for the last time, when his prediction was in part fulfilled, for his playing was too delicate to create enthusiasm, and I felt truly sorry for him.

When he played the "Funeral March" Sonata in Manchester, a curious incident occurred. He had played the first movement and the Scherzo when he suddenly rose from his chair and disappeared. What was wrong? Had he forgotten the music? Had he suffered a coughing

attack? He reappeared almost immediately and finished playing the
Sonata. The *Manchester Guardian* commented on the incident. The
explanation is contained in a letter to Solange:

> September 9, 1848
> A strange adventure befell me while I was playing my Sonata in B-flat
> minor before some English friends. I had played the Allegro and the
> Scherzo more or less correctly. I was about to attack the March, when
> suddenly I saw arising from the body of my piano those cursed creatures
> which had appeared to me one lugubrious night at the Chartreuse
> [Majorca]. I had to leave for one instant to pull myself together, after
> which I continued without saying anything. . . .*

George Sand. Majorca. Specters. Visitations. Recollection of dead
love.

(4)

From Manchester he went to Johnstone Castle, near Glasgow, owned
by Anna Houstoun, another sister of Jane Stirling. He rested there
before a recital in Glasgow's Merchant Hall on September 27. This was
a matinee and the tickets were a half guinea. The men were busy during
the day and "half a guinea was considered too high a sum for their wives
and daughters." And the hall was only one-third full. Chopin seems to
have played superbly.

He then proceeded to Keir in Pertshire to the castle owned by
Stirling-Maxwell.** His peregrinations took him from one castle to another—and nowhere did he find surcease. On a gloomy, typically Scottish Sunday, on which there was "no post, no trains, no carriages (even
to take the air), not a boat, not even a dog to whistle at," he wrote to
Grzymala:

---

*This letter is owned by Bernard Gavoty. It has not been included in any compilation
of Chopin's correspondence.

**William Stirling-Maxwell was a cousin of James Stirling, Jane's father. He was a
historian, specializing in Spanish history. He had married Caroline Norton, "the Hon. Mrs.
Norton," one of the three granddaughters of Richard Brinsley Sheridan. She became
famous for her liberal attitude toward divorce and served George Meredith as his model
for *Diana of the Crossways*.

October 1, 1848

At the same time as your letter to Johnstone Castel [*sic*]—the one in which you said you had been to the Gymnase Theater with Solange—I received another from Edinburgh, announcing that Prince and Princess Alexander [Czartoryski] had arrived and would be glad to see me. Although tired, I jumped into the train and caught them still in Edinburgh. Princess Marcellina is kindness itself, just as she was last year. I revived somewhat under the influence of their Polish spirit, and it gave me strength to play at Glasgow where a few score of the nobility drove in to hear me. The weather was fine and the Prince and Princess also came by train from Edinburgh, bringing little Marcel who is growing into a fine boy. (He can sing my compositions, and if anyone doesn't play them quite correctly he sings to show them how.) It was on Wednesday afternoon at three o'clock; and the Prince and Princess were kind enough to accept an invitation to dinner at Johnstone Castel (12 English miles from Glasgow). So we spent the whole day together. . . .

You can't imagine how that day brought new life to me. But I am already depressed again—this fog! Although, from the window I am writing at, I have under my very nose a most lovely view of Stirling Castle (that castle near the town of Stirling—the one in *Robert Bruce,* at night, on the top of the cliff—you remember?), and of the mountains and lakes and splendid parks—in short, one of the finest views in Scotland—well, of all this I can see nothing, except when the fog is now and then so obliging as to give way to the sun for a few minutes—a sun which shows very little fight here. The owner of the house is called Stirling. He is the uncle, on the father's side, of our Scots ladies, and is the head of the family. I made his acquaintance in London. He is a rich bachelor and has here numerous fine pictures—many Murillos and paintings of the Spanish school. He has lately published an expensive volume (you know how well they do that sort of thing here) on the Spanish School. He has traveled widely and has been in the East: he is an intelligent man. Whenever members of English society are visiting Scotland they come to see him. He keeps open house and there are usually about thirty people to lunch. . . .

I shall soon be forgetting Polish. I shall talk French like an Englishman, and I shall learn to talk English like a Scotsman, resembling old Jawurek [a piano teacher at the Warsaw Conservatory], who used to talk five languages at the same time. . . .

Nowadays I am not fit for anything during the whole morning, until two o'clock—and after that, when I have dressed, everything irritates me and I go on gasping until dinnertime. Dinner over, I have to remain at table with the menfolk, *watching* them talk and *listening* to them drinking. Bored to death (thinking of quite different things from them, in spite of all their politeness and explanatory remarks in French around the table), I must call up all my strength of mind, for they are by that time curious to hear me. Afterward my good Daniel *carries* me off upstairs to my bedroom (as you know, bedrooms are usually upstairs in English houses), helps me to undress, puts me to bed, leaves a candle, and then I am free to gasp and dream until morning, when it starts all over again. As soon as I have got somewhat used to being in one place I have to go off somewhere else; for my Scots ladies give me no peace. They either turn up to fetch me or cart me around to their families; but note that I always insist on a pressing personal invitation. They will suffocate me out of *kindness* and I, out of *politeness,* will not refuse to let them do it.

On the fourth of October Chopin gave an evening recital in Edinburgh. This time he undertook the entire program. Never before had he appeared that often within a space of three months and never before had he cared so little. The day before, he said, he had not visited the room where he was to play, nor settled on his program. He seems to have worked in a half-somnolent state—until he sat at the piano. Again the tickets were priced at a half guinea. Jane Stirling feared that not enough of them would be sold to a public to whom Chopin was largely unfamiliar, so she secretly bought fifty pounds' worth of tickets and gave them to her friends. So generous an action could not be kept quiet and rumors were now flying that Chopin was going to marry Jane. Chopin protested: Could Jane "marry a cadaver"? To marry "there must be some sort of physical attraction; the unmarried one is far too much like me. How can one kiss oneself?"

He was longing to get away, back to Paris, revolution or no revolution. He was weary of Scotland, sick to death of travel, tired of Jane, to whom, however great her kindness, he really could not warm. He spent a few more weeks in Scotland, dividing his time between Calder House and the homes of other acquaintances, and at the end of October he returned to London. He was now seriously ill, took to his bed, and feared he would die "in the presence of an indifferent doctor and a servant." The Stirling sisters followed him to London; but their solicitude was cold comfort. Marcellina Czartoryska, who happened to be in London, came to see him almost every day; those visits he loved. After two weeks he recovered physically, if not spiritually. On November 16 he played at a benefit given for Polish refugees. He consented to do so

out of a sense of patriotism: it was a mistake. He played in a small room,*
while in a large room nearby a dance orchestra officiated. The people
drifted away; they wanted to dance, to have a good time, not to listen
to a serious, subdued pianist. That was Chopin's last concert.

The next day he began a letter to Grzymala, once more pouring out
his grief—"why doesn't God finish me off at once instead of killing me
by inches?"—but this time old resentment, still fresh, rose to the surface:

> London, 17–18 [November, 1848]
> I have never cursed anyone, but everything is so unbearable that I
> should feel easier if I could curse Lucrezia. But they too must be suffer-
> ing down there [at Nohant], suffering all the more since they are grow-
> ing old in their fury.

The fact that he called George Sand Lucrezia suggests that he had
known the meaning of *Lucrezia Floriani* all along.

Three days later he had made up his mind to leave "beastly" London
and return to Paris. He wrote to Grzymala:

> [November 21, 1848]
> I shall spend the night from Thursday to Friday at Boulogne, and on
> Friday I shall reach the Place d'Orléans in daylight—reach it to go
> straight to bed. Besides my usual troubles I have neuralgia and my face
> is all swollen. Please get them to air the bedclothes and pillows. See that
> they buy plenty of fir cones—Mme. Etienne must not try to economize
> —so that I can get warmed right through as soon as I arrive. I have
> written to Rozières. Have the carpets laid and the curtains hung. I will
> pay Perricher, the furnisher, at once. You might even tell Pleyel to send
> me any kind of piano on Thursday evening—see that he is paid for the
> transport. On Friday, get them to buy a bunch of violets to scent my
> drawing room—let me find a little poetry when I come home, just for
> a moment as I go through on my way to the bedroom, where I know I
> am going to lie a long, long time.
>
> Well, then, by midday on Friday I shall be in Paris. One more day
> here—and I shall not die but GO MAD—my Scots ladies are so tiresome!
> May the hand of God protect them! . . .
>
> P.S. Get them to light the fires, warm my rooms and dust them—I may
> yet recover.

---

*At the Old Council Chamber, not, as is usually stated, the Guildhall.

He left London on November 23, in company of a Polish acquaintance. Broadwood had made the same kind arrangement as for the journey to Scotland: the seat opposite Chopin was reserved and he could stretch his legs. As the train moved out of the station and friends waved good-bye, Chopin suffered a terrible spasm. His companion thought he was going to die. But he recovered, looked calmly at the English countryside, and when he reached Folkestone ate with appetite. The Channel was easy and they spent the night at Boulogne. At noon of November 24 he reached Paris.

He was home, with his own curtains, in his own bed, his own fire, and the scent of violets. One of the first things he did was to write Solange, who was away from the city, at Guillery. She was pregnant again and she and Clésinger were deeply in debt. She needed help; Chopin gave it.

He could no longer give lessons, nor did he have new compositions to sell. A concert was out of the question. His expenses increased, if anything, what with the fees for all the doctors he consulted, the money he sent Solange, the fresh flowers daily, the cost of Daniel, the Paris inflation. For the first time since his youth he was financially hard pressed. That worried him. The doctors advised sunshine and rest. "Rest!" he wrote to Solange. "I shall have that one day without their help!" Regardless of expense, in the spring of 1849 he moved to a fine little country house, in Chaillot, a suburb of Paris. He longed for good air, though most of the time he could breathe it only by opening the window; he sat there and looked out over the city he had come to understand. Friends came to his aid with a generosity which indicates how much they loved him and a delicacy which shows they respected his pride. Countess Natalie Obreskoff, a long-time friend, arranged the rental of the villa and lied to him about the cost: the rent was four hundred francs but she told him two hundred, and paid the other two hundred herself. He could hardly believe this extraordinary bargain, but she made up some taradiddle of a story about the summer rents in Paris being cheaper. Presently he could ill afford even two hundred, in addition to the Place d'Orléans apartment. Franchomme sent one thousand francs, as did the Rothschilds; the Czartoryskis contributed various sums; and Marcellina saw to it that a nurse was in attendance, whose salary she probably paid. The most munificent gift came from the Stirlings: Mrs. Erskine sent a messenger with twenty five thousand francs —a sum which could have lifted any money worries from Chopin's shoulders—in an unmarked envelope. The messenger left it with Mme. Etienne, the concierge of the Place d'Orléans house. The romantic notion of delivering cash without the name of the donor seems to have been Jane's: she wanted to play the part of the good fairy who gives mysterious gifts. Mme. Etienne did not deliver the packet, claiming that she forgot about it; however, she kept it carefully, somewhere in her lodging. This happened in March. Four months later, when Chopin continued to complain of his straitened circumstances, saying never a word about the anonymous gift, the Stirlings began to wonder if he had received the money. Mrs. Erskine wrote Grzymala, putting him in the picture, he in turn wrote to Chopin, and a little investigation was begun.

Chopin from Chaillot to Grzymala in Paris:

July 28 [1849]

After your reply to her [Mrs. Erskine's] letter I let my hands drop in amazement, and I did not know whether to suspect her of suffering from hallucinations, or her messenger or Mme. Etienne of being a thief. And I did not know whether to think I had lost my memory or whether I was a lunatic: in short, my head was fit to burst. She came and confessed, and answered so stupidly—her sister [Jane Stirling] being supposed to know nothing of it—that I was forced to tell her a few truths: for example, that from no one except the Queen of England . . . would I consent to receive such lavish gifts, etc. But here is what happened: the individual to whom they entrusted such a sum without his being aware of it, and who did not even get a receipt from Mme. Etienne showing that he had delivered that letter or parcel, well, that person went to Alexis, the medium. This is where the drama begins.

Alexis tells him that on a Thursday in March (the 8th) he had taken some very important papers to a certain address (he wrote down my name), that the packet had not reached its destination, that he has not got it, that in fact he handed it over in some small room, where you go down two flights of steps, to some woman—there were two of them, and the taller one took it. She had a letter in her hand which the postman had delivered to her and, taking also the packet in question from the aforementioned individual, she told him she would deliver it at once. But, added Alexis, she took it downstairs and did not even show it to me; and he said that I have never seen the packet.

When he was asked whether he could see what had happened to the packet, he said he could not, but that if they brought him a lock of hair, or a handkerchief, or a pair of gloves belonging to the person who had accepted the packet, he would be able to tell. Mrs. Erskine was present at the séance with Alexis, and she came yesterday to tell me about it and to ask how she could manage to get hold of something belonging to Mme. Etienne, so as to be able to give it to Alexis. I sent for Mme. Etienne, on the pretext of asking her to fetch the Boiste [French] dictionary and some handkerchiefs, and when she came I pretended to want to get rid of Mrs. Erskine who was supposed to want a lock of my hair for some spiritualist at Saint-Germain (where the Scots ladies are living just now) who cures sick people. Well, pretending to get rid of her, I said that if the spiritualist recognized where the hair came from—for I should send some of Mme. Etienne's hair—then I would believe it and send some of mine; but I said I was sure the spiritualist would not know the difference between healthy hair and hair clipped from a sick person. So at my request Mme. Etienne cut off a lock of hair, wrapped it up, and Mrs. Erskine took it away.

This morning Mrs. Erskine and the messenger came here after seeing Alexis. Alexis had recognized the hair as being that of the person to whom the packet had been given. He said she had placed the packet, sealed, in some cabinet near the bed, and that it was still in her house and neither lost, delivered nor unsealed. He said that if the messenger went about it prudently she would hand it over, but he must use caution. So the man went straight from here at twelve o'clock to the Square d'Orléans, found Mme. Etienne alone and reminded her that in March he had given her a packet for me—he had told her it was very important. She recognized him and handed over the packet which he had delivered so many months ago. It was not unsealed and the twenty-five thousand francs in it were untouched. Mrs. Erskine unsealed it in the presence of the man and myself. What do you make of it? That medium!!! The occurrence makes my head whirl. Please note that I did not accept the gift—and I could say a great deal about it. I prefer to tell it to you some other time. You may now believe in magnetism [sic]. Thank God the money was found. . . .

Chopin began to doubt the Alexis the Medium story soon enough and wondered whether it was humbug trumped up by Jane Stirling, who had sent the money only a few days before the séance—not in March but in July—her motive being that she wanted the gift to be anonymous, yet one of so transparent an anonymity that Chopin would quickly discover the donor. Hence the business of the disappearing and reappearing packet and the complicated ritual, all invented by Jane to impress Chopin. Considering Jane's romantic temperament, her mystification was not impossible, being the kind of storybook gesture of which she was fond. And if it was a hoax, it was well calculated to appeal to the moribund Chopin, the mystic who saw apparitions arise from the piano. After suspecting the tale, Chopin wrote, "I can't get that Alexis out of my mind"; he half believed.

Perhaps there is a simpler explanation. Very likely Jane had nothing to do with the disappearance of the money. Mme. Etienne may have attempted a fraud, highly profitable if successful. She may have known that there was money in that envelope. She knew Chopin to be a very sick man. He might die shortly and the money might remain unclaimed. At worst she could always "find" it and, if questioned, apologize for "forgetting" to deliver it, producing a convenient soothsayer to show her where it was. When in July she *was* questioned, she did just that, using the messenger as her helper. A devious scheme—but well within the capacity of a Mme. Etienne. Chopin may not have been far from the mark when he suspected her of "being a thief."

Chopin at first refused the large sum altogether. It was probably Grzymala who persuaded him to keep fifteen of the twenty-five thousand. The fifteen thousand was more than enough to save him from penury for the brief span he had yet to traverse. But the gift did nothing to bring him closer to Jane Stirling; we hardly ever forgive our benefactors.

CHAPTER

XII

"NO MORE"

SICKROOM CALLS are at best embarrassing, at worst heartbreaking. But such considerations did not prevent Chopin's friends from making their way to Chaillot and spending time with him. Jenny Lind, however nomadic her life, came to sing for him. Delacroix, Franchomme, and Grzymala brought him the news and gossip.* Delfina Potocka, as beautiful as ever, had herself driven over from Versailles. Her sister, Princess Ludmilla Beauveau, brought the violets Chopin liked. The Baroness Rothschild appeared before leaving Paris for Sweden. They all emerged from isolation to see Chopin, ignoring the epidemic of cholera which was raging in most of Europe and which, on June 10, killed the old pianist Kalkbrenner and two days later the singer Angelica Catalani, who had been one of the first to recognize Chopin's talent. Even Berlioz came to see Chopin, though Harriet Berlioz, very ill, needed continuous nursing. She, too, contracted cholera, but recovered.

In defiance of doctors' orders, Chopin indulged himself once more in his love for opera, and went to the premiere of Meyerbeer's *Le Prophète* on April 16, when Pauline Viardot sang the role of Fidès, which Meyerbeer had created for her. Delacroix noted in the *Journal* on April 22, 1849:

---

*Grzymala did not come often. He was afraid to go out. Several members of the Polish society in Paris were accused of having taken part in the 1848 revolution and were expelled by the new government.

To Chopin after dinner. He is another man it does one's heart good to be with, and one's mind as well, needless to say. . . . He had dragged himself to see the first performance of Meyerbeer's *Le Prophète*. His horror at that rhapsody!

His disease followed the classic course of consumption: days of misery, days when he felt well, and days when he hoped he would recover, as Verdi's Violetta hoped—*"Rinasce, rinasce!"* His favorite physician, Dr. Molin, had died and he now consulted doctors Louis, Roth, Simon, Blache, Fraenkel, and the well-known Dr. Jean Cruveilhier. They all gave him the usual false encouragement. As he sat in his armchair, unable to work but hoping for a brighter future, his mind reviewed the past, and though surrounded by affection, he longed for the friends of his young days and most of all, a feeling stronger than all others, for the bond of family. After twenty years in Russian-dominated Poland, Titus Woyciechowski had at last obtained permission to come to Belgium. He was now at Ostend, relatively near. Could he come to see Chopin? It would be wonderful. But the French frontier was closed to Russian subjects. Chopin at once asked "an influential friend" to obtain an entry permit for Titus. Seeing Titus after all those years—it would do him more good "than all the medicines in the world!" Alas! the permit was refused.

But another wish near to his heart was granted: to see his sister Louise. Here, too, a travel permit presented a problem. From Würzburg, Marcellina Czartoryska wrote to Ladislas Czartoryski in Paris:

May 16 [1849]

Go and see Mme. Kiseleff [wife of the Russian ambassador]. I have asked her to get someone to write to Warsaw and apply for a passport for Chopin's sister and brother-in-law. Ask what is happening, and request Mme. Kiseleff not to mention it until a satisfactory answer is obtained, for I should not like poor Chopin to torment himself unnecessarily over the business.

Not only the Princess Marcellina but Delfina went to work, as well as the ever helpful Mme. Obreskoff. Strings were pulled, and after the usual bureaucratic delay, permission was granted. Louise, her husband, and their daughter, Louise, arrived at Chaillot the first week in August.

In inviting her, Chopin had fooled himself about the seriousness of his condition, believing he would be strong enough to play the active host:

Chaillot, June 25, 1849

My dearest: Can you come? Please do! I am ill and no doctors will do me so much good as you. If you are short of money, borrow some; when I get better I shall easily earn money and I shall pay back whoever has made you the loan. At the moment I am too hard up to send you anything. My place here at Chaillot is large enough to take you both, even with two children. It would be beneficial in every way for little Louise. Father Kalasanty could find plenty to do all day—there is a horticultural exhibition close at hand—in fact he will have more free time to himself than he did last time, because I am weaker and shall stay at home with Louise.

My friends and well-wishers consider that Louise's arrival would be the best possible medicine for me. She has probably realized that herself from Mme. Obreskoff's letter, so try to obtain passports. Two different persons—one from the north and one from the south—told me, without knowing Louise personally, that it would not only be good for *my* health but for *hers*. Come along then, Mother Louise and Daughter Louise, bring your thimbles and needles and I shall give you handkerchiefs to embroider with my initials and stockings to knit; and you shall spend a few months here in the fresh air with your old brother and uncle. Besides, traveling is easier now. You don't need a lot of luggage. We shall live here as cheaply as can be. Your board and lodging will be provided. And even if Kalasanty sometimes finds it too far into town from the Champs Élysées he can stay at my apartment in the Square d'Orléans. The omnibuses come directly from the Square to my very door here.

I don't know myself why I am so eager to have Louise, but it is almost as though I were in an "interesting condition." I guarantee the trip will do her good as well. I hope the family council will send her, and who knows but what I shall bring her back home if I get better. And then, shouldn't we all embrace each other, as I wrote once before, without wigs on our heads and with all our own teeth! A wife owes her husband obedience, so now I must apply to the husband to bring his wife. Let me therefore beg him earnestly to do so. If he weighs the matter, he will realize that he can do nothing more pleasurable or useful either to me or to her, or even to the children, if any are brought (I have no doubt that the little girl will come). It will mean spending money, of course, but no better use could be made of it, and one could not have a cheaper trip. Once you are here, you will find a home awaiting you. Let me know soon. . . .

So now get a move on, expeditiously but without rushing, about your passport and the money. Send me a few lines at once. They say that "Even a cypress has its caprices." Well, my caprice today is to see you here. God will perhaps allow all to be well, but if He does not, never mind—act as though He were going to allow it. I am hopeful; for I don't often ask for much, and indeed I would have refrained from asking this, if I had not been urged to it by everyone who has my interest at heart. Get a move on then, Mr. Kalasanty, and you shall have a fine large cigar —I know someone who smokes famous ones—but please note, *in the garden.*

I hope Mamma received the letter I sent for her name day and that she did not miss me. I won't let myself think about it all, for I should be thrown into a fever, whereas, thank God, I am not at all feverish—a fact which baffles and annoys all my doctors-in-ordinary.

Your devoted but frail brother,
CH.

Louise came. She spent his final months with her brother. Her presence was a joy to him. Together they conjured up their childhood, sprinkled with smiles. Cyprian Norwid, the Polish poet, visited them:

The French servant said that he was asleep, so I muted my steps, left a card, and walked out. I had hardly descended a few stairs when the servant called me back, saying that upon learning who it was Chopin had asked that I come in—in brief, he had not been asleep but was not receiving anyone. So I entered the room next to the drawing room—in which Chopin slept—very thankful that he had consented to see me. I found him dressed, but reclining on his bed, with swollen legs; this could be perceived at once, although he wore stockings and shoes. The artist's sister was sitting next to him, strangely resembling him in profile. . . . He was in the shadow of the deep bed with curtains, leaning on his pillows, and wrapped in a shawl, and he was very beautiful, and as always there was something perfect, something classical, in his most casual gestures. . . . Then, in a voice broken by his coughing and choking, he began to reproach me for not having come to him for such a long time. After that he spoke jestingly and wanted to tease me about my mystical tendencies, and since it gave him pleasure, I let him do it. I talked with his sister; he had fits of coughing, and then the moment came when he had to be left alone. I said farewell to him, and he, pressing my hand, threw his hair back from his forehead, and said, "I am going . . ." and began to cough. Upon hearing this, I kissed him on the arm and, knowing that he was pleased when sharply contradicted, I said in a tone that one uses with a strong and courageous person, "You have been going in this way every year, and yet, thank God, we still see you alive." To this Chopin, finishing the sentence that was interrupted by the coughing, said, "I was trying to tell you—I am going to leave this apartment and move to the Place Vendôme."

(2)

In July George Sand received a letter from a Mme. Grille de Beuzelin. The lady was a friend of Marie de Rozières and a closer friend of Solange, who kept in touch with her all her life; Chopin, too, knew her, though Sand's acquaintance with her was of the slightest. Mme. Grille wrote:

> July 1849
>
> Madame: I am venturing to take a step which may strike you as very strange, and for which I beg your forgiveness. You have probably forgotten my name, Madame, but a mutual acquaintance [Mlle. Rozières] had brought me to your notice, and I possess two of your books which you presented to me.
>
> I will not describe the feelings which your admirable talent has aroused in me, or say how natural it was that my lively interest should have given me the desire to know more of you. All of which brings me to say that, knowing your long friendship for the illustrious person now cruelly struck down by illness, I feel that I am not mistaken when I say that he grievously realizes how much he misses you. And as he is, Madame, at the last stage of his long sufferings, if you, through ignorance, did not give him the consolation of receiving some mark of remembrance, *you* would lament it and *he* might die in despair. I make so bold as to send this note, Madame, and beg to assure you that no one in the world shall know of this approach.
>
> I venture to express the wish that I may not incur your censure, and also implore you not to mention this warning of mine to a soul.

George Sand answered forthwith. Her letter, long as it is, needs to be quoted in full, not only since it reveals once again a desire for self-justification so strong as to make her spin threads of untruth, but because the letter indicates by its tone, "the lady doth protest too much," that the separation had left an unhealed wound.

> Nohant, July 19, 1849
>
> Madame, I appreciate the kind feeling which dictated the step you have taken. It cannot but be echoed in a mother's broken heart, and I can make a confident reply. But what can I do, Madame, for the moral relief of the unhappy friend to whom you refer? I am compelled to live where I am at the moment, and even supposing that the connection between us had not been voluntarily and mutually broken, circumstances would inevitably have separated us.

An extreme partiality on his side for one of my children has es-
tranged the other, and in my view the latter was in no way in the wrong.
Things had reached the point where I had to choose between my son
and my friend. I believe you would have done what I did.

That is the fundamental truth of the matter, and one which has
brought some bitterness and much pain into our separation. But sooner
or later, and indeed before long, lack of financial resources must have
put an end to my residing in Paris, while lack of strength must have
similarly ended my friend's visits to the country. It was in fear and
trembling that I kept him so distant from the attentions of celebrated
doctors while leading a life which he found disagreeable in itself: he did
not hide this from us, for he used to leave us with the first days of
autumn, only to return as late as possible with the beginning of summer.

For a long period he had had the benefit of my care and attention;
they never failed him, but they were becoming insufficient, and worse
than that, harmful. The best doctor, who was also the best friend he had
in this part of the world, had long advised me to loosen the bonds of this
friendship until they ceased to be bonds. I had long worked to achieve
that, and it was no fault of mine that it was not smoothly accomplished.
But with a nervous constitution like his, with a character so strange and
unhappy (albeit a noble one), it proved to be impossible; and I myself
often lost patience when confronted with inexplicable and unjust reproaches.

I am here putting forward neither accusations nor justifications,
Madame, for they would be of little interest to you, and moreover, I feel
no need to justify myself in any respect whatsoever, or to accuse myself
unnecessarily.

Most wrongs in this world are the result of an inescapable destiny,
itself created by the outside world. But you have given me a piece of
advice, and it is for me to make clear to you a situation which gives you
concern, so that you may consider what can be done to lessen the
harshness of that situation in the interests of the sick man.

Had I sought your judgment at the time of the breach, and had you
seen things as they really were, you would have said: "You must part
without bitterness and without breaking the bond of affection." I repeat,
it did not depend on him or on me, but on *others*. For it is others who
have come between us. There was not even a cooling off in the friendship between the two of us. But, you will say, even when it was over,
there was still time for us to come to an understanding and to console
each other with tender words and lasting pledges of mutual esteem. I
asked for nothing better. I have met him since then, and offered him my
hand. . . . One would have said he hastened to avoid me; I sent someone
after him, and he came back unwillingly, to speak neither of himself nor

me, but to show in his attitude and looks anger and indeed almost hatred.

Since then he has unburdened himself of bitter confidences and frightful accusations leveled at me. I have taken it all, as I was bound to, for mere raving; and I swear I have forgiven him everything, and from the bottom of my heart. But when confronted with this rancor and aversion, what could I do, for my part? Nothing.

Had he but called me to him during my brief visits to Paris, I should have gone. Had he but written himself, or got someone to write some affectionate note, I should have replied. But *now,* does he really wish to have from me a word of friendship, of pardon, or any sign of interest? If so, I am ready. But you tell me, Madame, that *no one in the world* knows of the approach that you have been pleased to make. It is, therefore, neither he nor any of his friends who have urged you to it, for I believe you do not know him personally. Do not imagine that I am in the slightest degree making this a question of pride—pride is out of place where a sufferer so gravely threatened is concerned. But were I to write, I should fear to provoke an emotional reaction more harmful than salutary. And again, I scarcely know what pretext for writing I can find; for were I to reveal the anxiety I feel, I should only arouse his own anxiety over his state of health. Go and see him? That is absolutely out of the question at this moment and would, I believe, make matters worse. I still hope he will live, for I have so often seen him apparently at the point of death that I never despair of him. However, if the state of siege were over and if I could spend a few days in Paris without being persecuted or arrested, I would certainly not refuse if he wished to see me.

But I have the inward conviction that he does not wish it. His affection has long been dead, and if he is tormented by the memory of me it is because he feels in his own heart a pang of self-reproach. If he may be given to understand that I feel no resentment, find a way to let him be assured of it, without taking the risk of subjecting him to a fresh emotional shock.

Forgive this long letter, Madame, but I could not answer with a few words in a matter of such delicacy. I thank you for the secrecy you promise, but for me there is nothing secret in all this. It is a long and painful family story, and my friends have well understood the suffering it has caused me. As you see, I am treating you as a friend in speaking so very freely. The friendly solicitude you have shown must be my excuse. Believe me, Madame, when I say that it has called forth my profound and sincere gratitude.

GEORGE SAND

Even in a cursory reading of this letter one bumps against several falsehoods: it was not true that Chopin found life in Nohant "disagreeable," nor that she was threatened with arrest in Paris, nor that she "offered him my hand" and "sent someone after him."

The following month George Sand learned of Louise's presence in Paris. The woman whom she had liked so much and who had been so sympathetic to her? Here was an opportunity to approach Chopin through his sister. At the same time she very much wanted to show Mme. Grille that she was capable of the consolatory gesture. She chose a roundabout way: instead of writing to Louise directly, she wrote to Mme. Grille and asked *her* to ask Marie de Rozières to hand Louise a note she enclosed. She asked that the enclosure not be given to Louise "in the sick man's presence." Louise would "be the best judge" whether to mention the note to Chopin or keep silent.

> Nohant, September 1 [1849]
>
> Dear Louise,
> I learn now that you are in Paris—I was not aware of it before. At last I shall have through you some true news of Frédéric. Some people write that he is much worse than usual, others that he is only weak and fretful as I have always seen him. I venture to ask you to send me word, for one can be misunderstood and abandoned by one's children without ceasing to love them. Tell me also about yourself, and do not think that I have spent a single day since the time I first knew you when I have not thought of you and cherished your memory. Others must have spoilt the memory of me which you preserved in your heart, but I do not think I have deserved all I have suffered.
>
> > Yours from the bottom of my heart,
> > GEORGE
>
> Regards to your husband.

No answer from Louise is extant.

In September Chopin's physicians advised him to move back to Paris with the coming of autumnal weather. He was tired of the Square d'Orléans lodging, with the memories of George Sand which blew through its rooms, and at his request two friends found for him a luxurious apartment in Paris's finest and most central quarter, at No. 12 Place Vendôme. It was as if expense no longer mattered to him. Why should he not make it convenient for his friends to call on him? He was looking forward to receiving them during the winter.

Toward the end of September he took a turn for the worse. He spat blood almost daily, speaking became so painful that he whispered, he was so weak that he could just about manage to walk from the bed to the window. Yet he insisted that his valet shave and dress him and arrange his hair every morning, and he was to adhere to this routine until his last few days.

When October came, he could no longer sit up in bed without being held. He conversed by signs and smiles. Louise remained with him day and night, while her husband returned to Warsaw. To relieve the boredom of silence and the attacks of pain, Chopin, his mind perfectly clear, asked a friend to read to him: the book he chose was Voltaire's *Dictionnaire philosophique*. The friend, Charles Gavard, was the brother of one of Chopin's pupils, Élise, to whom he had dedicated the Berceuse Opus 57, and immediately after Chopin's death Gavard wrote down his recollection of Chopin's last days, and his is probably the most reliable account.

> Among the persons who came to visit him but were not admitted there was a certain Mme. M. [Charlotte Marliani?], who said that she came at the behest of Mme. Sand, who at the moment was very occupied with the staging of one of her plays, and who wanted to inquire about the state of Chopin's health. None of us wanted to disturb the last moments of his life by telling him of this belated solicitude.

During the fourteenth or fifteenth of October a final medical consultation took place. On the morning of the sixteenth a Polish priest was called, who administered extreme unction. Chopin accepted it without much emotion. A few days earlier Delfina Potocka arrived from Nice. Gavard reported:

> When this dear friend of his approached his bed, Chopin said: "Now I know why God has waited so long to call me. He wanted to offer me the pleasure of seeing you once more." As she bent over him, he expressed the desire to hear again that voice he had loved so much. A priest was praying at the side of the bed; he agreed that the wish of the dying man ought to be fulfilled. They pushed the piano in from the next room and the sorrow-stricken Countess mastered her grief and, swallowing her tears, mustered the strength to sing—right next to the bed where her friend was breathing out his soul. I neither listened to nor remember what she sang.

Because Chopin complained of pain in his limbs, Gutmann tried to relieve it by vigorously massaging his wrists and ankles. Chopin was grateful for this service, but when he tried to express his thanks, he broke into a racking cough. He vomited blood and shuddered when he saw his bed linen soiled. Then he lay quiet. Toward evening Dr. Cruveilhier held a lighted candle in front of Chopin's eyes; he no longer reacted. Yet when the physician asked him if he was in pain, he answered distinctly, "No more." Louise, Marcellina Czartoryska, and Solange were in the room. (Whether Adolf Gutmann was there remains uncertain.) They kept the vigil. At 2 A.M. of the night of October 17, Chopin died.

When the nobles of England assemble to mourn the death of King Henry V, "too famous to live long," the Duke of Exeter speaks of

> . . . death's dishonourable victory
> We with our stately presence glorify
> Like captives bound to a
>   triumphant car.
>   SHAKESPEARE, *Henry VI,*
>   Part I, Act 1, Scene 1

It is remarkable how many men and women claimed their stately presence at Chopin's death. Their recollections exceed in number and variety the usual tales of the death of kings. They are almost all unreliable. Gutmann said that George Sand came to the Place Vendôme, was refused admittance, and went sadly away. A touching story, but almost certainly untrue. Franchomme told Chopin's early biographer Niecks that Chopin said to him, two days before his death: "She [George Sand] promised me that I would die in her arms. Has she perhaps come to keep her promise or at least to take leave of her friend of many years?" This is most unlikely. The Polish priest Alexander Jelowicki wrote a long letter describing in detail how Chopin first refused to take the sacrament, how Jelowicki begged him to give him a gift, and when Chopin asked, "What gift?" Jelowicki answered, "Your soul," how Chopin finally was persuaded to make his peace with the Church, confessing, "Without your help I would have died like a pig," how Chopin murmured, "I have arrived at the source of felicity" and died—all self-admiring propaganda, with hardly a word of truth. Chopin had no quarrel with the Church, nor did any of those present confirm the priest's tale. Mrs. Erskine wrote Louise that Chopin in his last night screamed, " 'My mother, my mother.' . . . I am certain that I will never obliterate from my memory this moving cry during that solemn last night." But she wasn't there and Louise was, and Louise did not mention her brother's screaming. What did Delfina sing to him shortly before he died? Liszt wrote that she sang a hymn by Stradella and one by Marcello. " 'How beautiful it is!' Chopin was supposed to have exclaimed. 'My God, how very beautiful! Again! Again!' " Gutmann said she sang the selection by Marcello and an aria by Pergolesi, Franchomme that she sang only one aria from Bellini's *Beatrice di Tenda*, while Grzymala recorded she sang three selections by Bellini and Rossini. Grzymala, too, indulged in a fanciful tale when he wrote to the banker Auguste Léo:

[October 1849]
. . . Never did the greatest Stoic of antiquity leave behind the example of a finer death or of a nobler, purer or more Christian soul. His death struggle, after Confession and the administration of the Holy Sacraments, lasted three days and three nights; and never has a more tenacious vitality been seen. The doctors could not get over it. And at such moments my mind was crushed by the thought that if he had not had the ill luck to know G. Sand, who poisoned his whole life, he might have lived to be as old as Cherubini. On the last day and at the last hour of his life his mind was as clear as ever. He often sat up in bed and addressed to twenty persons at least, his adorers in ermine or rags who for four days and nights had been kneeling and praying, he addressed to them, I say, words of advice, of pleading, of consolation almost, with a propriety, a decency and a tact which pass belief—with a kindness and tenderness far removed from this world. He recognized everyone, remembered all their little characteristics, and dictated his last wishes regarding his works with the same loftiness of mind that had inspired them.

"There will be found," he said, "many compositions more or less sketched. In the name of the friendship you bear me I ask that they should all be burnt, with the exception of a piano method which I bequeath to Alkan and Reber to see whether any use can be made of it. The rest, without exception, must be consigned to the flames, for I have always had a great respect for the public and whatever I have published has always been as perfect as I could make it. I do not wish that under the cover of my name works which are unworthy of the public should be spread abroad."

Chopin surely did not make any exhortatory speeches to twenty listeners. Grzymala's flash of anger at George Sand is understandable, however unwarranted. Grzymala had loved his compatriot with all his heart.

Charlotte Marliani was at home the next evening. At nine-thirty a young woman entered whom at first she did not recognize. It was Solange. She was so agitated as to appear half mad. She spoke of having kept the watch with Chopin in his last hours and of having closed his eyes. Chopin wanted, she said, to have an autopsy performed and to give his body to science. His sister "was in despair and changed beyond recognition." Rambling on, Solange then launched into a bitter tirade against her mother: "She spoiled me without loving me. I didn't need a horse or those clothes, I needed affection." She remained for forty minutes, then left as abruptly as she had come.

Marliani reported all this to Sand the same night, October 18. Sand's answer to this letter was unfortunately burned with other documents when Charlotte died a year later.

In November George Sand wrote to Etienne Arago, the uncle of her friend Emmanuel and editor of the radical newspaper *La Réforme*. (Hence the anti-aristocratic tone of her letter?)

> November 11, 1849
>
> My poor sick one died in the arms of priests and lady devotees. He loved devotion, though he believed in nothing. I have never known a poet who was more of an atheist, nor an atheist who was more of a poet. He believed that he believed. He believed in a kind of divinity and a fantastic immortality. This was the undercurrent of genius, a nothingness of reflection. In his last moments, though they made him kiss the relics of all the saints, what he really thought of was a fine funeral with music. Little by little his heart had died and it seems that he never gave a thought to me who had cared for him like a son for nine years. My opinions shocked him—and his entourage, and his entourage got possession of him. Poland will never be revived by its aristocracy, to which it delivered itself through instinct and habit. That aristocracy—I know it —it is worse than ours. Is there such a thing as "a people" in that country? One says so, but I don't know.

Such was George Sand's equivocal valedictory. She had characterized him better when she wrote *Lucrezia Floriani* and there described him in the fictional guise of Prince Karol:

> Nothing was more exalted than his thoughts. Nothing more steadfast, centered and devoted than his affection. Yet he could understand only

what was identical with his own nature; all else was to him a vexing dream from which he tried to abstract himself. Lost in his reveries, reality bothered him. He was unable to face a person different from himself, being bruised by any living contradiction. . . . What saved him from perpetual anger was his habit, conscious and inveterate, of sloughing off everything that displeased him. He simply did not notice it. . . . It is strange enough that with such a character he could make friends. Yet he had them, Nature bestowing on him the gift of pleasing. People of lesser mettle were enchanted by his exquisite politeness, all the more so because in their innocence they did not realize that it was but a conventional exercise, lacking true sympathy. He was more lovable than loving [*plus aimable qu'aimant*]. . . .

(3)

Many of the French Romantics mourned him, not only as a man and artist they had admired, but because his death seemed to signal the end of a period of exuberance and hope. Things were moving toward the right, revolution had once again become brackish, and only three years elapsed before the republic changed to a second monarchy, under Napoleon III. Balzac died the year after Chopin, Mickiewicz six years after, and Musset within eight years. Some of those who eulogized Chopin in sad accents were depressed over the state of their world, doubting their own future. Berlioz saw black. He hit out against the increasing number of functionaries and their hectoring: "These people are our enemies." And Delacroix wrote in his *Journal* on October 20:

> It was after lunch that I learned of the death of poor Chopin. Strangely enough, I had a presentiment of it before I got up this morning. I have now had such premonitions on several occasions. What a loss he will be! What miserable rascals are left to clutter the earth, yet that fine soul is extinguished!

Paris then as now had many newspapers, of which six were influential, ranging from *Le Siècle* to *Le Courrier Français.* One and all they published florid necrologies, like the tribute the celebrated journalist Jules Janin paid him in the *Journal des Débats:* "He was music itself, inspiration itself; he hardly touched the earth we walk on," etc., etc. Théophile Gautier in *La Presse,* October 22: "Grace, melancholy, reverie, a strong style formed by his study of the classics as well as by his response to passionate modern poetry—these qualities turned any one of Chopin's works into an exquisite and precious substance. . . . Those who had the joy of seeing and hearing him mourn the loss of an eminent artist, a noble heart, an extraordinary mind."

Ernest Legouvé reminisced:

> This genius was sleepy until one o'clock in the morning. Before that hour, he was only a charming pianist. . . . The slightest unpleasant detail was enough to put him off. I still remember one day when his playing seemed somewhat nervous, he turned to me and secretly showed me a lady sitting opposite him, saying: "It's the lady's feather hat! If this feather doesn't leave, I can't carry on." Once he started playing, he never stopped. . . . There was, however, one way of drawing him away from the piano: if you asked him to play the March he had composed after the Polish disaster, he would never refuse, but once the last note was played, he took his hat and left. This piece, which was like the song of his country's agony, affected him deeply.

So many flowers arrived that Liszt was moved to say that he "seemed to sleep in a rose garden." Louise kept the vigil at Place Vendôme. A few minutes after her brother died, she had dispatched the briefest of notes to her husband: "Oh my darling—he has gone—" She had just strength enough to scrawl: "Comfort Mother and Isabella," but then broke off, and Marcellina Czartoryska continued the letter, writing: "She begs you not to be anxious on her behalf. Chopin's friends will help her to settle everything."

But Louise now had to cope with the journalists and with the many curiosity seekers who came to gape or to snatch souvenirs. Clésinger arrived to make the death mask and to take a cast of the left hand. (Jane Stirling bought the mask and later sent it to Louise.) A Polish artist, Theophile Kwiatkowski, made sketches of his compatriot, most of which were destroyed by German soldiers in World War II. The only photograph of Chopin was taken about the middle of 1849 and shows, more lifelike than the painted portraits, the disturbed eyes and the weary mouth of the ill man.*

The funeral did not take place until October 30. Because Mozart's

---

*The photograph, which Louise took back to Poland, was saved from the Nazis, along with other historic documents, by being smuggled out of Poland and sent, by way of Rumania, Italy, France, and England, to the Bank of Montreal. It remained there until long after the war. It is now back in Warsaw.

Requiem was to be performed—whether at Chopin's express wish or not is uncertain—permission had to be obtained for the female singers to be allowed in the Madeleine. And where but in the Madeleine should the obsequies for so famous an artist be held? Permission was obtained —by compromise. With the help of Pauline Viardot, stellar singers were enlisted: in addition to herself, the soprano Jeanne Castellan, the tenor Alexis Dupont, and the bass Luigi Lablache. He, the greatest bass of the era, had sung in a performance of the same Mozart music at Beethoven's funeral in 1827 and eight years later had taken part in Bellini's funeral. The singers volunteered their services, but the orchestra and chorus of the Conservatoire insisted on being paid. This disgusted Grzymala, but there was nothing to be done: Louise borrowed five thousand francs from the ever generous Jane Stirling and paid them two thousand, no doubt using the rest of the money for other expenses of the ceremony.

Chopin's friends foresaw that a huge number of the celebrity mad would try to witness the spectacle. Therefore printed invitations were issued—under Louise's name—and without them one was not admitted. The usual recriminations followed: some important people were forgotten and many musicians protested that they had a right to say farewell to a fellow musician even without an invitation. Soon after 11 A.M., about three thousand persons had filled the church, while a mass of people gathered outside and on the adjoining streets. Traffic came to a standstill. The great portal of the Madeleine was draped in black cloth, as was the catafalque, the initials "F.C." shining in silver on the cloth. The service began at noon.

While the coffin was being carried up the aisle and placed on the catafalque, the orchestra played the "Funeral March" from the B-flat Sonata. The organist of the Madeleine performed transcriptions of two Chopin Preludes. The singers stood at the back of the church, hidden behind a dark curtain. When Mozart's *Requiem* began, the curtain was partially drawn aside, leaving the male singers visible but the two women concealed; they could be heard but not seen. After about an hour, the procession formed to carry Chopin the three miles to Père Lachaise Cemetery. Old Prince Adam Czartoryski, acknowledged leader of the Polish colony, led the procession, followed by his son Alexander, husband of Marcellina, by Franchomme, Delacroix, Camille Pleyel, and Gutmann. Meyerbeer represented the musicians. Louise, veiled in black, walked at first alone, but after a while somebody, proba-

bly Grzymala, took her arm. Solange was supported by her husband.
George Sand remained in Nohant. Was it out of tact? Was it because
Louise had not answered her letter? Was it because she could not bear
to show herself to the thousands who lined the streets and the hundreds
who followed the coffin?

There were no speeches at the grave. Those who stood around it
threw flowers. The sky was gray and a small but cold wind blew across
the cemetery. The friends shivered, Louise wept quietly. Soon everybody went home.

> The leaves they were withering and sere;
> It was night in the lonesome October
> Of my most immemorial year.
> POE, "Ulalume"

Edgar Allan Poe died in the same year as Chopin.

A few days after Chopin's death a committee was formed, Pleyel and
Grzymala taking the initiative, to collect money for a monument to
mark his grave. Again thanks to Jane Stirling, the necessary sum was
subscribed and Clésinger was entrusted with the commission—Clésinger, whom Chopin could not endure. The unveiling took place on the
first anniversary of Chopin's death. (That the statue was utterly mediocre was soon recognized—yet it is still there.) Jane Stirling, having
bought all the violets she could find, covered the grave with them. A
Polish priest sprinkled Polish earth from an urn which Chopin's family
had sent. Louise was not present; she had returned to Warsaw at the
beginning of 1850.

(4)

In Chopin's pocketbook Louise found a lock of George Sand's hair and
among his belongings, as carefully wrapped as Maria Wodzinska's letters, were all the letters George had written him. Louise intended to
take these mementos back to Warsaw. As she traveled homeward in the
dead of winter, the George Sand letters were in her suitcase. Hidden
in her clothing she carried a little urn containing her brother's heart.
As she neared the border she began to be afraid. The letters were in
French, a language with which the Russian customs official was proba-

bly unfamiliar. She knew he would be highly suspicious, the letters would have to be turned over to somebody for translation to make sure that they contained no subversive matter, and she thought it possible that she herself would be detained until the correspondence could be proved harmless. She decided, therefore, to leave the packet with an acquaintance who kept an inn near the border, planning to retrieve the letters at a more convenient time. Five months later Alexandre Dumas *fils* arrived at the same place; he was pursuing one of Europe's most desirable women, the ravishing, capricious, wildly extravagant wife of Count Dimitri Nesselrode. He called her "The Lady of the Pearls." When he arrived at the Russian border he found it locked and bolted against him. Count Nesselrode had seen to that. So there Alexandre was, stymied and fuming, and to entertain his guest the innkeeper showed him the packet of letters. He fell on them and devoured them:

> Myslowitz, May 1851
>
> While you, my dear father, were dining with Madame Sand, I too was occupied with her. . . . Just imagine! I have here, in my hands, the whole of her correspondence with Chopin, covering a period of ten years! I let you guess whether I copied these letters which are a lot more interesting than those now proverbially famous letters by Mme. de Sévigné! I send you a notebook full of them, because, unfortunately, these letters have only been lent to me. How comes it, you will ask, that here, at Myslowitz, in the depths of Silesia, I should have found a collection of letters which had their origin in Berry? The explanation is quite simple. Chopin was a Pole, as you may or may not know. After his death, his sister found them among his papers, kept, docketed and put away in their envelopes, with the most loving care. She took them away with her, and, when about to enter Poland, where the police, without showing her the slightest consideration, read everything readable which she had with her, left them with one of her friends who lived in Myslowitz. This, however, did not save them from profanation, as is proved by the fact that I have had access to them. Nothing could be sadder, more touching, believe me, than these letters, with the ink already faded, which once were handled and rapturously received by one now dead! . . . For a moment I was tempted to wish that the man who held these letters in trust, who is a friend of mine, might die suddenly, and I, being left with them, might offer them to Madame Sand, who, perhaps, would find some pleasure in reliving one small part of her dead yesterdays. The wretch (my friend), however, is terribly hale and hearty. Thinking that I should be off on the 15th, I returned to him all the papers—which he has not had the curios-

ity even to read. This indifference may not seem so incredible when I tell you that he is junior partner in an export business.

Dumas *père* informed George Sand of the find, at the same time telling her that his son was most anxious to make her acquaintance. Sand answered that she very badly wanted those letters. Dumas *fils* to George Sand:

> Myslowitz, June 3, 1851
>
> In a few days' time I shall be back in France, and shall bring you, in person, with or without the consent of Madame Jedrzeiewice [*sic;* i.e., Louise] the letters you so much want to have back. Some actions are so obviously just that they require no authorization. It is understood that the copies will be restored to you simultaneously. Of all the indiscretions nothing now remains but a happy result. Believe me, Madame, there has been no profanation. The heart, so indiscreetly and after so long a lapse of time made the recipient of your confidences, has long been devoted to you. . . .

However, Alexandre didn't show up in Nohant during July, and George, becoming worried, wrote again to the elder Dumas, who reported that his son was on the point of departure when "he was detained by Solange." This news frightened Sand. She didn't want Solange to read the letters. She wrote directly to Alexandre:

> If you can come here the 25th [of August] I would be happy and grateful. If you can't, be so kind as to consign the packet, firmly sealed, to Mr. Falampin [a lawyer].

Alexandre answered that he was still hoping to come to Nohant. But on September 27 he wrote Sand saying that the letters were in the possession of Falampin. Evidently Sand had not been informed of that; Dumas apologized:

> I regretted having fulfilled my mission badly, but it is evident from the letter you wrote to Mme. Clésinger that Falampin is the guilty one. I put the packet in a box, wrapped in paper, and covered with oilcloth. That box nobody, not even Pandora, would have opened.

What happened then is unclear. Presumably Alexandre recovered the box from Falampin and brought it to Nohant. George Sand grabbed it and threw it into the fire. Like Hedda Gabler, she watched the paper being consumed by the flame. When only the ashes were left, George wrote young Dumas:

Nohant, October 1851

Now you know that maternal tenderness which filled nine years of my life. No—there are no secrets here and I could rather have prided myself than blushed to have nursed and consoled that noble and incurable being as if he had been my own child. Well, you have read the secret part of the correspondence. It is not too frightful, but it would have displeased me to have it commented upon and blown up. . . .

These family revelations would loom important in certain malevolent eyes; I would have suffered had I opened to the whole world a mysterious book of my intimate life, just at that page where, between smiles and tears, the name of my daughter appears so often. . . .

Blame Louise, blame Dumas, blame Falampin, blame George Sand —the fact remains that virtually all the letters from the indefatigable scrivener to her lover are lost to posterity.

(5)

The pomp of the funeral, the fullness of the encomiums, the memoirs and the monument—none was a truer tribute than the modest letter from Pauline Viardot, who loved Chopin with an uncalculating love. Some time after the funeral, she wrote to George Sand:

A long time has passed since I let you have news of me, but it is even longer that you haven't written to me. As for myself, my dear one, I felt such sorrow over the death of poor little Chopin that I did not know how to begin my letter. I am sure that you too must have been stricken and that, had you known that his end was so near, you would have come to clasp his hand for the last time. I did not know on what date he returned to Paris nor what agonies he suffered. I was apprised of his death by strangers who came and with great ceremony asked me whether I would take part in a Requiem which was to be held at the Madeleine. It was at that moment that I realized how much love I bore him. Poor fellow—he died martyred by priests who forced him to kiss reliquaries for six hours, till his very last sigh. He was surrounded by a bunch of people he knew or did not know, who had come to sob at his bedside. True, his sister was there, but the poor woman was too dissolved in her grief to think of chasing away those importunate intruders.

All the *grandes dames* of Paris felt the urge to come and swoon in his room. His apartment was filled with artists sketching away; a photographer wanted the bed pushed near the window to photograph the dying man in sunlight. At that the good Gutmann got mad and showed those "merchants" the door.

In the midst of all this Chopin found the strength to say an affectionate word to everyone and to console his friends. He begged Gutmann, Franchomme, and the other musicians to play only good music [at his funeral]. "Do this for me—I'm sure I'll hear it—and it will give me pleasure."

Moments before his death he asked Mme. de Potocka to sing him a psalm by Marcello and with its last note he expired.

Perhaps he had his peculiarities, underscored by his disease, but he was a noble being. I am happy to have known him, happy to have obtained a little of his friendship.

PAULINE

The recipient of this letter, the woman who had owned much of his friendship and most of his love, looked back over the years: she wrote to her editor, Pierre-Jules Hetzel:

[Nohant, November 9, 1849]

... I have lost my health. I am ill. This death has affected me profoundly.

She hoped that were they to meet in eternity—"whether above or below, but certainly where one has a clearer view"—he would understand her love. Once again she blamed all the ugliness on that daughter who "plunged the poniard into his heart and poured gall into his mind." She would henceforth live only for her son. Her own life had become "a mockery." It was not so: she lived for another twenty-seven years and published nineteen more books and plays.

(6)

How did it happen that the contents of Chopin's apartment in the Place Vendôme* were dispersed? How was it possible that most of the possessions of so famous a man were not kept together but scattered hither and yon—and this in the age of Romanticism with its worship of the

---

*The plaque affixed to No. 12 Place Vendôme gives the wrong birth date and the apartment pointed out as Chopin's could not have been his. On the basis of plans found in the Paris City Archives, the musicologist Henri Musielak has proved that the so-called Chopin Apartment had northern exposure and no room where Louise could have stayed. The correct apartment had southern exposure (as the doctor advised Chopin) and an extra bedroom for Louise. (*Ruch Muzyczny,* No. 14, Warsaw, 1978)

artist? In Nohant every stick of furniture, every kettle and vase belonging to George Sand was piously preserved. Similarly, when Balzac died less than a year after Chopin, a Balzac museum was immediately planned. Yet not only were Chopin's belongings relegated to miscellaneous collectors—and many lost in the course of time—but even some of his manuscripts went to diverse destinations, including a late edition of his works which he had corrected and furnished with notations, the whereabouts of which is now unknown.

The explanation of what seems superficially like indifference sounds almost unbelievable, except that it happens to be the truth.

As in those medieval paintings which show a young girl in the fullness of her beauty but reveal a frightening hag when the canvas is shifted, the love which had surrounded Chopin was shadowed by the hatred Louise's husband felt for him.

The story can be reconstructed from a long, long letter Louise wrote her husband, Kalasanty. It is a desperate and despairing letter, sentences broken, confused punctuation, chaotic repetitions, incomplete phrases, as if it had been pressed out between sobs during a midnight quarrel. The letter is undated and we do not know when, if ever, she sent it. Louise called it her "Confession."*

First, she reviewed their going to Paris to see her brother:

> I was in the country when letters came from F. and Mme. Obr[eskoff] asking if it would be possible for us to come and be with him. I learned about this only several weeks later when you came to fetch me; then you brought the letters and told me you had applied for passports. Mme. Ob. wrote that things were very bad. I was shattered. I wanted to leave at once, although the thought of a long separation from the children distressed me. . . .
>
> You now announced that should you not be granted a passport, you would forbid me to go alone or with my sister. Let *her* go with mother, though Frederic had specifically asked for me. You then declared categorically that I could not go unless mother paid for the voyage. She did not hesitate. She longed to comply with the will of that ailing Frederic, so that I could nurse him.
>
> You then forbade my mother and sister to go. . . . Isabella remained

---

*In quoting excerpts from the letter, we have clarified the syntax and eliminated some of the tearful cries, but in no way changed its meaning. The letter was first published by Krystyna Kobylańska in *Ruch Muzyczny,* Nos. 20 and 21, Warsaw, 1968.

and you went instead. To this day I have it on my conscience that I deprived her of the last consolation of seeing him again. It would have been a great solace to him, too, to see us both.

So you and I left, Mama and the Bar[cinskis, Isabella's married name] taking charge of the children, Mama giving you 5,000 zlotys, for which she never asked you for an accounting.

During our stay with Fr., who seemed to have taken a new lease on life, I noticed how many incidents aggravated you, how little sympathy you showed for his idiosyncrasies and habits. Do you recall how angry you were when I spent long evenings with him, how you reproached me because he prevented me from getting enough sleep? Perhaps you were motivated by concern for me—yet it was painful to him, an ordeal for me. I had come to take care of him, console him, endure anything as long as I could bring him one moment of relief. He liked to chat late at night and tell me of his sorrows, pouring his troubles into a loving and under-standing heart. Until the very end I harbored illusions of hope.

Kalasanty had no such illusions, and becoming impatient with Chopin's coughing, being bored and annoyed, he decided to return home.

The hour came when God struck most dreadfully. I needed all my strength to drink the chalice of bitterness to the last drop. While nursing him I swallowed my tears, so that he would not suspect that my pain was due to his pain. At the crucial moment you were not here.

She turned to her brother's friends, "those friends whom he loved and whom you could not bear." His condition was worsening: she knew it would soon be over. Should she ask her husband to return?

I realized that all would be over by the time you could arrive here (considering the length of time required to obtain another permit), that you did not have the means for the voyage, and that Fr. would no longer benefit by it. I told the Princess [Marcellina Czartoryska] that I saw no real necessity for you to return. At any rate, you yourself should decide. You misunderstood my intention. Your self-love was offended, you gave no thought to my suffering. And from that moment you behaved as a man deeply insulted, not as my husband and friend. Did I receive a single word of consolation from you? Did you shed a single tear? Every one of your letters contained nothing but bitter reproaches and words degrading the memory of my beloved brother.

Yet in previous years, when Kalasanty visited Nohant, Chopin and he had been friends. They had joked and laughed together. What now made him turn against Louise's brother?

You knew the story of Mme. E. [Etienne—undoubtedly the story of the gift from the Stirlings]. In your fury you bruited it about that he had enormous debts—which he did not have. How dreadful it was for me to learn that the man who is closest to me was besmirching the reputation of my brother. . . .

I know he did not have the debts you thought he had: the money had been paid. There was one loan outstanding which could easily be repaid. F. mentioned it on more than one occasion. He worried about it and I had to plead with him not to worry. It was a sum that could be easily raised. After his death I told his devoted friends that I considered it my most sacred duty to repay this sum. They first denied that he owed anything at all and then begged me not to give it a second thought, not to mention it again.

Obviously, Kalasanty was violently jealous, jealous of his wife's love for her brother and envious of the fact that his brother-in-law was famous while he remained obscure. The image of Chopin oppressed him like an incubus and he wished to obliterate as much of his glory as possible. To his possessiveness another and grosser motive needs to be added: cupidity. He wanted to realize as much money as possible from Chopin's belongings: they were worth a good deal and he wanted every franc of it.

Louise had to grapple with the problem of what to do with Chopin's possessions. He had died intestate. In this situation, according to French law, an inventory had to be made of the deceased's possessions and his or her dwelling sealed by the police within twenty-four hours. Nothing was to be touched until the inventory was officially approved; then the estate would be released to the next of kin—which in Chopin's case was his mother—after an inheritance tax was paid. The triple purpose of the law was to prevent theft, to collect taxes, and to see that outstanding debts were paid.* Louise, representing her mother, was advised by Chopin's friends that once the necessary formalities had been completed, she should agree to keep his possessions intact, and to establish a Chopin museum. "They thought of preserving all the furniture and the apartment exactly as it had been in his lifetime—as it was done with

---

*According to the Napoleonic Code, "Formalities Required" were: "All natural relations as well as the conjunct, coming into a succession, are bound to cause seals to be affixed; and when the seals are taken off to preserve an inventory." Quoted from *An Essay on Intestate Successions According to the French Code* by Barthelemy Hardy Colin (London, 1876).

Voltaire in Ferney. It was a plan conceived by kind hearts. But it could not be carried out," wrote Louise.

It could not because Kalasanty would not have it. He wouldn't consider it! And Louise had no legal right to go against her husband's wishes. As a compromise the friends suggested that she lay claim to "all the mementos the shipment of which would not be too expensive," and have them transported to Warsaw.

> To this I received the most painful letter of my life. You commanded me to sell everything, absolutely everything, and you sent me an authorization signed by all of you. You added: *"Do not keep anything, not one rag will I let into my house."* Oh—I shed tears of blood.

She pleaded with him to reconsider. He would not.

> You met me only with suspicion and mistrust and you wrote a highly improper letter to Alb [Grzymala], who had been helping me with the greatest conscientiousness. How I wish he had remained ignorant of your attitude!

But the command remained: "Sell!"

Faced with her husband's intransigence, Louise committed a bit of thievery. She couldn't bear letting everything go. A few hours still remained of the night during which Chopin died. She went into his room, accompanied by Marcellina Czartoryska.* Together the two weeping women filled two small cases with Chopin's manuscripts and letters and before dawn transported them to Louise's room. The police, they thought, would not examine her room, and Louise swore that everything in that room belonged to her. She confessed her "theft" to Kalasanty:

> Before they left, his friends suggested that I put away what I could of his papers and other items. The next day everything would be sealed and perhaps the [Russian] Consul himself would go over the papers. Only somebody who has undergone a similar experience would understand what it is like to have to gather and classify papers when your heart is close to bursting. He had Mme. S[and]'s papers in a safe: I took them. I also took the watch which had accompanied him for years. I didn't want these things sealed, nobody knowing what would happen to

---

*Marcellina had decided to stay at No. 6 Place Vendôme to be near Louise.

them eventually. Later people accused me of selfishness. You accused me of exactly the opposite.

Louise consulted Thomas Albrecht, a wine merchant who lived in the same building and had been a friend of Chopin's. (Chopin was godfather to Albrecht's daughter.) Albrecht proved helpful to Louise in more ways than one, reporting the death and seeing to the other formalities. He advised an auction:

> When everything was catalogued, they asked me where I wished the sale to be held—at his home or at the auction house. I was told that if it took place at home it would be more profitable, while the alternative would satisfy the requirements of the law, but would bring less.

She could have held the auction in Chopin's rooms, but she couldn't face the prospect of strangers swarming all over, and on Albrecht's counsel, she decided on an "anonymous" public auction. The name of the owner would not be disclosed, only Chopin's friends knowing about it. By that means the friends could acquire the mementos more cheaply: this was her way of thanking them. The announcement of the auction is extant: it gives no hint of the identity of the possessor of "the fine furniture, bronzes, clocks, *objets d'art et de curiosité,* antique porcelain, silver, crystal, rugs, linen, male wardrobe, drapes, etc. . . . to be sold November 30, 1849, at Rue des Jeuneurs 42." A piano rented by Chopin was later bought by Jane Stirling; she had it inscribed *"Pour Louise"* and transported to Warsaw. (It is at the Chopin Society in Warsaw.)

Kalasanty's anger redoubled when he heard about the auction. He accused his wife of handling money carelessly, since she spent it on such unnecessary frills as printed invitations to the funeral, and letting friends have "bargains" instead of trying to get the best prices for Chopin's estate. He asked her for an accounting:

> I gave 6,000 frs. of his money toward the expenses of the funeral. It is not customary here to make announcements by posters; one has to send printed individual invitations.
>
> The contractors [for work on the apartment] and the tradesmen had to be told that they would be paid. Only then would I know where we stood. He had asked me to refund 400 frs. to G. [Grzymala?] which I did the next day. As to the 1,000 frs. which he asked me to give to Mme. E[tienne] for her services, I did not give them to her immediately, but

advised her I was holding them for her, since she would be needed until the funeral was over.

I mentioned in my first letter to you that I could not give you an accurate accounting since I had no way of estimating what the expenses were.

On the day of the auction Louise went to the country so as not to be accused of interfering. Now it was over, and Louise, sick at heart, was anxious to go home. In the meantime, Kalasanty had broken with her family. He wrote that he was going to meet her at the Polish border and they would then decide their future course. She was delayed; he got tired of waiting for her and returned to Warsaw.

Before Louise left Paris, she decided that she would bring with her a woman who for a time had been Chopin's nurse, a Mrs. Matuszewska. Louise thought she could be useful as a governess for her children; she would "polish their French." Then, too, she wanted somebody to accompany her on the difficult journey to Poland in the middle of the winter. Apprised of her intention, Kalasanty replied: Under no condition would he allow the nurse to set foot in his house. Louise then asked her mother if she would be willing to employ the woman—she had been paid for some weeks in advance. Justyna said that of course she would be welcome. As a countermove of spite, Kalasanty got rid of a German maid they had had for years. Henceforth Louise was to do all the housework herself and take care of the children.

Louise was by no means a little ermine of a woman; she possessed will and strength. Yet in addition to the fact that a wife could not by law act independently, the nineteenth-century tradition of the husband as lord and master was deeply enough inculcated in her so that, while crying out against him, she could still write: "I was confident I could justify myself" and "I still believe in the kindness of your heart." Returned home, she attempted a rapprochement. He would not soften. Her dead brother destroyed a marriage which could never have been sound. They stayed together, probably "for the sake of the children," but there was no real reconciliation.

From a friend you became a tyrant. I, from your friend, became a slave.

She did not talk of her brother to him.

The slightest mention of him angered you—being with you I had to give up my memories.

Louise was forty-two when Chopin died; in a portrait made around that time she looks a weary sixty. Kalasanty died four years after Chopin; Louise outlived her husband by only two years. She died in 1855. Chopin's mother, Justyna, outlived three of her four children, dying in 1861, while his youngest sister, Isabella, only a year younger than her brother, reached the age of seventy. Jane Stirling devoted the rest of her life, some ten years, to the memory of the man she had fruitlessly loved. Her friends sometimes called her "Chopin's widow"; she did not think the gibe amusing. She died at Calder House in 1859.

XIII

AFTERWARD

CHOPIN, wrote Tolstoy's daughter Alexandra, was the composer whom her father "loved above all." Tolstoy said: "While I listened I became as one with Chopin; I felt as if I had composed the piece myself." Again: "In every art, I know this from personal experience, it is difficult to get rid of two extremes: inaccessibility and vulgarity. Chopin's greatness lies in this: when he is simple there is no trace of vulgarity, and when he is complicated he is still intelligible." Incidentally, Tolstoy compared the audience for music to a mountain. At the wide base are large numbers of people capable of appreciating popular music. In the middle are those who enjoy Mozart, Beethoven, and Chopin. The complexity of modern music is responsible for the diminishing number of listeners. "Finally there will come a composer who will be the only one to understand his own music." (Told to R. M. Meindorf, 1895.) However, shortly before Tolstoy's death, when he had abjured his own works, he complained bitterly: "True art should be comprehensible to everybody. Art today caters only to the higher classes, to us. Much as I like Chopin, I think he will not remain alive." He read Huneker's biography of Chopin and found it "only clever flamboyant writing, but Chopin is not there."

It didn't take long before Chopin was "not there."

Because he left little autobiographical material; because the apex of his story lay in the love affair with a brilliant and scintillating woman; because she gave the impression that in that affair he played a weakling's role; because he died of that most romantic of nineteenth-century diseases, which served Turgenev and Murger in literature, Verdi and Puccini in opera; and last but not least, because some of his music *is* sentimental—for all these reasons he was soon sentimentalized. A soft shimmering fabric covered the real figure. He was, so to speak, gift-wrapped. In our imagination he became the very model of the romantic artist, the languid genius with the pale brow, destined not to dwell long among us, and to expire picturesquely. A few months after his death a Parisian periodical published a caricature showing an elaborately dressed lady sunk in deep despondency, her tears flowing. "What ails her?" asks a bystander. "Ah—she is the only countess in whose arms Chopin did *not* die."

Legend rendered the real figure mawkish. It was forgotten that he enjoyed long periods of good health; that however cloud-capped his imagination, in furthering his career he proved down to earth; that he laughed and could be ironic, sardonic, and even caustic, as is evident by his mimicking of people's foibles: he was famous for that. Balzac in *Un Homme d'affaires* describes a character as being able "to mimic people with the same skill as Chopin."

Chopin is "not there" either when we are told of his "scant interests outside music."

He was a man of culture and education, though he did not carry his culture on his sleeve for biographers to peck at. Gautier was not the only one who remarked on his response to poetry. It was to be expected that he would read his Polish contemporaries—he set to music poems by Witwicki, Mickiewicz, and Krasinski—but he also read Hugo, Byron, Shakespeare, Scott, Musset, Voltaire. And surely he read George Sand, including that "most excellent" essay on Goethe, Byron, and Mickiewicz, as well as *Lucrezia Floriani.* Yet, because he never would express himself about books or plays, let alone pontificate about current literary tendencies, his biographers pictured him as practically an illiterate. Cecil Gray in his *History of Music* stated that Chopin "was never known even to read a book." Herbert Weinstock thought that he

> was not to any appreciable sense an intellectual at all. His letters are almost wholly devoid of any discussion of ideas, of books, of other arts than music, of any music but his own and that of a few operatic composers. He was unique among the composers of his era in not himself having

literary pretension: as an adult he wrote nothing but letters, letters charming in their complete spontaneity, but usually lacking in verbal graces. It would be impossible to prove that he understood, or for that matter that he even read, Sand's writings, not to mention those of a dozen other important literary figures whom he met.

Can one imagine that the man who lived with George Sand for almost nine years did *not* read her writings? Even supposing he didn't want to, would she not have coerced him to do so? An author is an author. At Nohant she used to read aloud in the morning what she had written during the night.

He was a Benvenuto Cellini of music; all the jewels he set were not of the purest water, yet the settings were of the finest workmanship. Self-critical, that casual little waltz caused him agony. George Sand described how he worked:

> His ideas came to him spontaneously, miraculously; he found them without searching, they arrived at the piano all at once, complete and sublime. Or they resounded in his head and he rushed to listen to them, by himself, trying them on the instrument. But then began the most exhausting struggle I have ever witnessed. It was a special kind of effort, of uncertainty, of impatience, reshaping the details of the theme of his imagination. That which he had conceived as a whole he now analyzed all too minutely. His grief at not finding the total perfection which he sought threw him into desperation. He locked himself in his room for days on end, weeping, walking up and down, breaking pens, repeating or changing one measure a hundred times, writing, crossing out over and over again, the next day commencing anew with a perseverance at once meticulous and frantic. He spent six weeks on one page, only to end by writing it in the form in which he had sketched it the very first time.

Histoire de ma vie

The countless corrections and erasures in his manuscripts indicate that this description is true, though he burned his preliminary sketches. Mozart's output was about ten times greater than Chopin's and he lived four years fewer. Mendelssohn composed twice as much as Chopin and died at thirty-eight, and Schubert, dying at thirty-one, far outreached Mendelssohn.

Chopin had an easy climb to fame. He witnessed a few thumbs-

down gestures, such as the review by the Berlin critic Ludwig Rellstab*
or the one in the London *Musical World,*** but the laurel wreaths were
plentiful and the bravos loud. He shared with Mendelssohn and Liszt
the satisfaction of being quickly appreciated both by cognoscenti and
plain music lovers. Even Wagner, who hated everything imported from
Paris (except perfume), enjoyed Chopin, as is apparent from Cosima's
diary:

> Richard asks him [Josef Rubinstein] to play a Chopin Polonaise to warm
> him. It delights him and he calls it a masterpiece.
>
> *February 5, 1882*

> Early in the morning after a fitful night Richard plays the melody of
> Chopin's Funeral March. At breakfast that leads to a discussion of the
> Poles and their charming characteristics.
>
> *February 26, 1881*

In retrospect, when we read all those dedications to Baroness X and
Countess Y (more than forty titled names are mentioned), we get the
impression that he was indeed "crazy about the aristocracy," as his
pupil George Mathias wrote. Chopin himself was a natural aristocrat,
walking nonchalantly on the waxed parquet of society and appearing
before Louis Philippe with the same insouciance with which he sipped
his morning chocolate. He saw clearly the poses and pretensions of the
titled Polish émigrés and the fustian impracticability of the world-sav-
ing schemes proposed by the Lerouxes and the Lamartines. Nor did his
predilection for the titled prevent him from giving his love to a woman
who affected a truculent plebeianism and must often have smelled of
tobacco.

He was scrupulous with himself, but he was a superficial critic of
other men's work. Creative ability and critical acumen—they are not

---

*"In search of ear-rending dissonances, torturous transitions, sharp modulations, re-
pugnant contortions of melody and rhythm, Chopin is altogether indefatigable. . . . Had
he submitted this music to a Master, one hopes that he would have torn it up and thrown
it at his feet—and this is what we symbolically wish to do." (July 5, 1833)

**"There is an excuse at present for Chopin's delinquencies; he is entrammeled in
the enthralling bonds of that arch-enchantress, George Sand, celebrated equally for the
number and excellence of her romances and her lovers; not less we wonder how she, who
once swayed the heart of the sublime and terrible religious democrat Lamennais, can be
content to wanton away her dream-like existence with an artistical nonentity like Chopin." (October 28, 1841)

usually functions of the same mind. As Oscar Wilde said: "A really great artist can never judge of other people's work. . . . The Gods are hidden from each other." Thus, Tchaikovsky: "Brahms does not possess melodic invention. His musical ideas never speak to the point." Brahms: "In everything I attempt I step on the heels of my predecessors, who shame me. But Wagner—he would not hinder me at all from proceeding with pleasure to the composing of an opera." Wagner about Brahms: "A stupid youngster." Chopin's understanding of Berlioz was so limited that he said Berlioz spattered ink on ruled paper and then transformed the accidental blots into notes. Of Schumann, who had so warmly welcomed him, he thought so little that he considered *Carnaval* "not music at all." Verdi's *Ernani* was not worth talking about.

Like most artists, he knew how to drive a good bargain with his publishers, and like most, he berated them. But he did not cheat them. Like most artists, he demanded complete devotion from his friends and when one failed to perform a service for which he asked, he would let loose with his favorite terms of opprobrium: "Pig" and "Jew." When he was rightly appealed to, when his feelings were stirred, he could be enlisted in a good cause, especially if it concerned Poland. In March 1838 he went to Rouen and gave what for him was a "monster" concert for the benefit of Anton Orlowski—friend and fellow student. (Both studied under Elsner.) Ernest Legouvé wrote that the audience of five hundred "was constantly quivering, constantly murmuring in ecstasy." That concert took a heavy toll of Chopin's nerves, not lightened by his having seen a chimney sweep on the way to the hall. (In Austria that meant good luck, in Poland bad luck.)

How superstitious he was! He managed to combine both Polish and French superstitions. His slippers had to lie exactly parallel before he could retire, seven and thirteen were bad-luck numbers (later twenty as well), and no enterprise could be begun on Mondays or Fridays. Always enter a new place with the right foot; never walk under a ladder; thirteen at table meant death. A hare jumping across your path meant sickness. One must never count the strokes of a church bell.

(2)

The misinterpretation of what was—in spite of superstitions and prejudices—a sensible and buoyant personality was followed by a misinterpretation of his music. Pianists began to oversugar the contents. They thought they played "soulfully," like him; but nobody could play like him, because his own interpretations were too flexible and too mercurial to be imitated. "I never play a piece twice in the same way," he said. We have some testimony from one of his pupils, F. H. Péru, of whom little is known except that he and Massenet were instrumental in commissioning a statue of Chopin which was erected in the Luxembourg Gardens in 1899:

> Reclining on a couch he listened to a piece I played. He got up and played it the way *he* felt it and I listened religiously. . . . I came to the next lesson having worked hard and being almost satisfied that I had succeeded in copying his interpretation. Again he got up and after a bit of banter sat down at the piano saying, "Now hear how this should be played," and then played the piece in a style entirely different from the previous occasion. I wept. . . . I was so discouraged. Then he was sorry for me and said, "Well, it was almost good, but it was not how I felt it."

Another pupil of his who tried to copy him was an American, Paul Emil Johns. Born in Austria, he emigrated to New Orleans at an early age, married a rich Creole, and started a business selling musical instruments. In 1832 he went to Paris to call on Pleyel: he wanted to obtain the U.S. and Canadian agency for Pleyel pianos. He did. Pleyel probably introduced him to Chopin, who liked him. Chopin gave lessons to Johns —he seems to have been a competent pianist—and dedicated his Five Mazurkas (Opus 7) to him. Johns returned home and began to tour the U.S. and Canada playing Chopin's works—and selling pianos. He let it be known that he was interpreting Chopin "the Chopin way." He aped Chopin's mannerisms and gestures. Those he had down pat. But as to his playing? "The way he clears his throat and the way he spits—that you have duly learned!" says the soldier about the sergeant who imitates the general in Schiller's *Wallenstein.* It is ironical that a better pianist than Johns, Henry Kowalski, toured the same cities a few years later but met with an icy reception; he was not "authentic." Johns died suddenly on one of his visits to Paris; he is buried in Père Lachaise Cemetery, not far from Chopin.

Inevitably, imitative playing led pianists to sentimentalized interpretation. When the storm of the A-flat major Polonaise did not make the windows rattle, the Swooning Style (Nocturne Department) took over—lots of pedal, long notes hugged too long, and everything hush-

hush. Quite contrary to Chopin's real way of playing, as described by one of his zealous scholars, Arthur Hedley:

> Chopin's own playing was the counterpart of his personality. Every characteristic which may be distinguished in the man came out in the piano—the same precision; the horror of excess and all that is "sloppy" and uncontrolled; the same good manners and high tone of breeding, combined with poetic warmth and a romantic fervour of expression. No one had ever heard such polished playing, although others could make a more overwhelming impression by their rush and violence. It is a mistake, encouraged by sentimental legend, to believe that Chopin's playing was invariably limited by a delicacy which was equivalent to weakness. The fact is that even in the last stages of consumption he could rally and summon the strength to play (as in Scotland in 1848) works like the F major Ballade with an energy that surprised the audience, who saw in front of them "a slight, frail-looking person."
>
> *The Interpretation of Chopin*

(3)

Immortality is subject to relativity. An immortal artist's work may make a greater impact on one generation than another, and the validity of his message may rise, dip, and rise again. During the generation following Chopin's death, music, or at least a substantial portion of it, seemed to be in search of poetic underpinning. Did music suggest a painting? A love poem? A philosophic idea? Such compositions appeared as Liszt's *Faust* and *Dante* Symphonies, the tone poems *Tasso, Mazeppa,* and *Hamlet;* Saint-Saëns' *Le Rouet d'Omphale, Phaëton,* and *Danse macabre;* Smetana's *Ma Vlast* symphonic cycle, Moussorgsky's *Pictures at an Exhibition,* Tchaikovsky's *Romeo and Juliet* Overture, Franck's *Les Éolides*—all between 1850 and 1875.

The result of this tendency, an outgrowth of Romanticism, was the notion that *all* music could be articulated in words. It had to "mean" something. Harold Schonberg has written amusingly about this: he points out that so serious a musician as Hans von Bülow supplied a set of programs for each of Chopin's twenty-four Preludes. This is what Bülow saw in the tiny C-sharp minor Prelude:

> A night moth is flying around the room—there! it has suddenly hidden itself (the sustained G sharp); only its wings twitch a little. In a moment

it takes flight anew and again settles down in darkness—its wings flutter (trill in the left hand). This happens several times, but at the last, just as the wings begin to quiver again, the busybody who lives in the room aims a stroke at the poor insect. It twitches once . . . and dies.

Schonberg comments: "But this is kid stuff compared to Bülow's surrealistic exegesis of No. 9 in E Major:"

Here Chopin has the conviction that he has lost his power of expression. With the determination to discover whether his brain can still originate ideas, he strikes his head with a hammer (here the sixteenths and thirty-seconds are to be carried out in exact time, indicating a double stroke of the hammer). In the third and fourth measures one can hear the blood trickle (trills in the left hand). He is desperate at finding no inspiration (fifth measure); he strikes again with the hammer and with greater force (thirty-second notes twice in succession during the crescendo). In the key of A flat he finds his powers again. Appeased, he seeks his former key and closes contentedly.

Schonberg: "One might well ask why a composer fearing loss of inspiration decides to hit himself on the head with a hammer. But . . . well, let's forget about it."

During Bülow's time and for some time after, when audiences were preoccupied with exploring Wagner's Valhalla, Chopin's "unphilosophic" work sank to the level of "salon music." Pretty, sentimental, but not much more. Proust commented sarcastically that he had "forfeited the esteem of 'really musical' people."

Today's pianists, modernists though they may be, cannot get away from him. The best of them play Chopin very well—that is, without overcoloring and overstraining, without spreading butter on their fingertips or executing a high dive into a chord. At the Touraine Festival of 1976 Sviatoslav Richter devoted half his program to Chopin. The London *Times* commented:

Except for a touch of teasing in the F major waltz, there was no conscious "presentation" of the music. Even the Polonaise-Fantaisie had no dramatic dynamic contrasts in the introduction, or rhetorical calls-to-arms in what followed. Half a century ago such an approach to Chopin might even have been called austere. Today it is better described as aristocratic; and on this occasion it amply proved the eloquence of understatement. It was affecting to recall that one or two of the pieces he played were composed at Nohant, near by. He could have been the composer himself, introducing them for the first time to a circle of intimates.

No one has played Chopin more beautifully than his compatriot Arthur Rubinstein. Here are a few quotations from an article Rubinstein wrote for the 150th anniversary of the composer's birth:

> Though it might be more dramatic to say that my discovery of Chopin took place in infancy and that once hearing his music I vowed in my crib to devote myself to his cause for eternity, the truth, as always, is more interesting. The awakening came relatively late—after I had been performing in public for ten years, as a matter of fact. . . .
>
> As you can imagine, however, I heard quite a bit of Chopin during my childhood in Poland—mazurkas, polonaises, nocturnes, the whole beloved repertory. All of it was played interminably, and most of it badly.
>
> Why badly?
>
> In those days both musicians and the public believed in the Chopin myth, as do many people today. That myth was a destructive one. Chopin, the man, was seen as weak and ineffectual; Chopin the artist, as an irrepressible romantic—effeminate if appealing, dreaming around, dipping his pen in moonlight to compose nocturnes for sentimental young women. Pianists whose heads were filled with such nonsense had to play Chopin badly. . . .
>
> Undeniably Chopin expressed his age in his art. To a great degree the surface facts of his life did satisfy the Romantic myth—his ascetic face, his dandyism, his affair with the leading novelist of the day, George Sand, his disease, tuberculosis, which was the fashionable disease of the nineteenth century. But these facts tend to obscure Chopin's lack of self-consciousness about Romanticism. Unlike many of his contemporaries, he could take or leave the Romantic Age. . . .
>
> As a matter of fact, Chopin's approach to music was more closely allied to the classicists than to his contemporaries. To the intense subjectivity of the ego-permeated people surrounding him . . . he opposed a scrupulous self-discipline, and purely musical content. . . .

(4)

How Polish is Chopin's music? His first composition was a Polonaise, his last a Mazurka, and both forms are based on Polish dances, the first a statelier and slower rhythm than the second. Yet neither is "folk music." Chopin drew on the rich treasure of Polish music—more than ten thousand folk tunes have been traced—only to transmute it. Couperin, Rameau, Johann Sebastian and Wilhelm Friedemann Bach used Polish modes as well. If we listened to Chopin's "Polish" compositions, ignorant of the title and the author's name and origin, would we recognize them as nationalistic? A few of them, no doubt. Of others—even some bearing a Polish title—one could not be sure, for they are fashioned with too subtle a craftsmanship to make the source apparent. And if this is true of the so-called Polish pieces, with how much less certainty could we trace Slavic elements in the Sonata Opus 35 or the Waltzes? Most of his music is not evocative of silver-buttoned spencers and tasseled boots and red-and-white sashes. Moussorgsky is Russian, De Falla Spanish, Ives American—but how importantly did the country of his childhood influence this man's thinking, who was taught the classical tradition by a German teacher and lived his life among the French Romantics? He loved "Poland," but what he knew of it was chiefly Warsaw and a home where half the conversation was in French. The wonderful Barcarolle is as Polish as the first "Rasoumovsky" Quartet is Russian.

He was more than Polish; he was in the best sense an artist without a country. Like the work of all vital composers, his work moves and exalts you, whether you were born in Tokyo or the Tatras. His finest music is so original that it seems to have been created by somebody who had no predecessor. That, of course, is not the case. He expanded the classical form of the Scherzo; he could be melancholy as well as truculent in a Scherzo. The Ballade in his sense *is* original, a composition of episodic character which is based on no extramusical idea, and tells no tales. The Nocturnes do derive from a form made popular by the Irish composer John Field, pupil of Clementi, who had great fame but whom alcohol ruined. But the difference between Chopin's and Field's "night pieces" is as great as between Mozart's *Eine Kleine Nachtmusik* and a good village serenade. In these Nocturnes, as in some other lyric compositions, Chopin created a new "bel canto" style for the piano: it sings as a matchless prima donna, free of throat troubles.

In spite of his "perseverance at once meticulous and frantic," which astonished George Sand, one can find pulpy passages and weak transitions in some of his works. Here and there he falls short of the architectural mastery of a Brahms, lacking Flaubert's instinct of inevitability.

What are his best works? Though opinions naturally differ, many musicians agree on the following:

		Date of Composition
Opus 9	Three Nocturnes: Nos. 1 and 2	1830–31
Opus 10	Twelve Etudes: Nos. 3, 10, 12	1829–33
Opus 15	Two Nocturnes	1830–31
Opus 23	Ballade in G Minor	1831–35
Opus 24	Four Mazurkas: No. 4	1834–35
Opus 25	Twelve Etudes: All twelve are superb, the last the greatest	1832–36
Opus 27	Two Nocturnes	1835–36
Opus 28	Twenty-Four Preludes: All, especially Nos. 11, 15, 16, 20, 23, 24	*Composed over a span of time, finished in 1839*
Opus 30	Four Mazurkas: No. 4	1836–37
Opus 31	Scherzo in B-flat minor	1837
Opus 35	Sonata in B-flat minor	1837 (March), 1839
Opus 37	Two Nocturnes: No. 2	1839
Opus 39	Scherzo in C-sharp minor	1839
Opus 40	Two Polonaises	1838–39
Opus 44	Polonaise in F-sharp minor	1840–41
Opus 47	Ballade in A-flat major	1840–41
Opus 48	Two Nocturnes: No. 1	1841
Opus 49	Fantaisie in F minor	1841
Opus 50	Three Mazurkas: No. 3	1841–42
Opus 52	Ballade in F minor	1841–42
Opus 53	Polonaise in A-flat major	1842
Opus 57	Berceuse in D-flat major	1843
Opus 58	Sonata in B minor	1844
Opus 59	Three Mazurkas: Nos. 2 and 3	1845
Opus 60	Barcarolle in F-sharp	1845–46
Opus 61	Polonaise-Fantaisie in A-flat major	1845–46
Opus 63	Three Mazurkas: No. 3	1846
Opus 64	Three Waltzes: No. 1	1846–47

Chopin is one of the few composers whose music can fill an evening-long concert and hold the audience. He is one of the composers most copiously represented by recordings; virtually all his music has been

recorded and "Selections" occupy fifty-one entries in one record catalogue, the performing artists ranging from Argerich to Zimerman.

He had no direct successor. He influenced Slavic music only a little,
very little Dvořák or Smetana or Bartok, more Scriabin and much more
Rachmaninoff, about whose performance of Chopin's B-flat-minor
Sonata the critic W. J. Henderson wrote that it was a case of "genius
understanding genius."* In an interview the following year Rachmaninoff said: "From the time when I was nineteen years old, I felt his
greatness, and I marvel at it still. He is today more modern than many
moderns."

Brahms made a close study of Chopin. Debussy was the composer
most influenced by him. "He was impregnated with the spirit of Chopin, inhabited by it," wrote Marguerite Long, a pianist and friend of
Debussy. In 1915 Debussy edited a new edition of Chopin's work for the
French publisher Durand, the German editions having become una-
vailable, and in the same year he composed his last work for the piano:
"Twelve Etudes, dedicated to the memory of Frederic Chopin."

As an innovator in pianistic terms, Chopin maintains a fame as firm
as that of the strongest pillars of music. As a man let us remember him
not always in infirm sadness, the way Delacroix saw him in the portrait.
As a contributor to living music let us think of him as a poet, accepting
Wordsworth's definition:

> What is a Poet? He is a man speaking to men: a man, it is true, endued
> with more lively sensibility, more enthusiasm and tenderness, who has
> a greater knowledge of human nature, and a more comprehensive soul,
> than are supposed to be common among mankind; a man pleased with
> his own passions and volitions, and who rejoices more than other men
> in the spirit of life that is in him.

---

*Rachmaninoff recorded this performance for Victor in 1930.

APPENDIX

1

SOME OF THE DELFINA LETTERS

Disagreements about the unlit areas in a man's life are pursued by his biographers with scarcely less acrimony than the war between the Guelphs and the Ghibellines. The question of Beethoven's Immortal Beloved, for example, has been debated by at least fourteen researchers, with no agreement. The Delfina affair has been discussed by more than a dozen scholars, with no agreement but much vituperation.

It began with the biography by Ferdinand Hoesick, *Chopin, His Life and Works,* published in 1910–11 in three volumes. Hoesick is regarded as a punctilious scholar, though in one man's opinion he "displays too much sympathy for legends and undocumented anecdotes." Hoesick devoted nine pages (pp. 70–79, Vol. II, 1965 edition) to a description of what he asserts to have been a love affair. "It was no secret either to the Polish émigrés or to fashionable French society." He mentions a "voluminous correspondence" between the two and he strongly implies that he knew some of this correspondence: "she was writing to Chopin exclusively in their native language and she could express herself quite correctly in Polish," while her later letters to the poet Krasinski were written in French, "pretending she did not write Polish adequately." Obviously to make such a statement Hoesick must have read her letters to Chopin and presumably Chopin's letters to her. Why, then, did he not copy and publish them? He hinted that he had promised not to use or divulge these letters. His daughter later confirmed this. The letters were owned by a Mme. Rose Raczynska, the daughter-in-law of the poet Krasinski. How did she get these letters? Hoesick did not say: he only quoted Madame Raczynska as swearing a solemn oath that she would never let them be published, some of the letters being "scabrous." But why such prudishness? What interest could she have had in protecting posthumously the reputation of Chopin and her father-in-law's mistress? Hoesick seems to have remembered some of the texts and later referred to them. Yet the original letters have never come to light; if they did exist, they may have perished in a fire which destroyed the Raczynska Palace in Warsaw in 1939.

Hoesick's belief that Chopin and Delfina were lovers was seconded by Bronisław E. Sydow, who edited Chopin's letters, devoting fifteen years to the task and dying before he could finish it. In the preface to his edition he wrote: "It is my opinion that a passionate relationship existed for many years between the great composer and the marvelously beautiful Delfina Potocka. Others, among them my collaborators Suzanne and Denise Chainaye, are of a different opinion." Several other Polish scholars agree, including Jaroslaw Iwaszkiewicz: "In actual fact we know nothing of that idyll. All that has been said belongs to tradition . . . a tradition, however, which is very strong."

Professor Matteo Glinski of Assumption University, Windsor, Canada, at one time executive director of the International Chopin Foundation, was also convinced of the romance.* Other scholars, disagreeing violently, believe that Delfina and Frederic were at most good friends: among these writers are Arthur Hedley, who wrote an impassioned essay on the subject; Herbert Weinstock, who throws out the baby with the bath water merely by a footnote: "I can find nothing to justify the belief . . ."; and Gastone Belotti, who in a three-volume biography, *F. Chopin l'uomo*, published in 1974, devotes a pedantic dissertation to "save others from the same error" committed by C. Wierzynski, a Polish poet and biographer (*The Life and Death of Chopin*, 1949), who accepted the affair and all the letters as true.

We offer herewith: (1) the fragments existing in photographs which the graphologist Ordway Hilton (see Appendix 2) judges as being probably genuine; (2) other photographic fragments, which Mr. Hilton has proved to be fakes; (3) three of the letters, existing only in the form of typescripts.

1. *Photographic fragments probably genuine*

I occasionally see Mickiewicz again. He visited me yesterday. He has changed a lot, become very gloomy so that I am no longer able to cheer him with songs or with Filon [allusion to an old Polish song], as I used to do. He comes and goes without having said a word, the only thing is that I know what he comes for, and I immediately sit down and play. I pretend I have a lesson and ask all visitors to be sent away because he does not like company. Last time I played for him for a long time, and I was afraid to look round at him because I heard him crying.

Later, when he was about to depart, I helped him put on his coat, as I did not want my servant to see him crying. Mick[iewicz] embraced me with affection, kissed my forehead and said the very first words of that afternoon: "May God bless thee, thou hast transported me . . ." he did not finish, because . . .

No. 87a and 87b

---

*See his *Chopin's Letters to Delfina* (1961) and *Chopin the Unknown* (1963).

They [Mickiewicz and the other Polish émigrés in Paris] keep dinning into my head that I should write symphonies and operas. They wish to have in me a Polish Rossini, Mozart and Beethoven. But I have a quiet laugh, and I think that one has to begin with small things. I am only a pianist, if I am worth anything so much the better, after me greater ones will come and, thanks to them, Polish music will expand and flourish. I think it is better to do little but to do it well, rather than do everything and do it badly. I shall never go back on that.

No. 55

2. *Photographic fragments probably fakes*

Dearest Findeleczko [a play on the diminutive of Delfina]:
I have been told that Slowacki [a Polish romantic poet] calls me a peacock and slanders me wherever he can. I have never been rude to him, keeping myself away from him. So I do not . . . [understand/know] what does this fool [want from me] . . . new, because I would like again to plop something down your little hole in D flat major. Do not refuse me. Your FC.

No. 24

The French horn player complained strongly about a poor solo phrase in the finale of my F minor Concerto. No rehearsals—he says—will help, because blowing time and again he will play clearly a few times, but at a concert he will blow once and, sure enough, will strike a false note. Offering many apologies he politely and in great detail explained the French horn to me, but in all this there was the unspoken accusation that I did not know how to score for instruments. I laugh at this and reply that I am a fool when it comes to scoring, but this phrase is not an error, and there may be a false note, for it represents the crowing of the cock before dawn.

No. 6

3. *Three letters existing only in typescript*

Fidelina, my one and only beloved:
I will bore you once again with my thoughts on the subject of inspiration and creativity, but as you will perceive these thoughts are directly connected with you.
I have long reflected on inspiration and creativity and slowly, slowly I think I have discovered the essential nature of these gifts.
To me inspiration and creativity come only when I have abstained from a woman for a long period. When, with passion, I have emptied my fluid into a woman until I am pumped dry then inspiration shuns me and ideas won't crawl into my head. Consider how strange and wonderful it is that the same forces which go to fertilize a woman and create a human being should go to create a work of art! Yet a man wastes this life-giving precious fluid for a moment of ecstasy.

The same is true of scholars who devote themselves to scientific pursuits or men who make discoveries. The formula is apparently a simple one: whatever his work, the creator must abjure woman: then the forces in his body will accumulate in his brain as inspiration, and he may give birth to a pure work of art.

Indeed, sexual temptation and desire can be transmuted into inspiration! Of course I am speaking only of those who have ability and talent. A fool, living without a woman, will merely be driven insane by frustration. He can't create anything worthy of god or man.

On the other hand unrequited love and unfulfilled passion, sharpened by the image of one's beloved and carrying unbearable frustration with it, can contribute to creativity. I have observed this in Norwid.

What about Mozart? I don't know, but I think his wife became ordinary food for him, his love and passion cooled, and he therefore was able to compose a great deal. I haven't heard of any love affairs in Mozart's life.

Sweetest Fidelina, how much of that precious fluid, how many forces have I wasted on you? I have not given you a child and God only knows how many excellent inspirations, how many musical ideas have gone to perdition.

Operam et oleum perdidi!!! Who knows what ballades, polonaises, perhaps an entire concerto, have been forever engulfed in your little D-flat major? I cannot reckon what might have been, since I have not composed anything for ever so long, immersed as I am in you and in love. Works which could have sprung to life, drowned in your sweetest little D-flat major, so that you are filled with music and pregnant with my compositions!

Time flies, life runs on, no one can recapture wasted moments. It is with reason that the saints call woman the gate to hell!

No, no, I take back this last sentence. I eat my words. I won't erase what I have just written because if I do you'll bother me until I tell you what the erased words were. And I don't have time to write another letter.

To me you are the gate of paradise. For you I will renounce fame, creativity, everything. Ah! Fidelina, Fidelina—I long for you intensely and frightfully!

I'm shivering as if ants were running up my spine to my head. When you finally arrive in your diligent-diligence I will glue myself to you, so that for a whole week you won't be able to tear me away from the little D-flat major, and to hell with inspiration and ideas. Let my composition disappear in the dark forever!

Ah! I have thought up a new musical name for the little D-flat major. Shall we call it "tacit"? I'll explain it to you at once! Isn't a pause a hole in the melody? So this name is a musical term quite appropriate for the little D-flat major.

Hoffman just came and scattered to the wind the possibility of writing a letter. The pupils will shortly arrive as well, I will therefore finish, so that my letter can leave by today's mail. I kiss your beloved little body all over.

Your most faithful Frederic

Your *most* gifted pupil, one who has

skillfully mastered the art of making love

P.S. I wasted time doing nothing yesterday and the letter did not leave, so I am adding to it.

I have just finished a Prelude in which I have "immortalized" [literally: "prolonged for centuries"; he means it ironically] our eleventh love-frolic. It contains eleven accents in honor of our sweetest frolic. I will explain it when I play it for you and you will fathom its real meaning. I know it will prove to be our favorite Prelude, just as our little frolic is.

P.S. They drove me mad yesterday. Imagine, the gossipmongers say that you are unable to have a baby, because you have had too many lovers, and grass does not grow on well-trodden paths. This is the kind of nonsense people spread. I almost burst into tears hearing it. Forgive me for repeating it to you. My dearest, when you return don't give me any more excuses for refusing to become pregnant. I will make you a baby and all those liars will have to eat their words.

Women of the world who have illegitimate children are not ashamed of them. Not at all. It is well known that illegitimate children possess outstanding aptitudes and talents. I'm obsessed with wild thoughts, with dreams that our child will become a very great musician and will emulate both of us in his art. You will see—all right, all right, I am finishing now and running to the post office.

Please respond promptly. These days your letters are my only delight.

F.F.C.

As you know I can be diplomatic and I am able to deal with people, yet I sometimes commit a *faux pas* so gross that later I cannot forgive myself. Such an unfortunate incident occurred with Norwid.

He came to see me and as usual I played for him. I noticed that the sleeves of his shabby linen jacket were badly shredded. I told him my concierge could mend them right away and I took the jacket to Mme. Etienne. In the meantime, Norwid sat wrapped in my warm dressing gown. When Mme. Etienne returned the jacket, repaired, I took it from her myself so that I could surreptitiously put a little money in one of the pockets. Norwid then put on the jacket without noticing anything and eventually departed.

Now he has not come to see me for ever so long. I am afraid he is offended because of the money. I know he has had to borrow money from others and that he has quite openly asked people for loans. Me he never asked for a sou. Money has never been mentioned between us. Perhaps he wished art to be our sole bond.

It is difficult to understand him. His nature is exceptional and today I realize one must make exceptional allowances for him. I can neither forgive myself nor explain to him that I acted purely on impulse.

Every time I recall the incident I grieve; I am inconsolable.

Each nation finds delight in a different kind of music. A Frenchman loves dazzling music of sophisticated elegance, reflecting his own tendency to take things lightly and amiably. A German admires erudition and emotionalism. We Poles are in love with patriotic sentimentality.

I have no idea what it is that an Englishman wants from music. He admires any and all music, old and new, as long as it is foreign. He lavishes money on it—after all music is a luxury—but, between ourselves, I think he is incapable of truly loving or feeling it. Today my new little pupil, an English girl, when I asked her to sing a phrase, squeaked as if someone had stepped on a nest of mice. I almost fainted.

Up to now I haven't heard an Englishman sing in tune. I think that the English have wooden ears and may never be able to create valuable music.

APPENDIX

2

THE HILTON REPORT:
REPORT OF AN EXAMINATION OF QUESTIONED
HANDWRITING—CHOPIN-POTOCKA

I have made an examination of the handwriting and other evidence contained in the photographs of fragments of five letters which are purported to have been written by Frederick Chopin to Madame Delfina Potocka. These documents were submitted as photographs, four of which are described and translated in an article, March 1973, by Adam Harasowski in *Music and Musicians*. The numbering used for these letters is that found in publications by J. M. Smoter.

1. An eleven-line text designated as Letter 6 and dealing with a horn solo in Chopin's F minor Concerto.
2. A collection of twelve fragments making up an incomplete letter beginning Dearest Findeleczko and signed with the initials F.C. This is Letter 24.
3. A ten-line text designated as Letter 55, reporting on friends urging Chopin to write symphonies and operas.
4. A four-line fragment designated as Letters 87a [and 87b], making reference [to] Mickiewicz.
5. Three fragments of writing consisting of the word Ponieolzialek and two additional fragments of almost one half the width of the paper containing 6 and 8 lines respectively. This has been designated as Letter 15.

PROBLEM

The purpose of this examination was to determine whether or not these letters were written by Frederick Chopin, whose known handwriting was available for study and comparison.

STANDARDS

Known specimens of Chopin's handwriting consisted principally of a photo-copy of a letter addressed to Jules Fontana, the original manuscript of which is found in the Pierpont Morgan Library Mary Flagler Cary Music Collection.

In addition, this examiner visited the Morgan Library and made further study of Chopin's writing from several other letters contained in this same collection.

OPINION AND REASONS

From an extensive examination of the handwriting and the reproductions of the five letters listed in the beginning of this report, it is my opinion that Letters 6 and 24 are not reproductions of any letter composed by Frederick Chopin, despite the fact that the two letters contain examples of his handwriting. It is my firm opinion that both of these letters were assembled in part by cutting words and letter combinations out of other Chopin material and pasting [them] together to form the text found in these two letters.

It is my opinion from a study of photographs of Letters 55 and 87a that these reproductions contain Chopin's authentic handwriting and since from the reproductions no evidence can be developed that the writing in Letter 87a was assembled in a manner comparable to Letters 6 and 24 that this fragment was prepared by Chopin. In the case of Letter 55, there is evidence in some portions of this reproduction that outlines of letters and words have been traced with a second writing instrument and consequently, from the available reproduction, I am unable to state positively that the letter was written in its present form by Chopin. There is no evidence which establishes positively that the letter was not his composition but in view of the background of other letters of this same collection, one is hesitant to declare the letter authentic from the present reproduction of it.

While the handwriting of Letter 15 appears to be completely that of Chopin, the upper-right-hand fragment with the single word on it does not appear definitely to be part of the two left-hand fragments.

Detailed analysis of each letter follows:

Letter 6—According to Harasowski's translation, Letter 6 is a fragment dealing with a French horn passage in Chopin's F minor Concerto. While this writing contains a good deal of Chopin's handwriting, there are within it apparent imitations and from available reproduction one can discern a number of assembled words. The outline of carefully cut-out combinations of letters and words can be seen in the photograph. They have been pasted up and then photocopied. For example, in the fifth line the word "koncercie" has been assembled. The "ko" may or may not be Chopin's writing. Then the "nc" and the "erci" have both been cut from some other documents in neat rectangles and pasted in. But the "o" and "n" were not accurately connected. It is not clear from the photograph whether the final "c" was pasted on with a third rectangle or added in ink. However, there is a gap between the "nc" and the "erci" rectangles and a short connection has been added between the two. There are a number of other words which have been found to be assembled in a similar manner. Apparently when particular letter combinations could not be found, these were made in imitation of Chopin's writing. The first word, "Walfornista," was probably partly written as an imitation of Chopin's writing, and partly pasted together. The "W," the "for" and the final "ta" lack the natural qualities of Chopin's writing while the "al" and "nis" may have been cut from other Chopin writing and pasted in. The "ta," for example, is slow and the handling of the connection between the staff of the "t" of the horizontal stroke and the "a" is not Chopin's way of doing this. At several points, as in this writing, some of the strokes are heavy and some of them are light within a single word, typical of two different width pens. So it is throughout the document, in other words Letter 6 is a completely assembled document using some [of] Chopin's writing with added letters and imitated words interspersed. Clearly this letter was not written by Chopin.

Letter 24—is described accurately by Harasowski as 12 fragments and incomplete. A study of the torn edges between fragments would indicate that adjacent fragments in most instances were not originally joined. They are of approximately the right size to make up the width of the sheet. But the torn edges cannot be fitted together. For example, when the bottom three fragments are rephotographed, cut up, and the bottom edge of the sheet properly aligned, the pattern of the torn edges would not fit together, and further the last line of writing is a little bit higher up on each fragment, in other words, not a continuous line of writing. Here again, there has been some assembling. Possibly a great deal more has been assembled than can be made out from the available reproduction. For example, and this is one of the clearest evidences of assembled words, the large right-hand central portion contains at the end of the bottom line the word "cymbal," made up of at least two or probably three cut-out rectangles which have been pasted up together. The first is "cyn," the second is what could be interpreted as the third downstroke of the "m" and the following "b," and finally a third island of paper containing the "al." With this interpretation the bar over the "l" was added as it ran off the right edge of the island. Other evidence of manipulation is found at the beginning of this letter. The first word, "Najukochansza," is written with one pen, and the second word, "Findeleczko," is written with a much broader pen. These do not match nor do the tear lines between the fragments match, suggesting that they were from two different writings. Since the tear through the middle of the second word does not appear to fit together, it would follow that this second word is actually an assembled word from two different sources. Granted the middle "l" has apparently been torn in half, but actually it is not the typical form of "l" as found in Chopin's writing and may represent some touching up to create the present letter. All in all the physical evidence contained in these fragments fail[s] to establish that Chopin wrote this letter in the form that it has been assembled. The reproduction is not of first-class quality at some points, but there is a suggestion several times that more than one pen was used in the writing on the different fragments. Again the evidence fails to establish that Chopin wrote the material as it has been assembled.

Letter 55—The photographic print of this letter does not display much background detail of the paper on which the writing appears. There is evidence when examination of this [is made] under magnification that a number of the words have been traced over with a second writing instrument, but it is not clear that any quantity of letters or words have been added or modified. Study of the writing reveals that this is consistent with Chopin's writing in the letters from the Morgan Library which served as a standard and there is no strong evidence within this document to say that it is not the writing of Chopin or that the letter was not written [in] its present form.

Letter 78a—This four-line fragment of writing, which according to Harasowski is part of a larger fragment designated as 87a and 87b, has all the qualities of Chopin's writing. The reproduction is highly contrasty, that is, black strokes on a very white background, and some of the finer lines in the original may have been lost in the course of photographing and recopying. The writing is consistent with Chopin's writing characteristics, and it is my best judgment that this is Chopin's original writing.

Letter 15—is a document made up of three fragments, two of which appear to be the left-hand edge or section of a letter, one containing six lines and the lower fragment containing eight. The third fragment is a single word in the upper-right-hand corner. Study of the torn edge between this upper-right-hand fragment and the one adjacent to it does not indicate a good match with the left-hand fragment, so that they may well not have been torn apart. Further, there is a suggestion that two different pens were used, but this cannot be positively established from the photograph. Nevertheless, the writing in the upper-right-hand corner is weaker than any of the other. There is no evidence of added words, strokes, or letters, nor is there evidence of any paste-ups. The writing does match Chopin's habits, and what we have here may well be his authentic handwriting.

Respectfully submitted,
[signed] ORDWAY HILTON

APPENDIX

3

SOME OF CHOPIN'S IDEAS FOR THE DEVELOPMENT
OF PIANO TECHNIQUE (FROM EVIDENCE
BY HIMSELF AND HIS PUPILS)

1. Every pupil, however advanced, should study Clementi's *Gradus ad Parnassum*.
2. Right hand should be placed on notes E, F sharp, G sharp, A sharp, B. Left hand on C, B flat, A flat, G flat, E. These positions help rapid performance of scale passages.
3. Hands should be held quite flat.
4. C major is the most difficult scale to play well. Let us begin with the scale of G-flat major, which tends to place the hand naturally, long fingers for the black keys.
5. Chromatic scale should be practiced with the thumb, forefinger, and middle finger.
6. Use pedals most sparingly, at least in the beginning. And even later on.
7. Compositions used by Chopin for instruction: Works of Beethoven, Hummel, Field, Dussek, Hiller, Scarlatti. "To study music": Bach, Mozart, Handel.
8. "Listen to great singers." From them you will learn how to phrase. "Beautiful sound" is the secret.
9. Practicing three hours a day is enough.
10. To lift your hands in the air is undignified: it is "catching pigeons."
11. A clean, even *staccato* helps to develop a clean, even *legato*.
12. Rhythm: "The left hand should act like an orchestra conductor. . . . It is the clock. . . . Rhythm must not be violated."
13. "Always practice on a good piano, not a second-rate one."
14. Don't play duets or chamber music with dilettantes.
15. "Interpret your own way, as long as you don't change what is written."

A CHOPIN CALENDAR

This calendar does not attempt to list all that was happening in the world during Chopin's life. It is merely an attempt to orient the reader by mentioning some of the political, social, and artistic events which may, directly or indirectly, have impinged on his life.

YEAR	LIFE AND WORKS	POLITICAL & SOCIAL EVENTS	ARTISTIC EVENTS
1810	Born March 1 at Zelazowa Wola, son of Nicolas, aged 39, and Justyna Krzyzanowska, aged 30. Family moves to Warsaw, October.	Napoleon marries Marie Louise, daughter of Franz I. Orders beginning of continental blockade.	G. de Staël: *De l'Allemagne* W. Scott: *The Lady of the Lake* Beethoven: Music for *Egmont*
1815		Battle of Waterloo; Napoleon banished to St. Helena. Czar Alexander I proclaims Poland to be part of Russia; issues a Polish constitution.	Schubert: "Erlkönig"
1816	Begins to take piano lessons from A. Zywny.		
1818	Plays at a charity concert in Warsaw. Receives invitations to many aristocratic homes.		Jane Austen: *Emma* Byron: *The Siege of Corinth* Coleridge: "Kubla Khan" Schubert: Fifth Symphony Rossini: *The Barber of Seville* Jane Austen: *Northanger Abbey* and *Persuasion* (posth.) Byron: *Don Juan* (begun) Keats: *Endymion*

YEAR	LIFE AND WORKS	POLITICAL & SOCIAL EVENTS	ARTISTIC EVENTS
1820	Hears Catalani, who gives him a gold watch. Plays for Duke Constantin.	Individual liberty curtailed in France (March 26).	Venus de Milo discovered Constable: *Harwich Lighthouse* Keats: *The Eve of St. Agnes* Lamartine: *Méditations poétiques* Pushkin: *Russlan and Ludmilla* Scott: *Ivanhoe* Shelley: *Prometheus Unbound* and "Ode to the West Wind" Weber: *Der Freischütz*
1821	First extant manuscript: Polonaise in A-flat major.	Greek rebellion against Turks. Napoleon dies.	
1822	Begins lessons in composition from J. Elsner.	Greece declares independence from Turkey; Turks massacre inhabitants of Chios.	Schubert: "Unfinished" Symphony Liszt, 11 years old, plays in Vienna
1824	At Warsaw Lyceum, where his father is professor of French.	Greek war. In France, Louis XVIII succeeded by reactionary Charles X.	Byron dies, aged 36 Delacroix: *Massacre at Chios* Beethoven: Ninth Symphony performed in Vienna. Composes *Missa Solemnis* and last String Quartets (to 1826)
1825	Plays at two charity concerts at Warsaw Conservatoire. Czar Alexander I hears him and gives him a diamond ring. Rondo Opus 1.	Alexander I dies (December 1); succeeded by Nicholas I, his younger son. Decembrist revolution in Russia, quickly crushed.	Manzoni: *I promessi sposi* Pushkin: *Boris Godunov*

YEAR	LIFE AND WORKS	POLITICAL & SOCIAL EVENTS	ARTISTIC EVENTS
1826	Studies with Elsner. *Don Giovanni Variations* (Opus 2) composed. Holiday at Reinerz, his health being delicate. *Rondo à la Mazur* (Opus 5).		Schubert: "Death and the Maiden" Quartet Weber: *Oberon* Mendelssohn: Overture to *A Midsummer Night's Dream*
1827	His younger sister, Emilia, dies. Composes many pieces, e.g., Sonata No. 1 (Opus 4). Visits Prince Anton Radziwill.	Turks in Athens. In French elections (November 17, 24) ultra-conservatives are defeated by liberals.	Beethoven dies Schubert: *Die Winterreise* Bellini: *Il Pirata*
1828	Visits Berlin. *Rondo à la Krakowiak* (Opus 14).	Russia declares war on Turkey.	Constable: *Dedham Vale* Delacroix: Illustrations for Goethe's *Faust* Schubert: "The Great" C Major Symphony Schubert dies Rossini: *Le Comte Ory*
1829	Meets Hummel, hears Paganini. Visits Vienna, where he meets musical and other celebrities and gives two concerts (August 11, 18) with great success. Returns to Warsaw via Prague, Teplitz, Dresden. Infatuation with the young singer C. Gladkowska.	Russo-Turkish war ends. Greece achieves independence.	Balzac begins *La Comédie humaine* Rossini: *William Tell*
1830	First public concert in Warsaw; plays his Concerto in F minor (Opus 21). Two more concerts: all acclaimed. Leaves Warsaw November 2 with his friend Titus, his goal Vienna; they arrive end of November.	July: Revolution in Paris. Louis Philippe succeeds Charles X. Discontent in Poland against Russian stringency grows, leading to insurrection November 29. Epidemic of cholera in Europe.	Stendhal: *Le Rouge et le noir* Hugo: *Hernani* Mendelssohn: "Reformation" Symphony Delacroix: *Liberty Leading the People* Berlioz: *Symphonie fantastique*

YEAR	LIFE AND WORKS	POLITICAL & SOCIAL EVENTS	ARTISTIC EVENTS
1831	Is unsuccessful in Vienna. Friendship with Dr. Malfatti. Leaves for Munich (July 20), then Stuttgart, where he hears of the failure of the Polish insurrection. "Revolutionary" Etude, in C minor (Opus 10), composed. Proceeds to Paris, arriving late September or early October. Meets Kalkbrenner. Friendship with Liszt begins.	Polish Diet declares independence (January 25); Russian troops defeat Poles (May 26); Warsaw occupied (September 8); revolt collapses. Riots by silk-weavers in Lyons (November). Revolutionary outbreaks in Papal States, Modena, Parma.	Balzac: *La Peau de chagrin* Hugo: *Notre Dame de Paris* Delaroche: *Princes in the Tower* Bellini: *Norma* Meyerbeer: *Robert le Diable*
1832	First Parisian concert appearance, February 26. Engagements and pupils come after a little while. Finishes composing Five Mazurkas (Opus 7). First publications in Paris and London.	Mazzini founds secret society "Young Italy." Radetzky and Austrian troops occupy Ancona, after new risings in Papal States.	Balzac: *Contes drolatiques* Goethe: *Faust*, Part II, completed Goethe dies Scott dies George Sand: *Indiana*
1833	Becomes popular in homes of Polish and French aristocracy. Successful as teacher. Plays with Liszt at benefit concert for Harriet Smithson. Opus 6 and Opus 7 published. Three Nocturnes (Opus 9) published. The great Opus 10, "Twelve Grand Etudes," published in full. Concerto in E minor published. Friendship with Bellini. Affair with Delfina Potocka?	British Factory Act: children under nine cannot be employed in factories.	Pushkin: *Eugene Onegin* published Musset: *André del Sarto* Sand: *Lélia* Mendelssohn: "Italian" Symphony

1834	Visits Rhenish Music Festival with F. Hiller. Friendly with Mendelssohn. Plays at Conservatoire at concert given by Berlioz. Three Nocturnes (Opus 15), four Mazurkas (Opus 17), Grande Valse Brillante (Opus 18), published.	Civil War in Spain. Abolition of slavery in Britain.	Mickiewicz: *Pan Tadeusz* Balzac: *Le Père Goriot* Schumann: *Carnaval* (Opus 9) Berlioz: *Harold in Italy* Lamennais: *Paroles d'un croyant*
1835	Travels to Karlsbad to meet parents. Visits Dresden, where he is attracted to Maria Wodzinska. Visits Leipzig to meet Mendelssohn, Schumann, Clara Wieck. Returns to Paris after illness. Scherzo Opus 20, four Mazurkas (Opus 24), published. First performance of Andante Spianato and Polonaise (with orchestra) at Conservatoire concert.	September Laws in France censor press and suppress radical movement, following July assassination attempt on Louis Philippe.	Gautier: *Mademoiselle de Maupin* Krasinski: *Undivine Comedy* Donizetti: *Lucia di Lammermoor*
1836	Visits Marienbad. Proposes to Maria. Her mother, Countess Wodzinska, pledges him to secrecy. Publications: F-minor Concerto (Opus 21); G-minor Ballade (Opus 23); Two Nocturnes (Opus 27).	Louis Napoleon (later Napoleon III) fails to seize power.	Dickens: *Pickwick Papers* (1836–37) Arc de Triomphe, Paris, completed Meyerbeer: *Les Huguenots*

A Chopin Calendar (cont'd)

YEAR	LIFE AND WORKS	POLITICAL & SOCIAL EVENTS	ARTISTIC EVENTS
1837	First meeting with George Sand. Maria Wodzinska severs engagement. Visits London with the Pleyels. Composes Scherzo in B-flat minor (published as Opus 31). Other publications: Four Mazurkas (Opus 30); Twelve Etudes (Opus 25).	Queen Victoria succeeds to British throne. Telegraph invented by Samuel Morse.	Dickens: *Oliver Twist* (1837–38) Carlyle: *French Revolution* Berlioz: *Requiem*
1838	Plays for Louis Philippe. Goes to Majorca with George Sand. Composition of 24 Preludes (Opus 28; published 1839) and Ballade in F major (Opus 38; published 1840) progresses.	Austrian troops withdraw from Papal States. Mexico declares war on France.	Schumann: *Kinderscenen* Jenny Lind's debut in Stockholm
1839	Ill in Valldemosa. Returns to Marseilles in spring. Summer at Nohant, cared for by Sand. Return to Paris. Appears with Moscheles at concert at Saint-Cloud. Composes Sonata in B-flat minor (Opus 35) at Nohant.	Opium War between China and Britain.	Darwin: *A Naturalist's Voyage on the Beagle.* Stendhal: *La Chartreuse de Parme* Turner: *The Fighting Téméraire* Berlioz: *Roméo et Juliette*
1840	"Funeral March" Sonata (Opus 35) published, then Opus 36 to Opus 42. Spends quiet year in Paris, composing extensively.	Queen Victoria marries Albert. Louis Napoleon's attempted coup d'état fails. Napoleon I's corpse brought to Les Invalides.	Dickens: *The Old Curiosity Shop* Schumann: *Dichterliebe*

1841	Summer at Nohant. Friendship with Pauline Viardot. Opus 43 to Opus 50 published, including F-minor Fantaisie (Opus 49). Happiness with George Sand.		Poe: *The Murders in the Rue Morgue* Carlyle: *On Heroes and Hero-Worship* Daumier: Lithographs
1842	Concert with Pauline Viardot and Franchomme (February 21). Delacroix visits at Nohant.	End of Opium War.	Tennyson: *Morte d'Arthur* Gogol: *Dead Souls* Stendhal dies Wagner: *Rienzi* Glinka: *Russlan and Ludmilla* Madeleine completed
1843	Opus 51 to Opus 54 published. Spends much time at Nohant.		Sand: *Consuelo* Dickens: *A Christmas Carol* Wagner: *The Flying Dutchman* Donizetti: *Don Pasquale*
1844	His father dies. His sister Louise visits him, is invited to Nohant by George Sand. Opus 55 and Opus 56 published.	French war in Morocco.	Dumas père: *The Three Musketeers, The Count of Monte Cristo* Mendelssohn: Violin Concerto Verdi: *Ernani* Berlioz: *Traité d'instrumentation*
1845	Sonata in B minor (Opus 58), composed in Nohant the previous summer, published.		Mérimée: *Carmen* Wagner: *Tannhäuser*
1846	Relationship with Sand begins to deteriorate. Opus 59 to Opus 62 published, including the Polonaise-Fantaisie (Opus 61).	Rising in Cracow; Austria annexes the city. U.S.-Mexican War. Potato famine in Ireland.	Sand: *Lucrezia Floriani* Berlioz: *The Damnation of Faust* Mendelssohn: *Elijah*

YEAR	LIFE AND WORKS	POLITICAL & SOCIAL EVENTS	ARTISTIC EVENTS
1847	Solange, Sand's daughter, marries. In bitter family quarrel, he takes Solange's part. Break with Sand. His health worsens. Opus 63 to Opus 65 published. Dedicates Opus 64 ("Minute" Waltz) to Delfina Potocka.	Severe unrest in France. Guizot becomes French premier.	E. Brontë: *Wuthering Heights* C. Brontë: *Jane Eyre* Thackeray: *Vanity Fair* (begun) L. Blanc: *History of the French Revolution* Mendelssohn dies Verdi: *Macbeth*
1848	Gives last concert in Paris, February 16. Leaves for London in April, protected and cared for by Jane Stirling. Plays at many aristocratic functions. Meets Jenny Lind. In May goes to Scotland, staying with Jane's brother-in-law Lord Torpichen till August. Plays in Manchester, Glasgow, Edinburgh. Returns to London, very ill, in November. Makes last public appearance at a Polish ball, November 16.	Year of revolution: Vienna, Berlin, Parma, Milan, Cracow, Prague, Budapest, etc., all in ferment. February 22: Revolt in Paris begins, forcing abdication of Louis Philippe. December 10: Louis Napoleon becomes president of the Republic of France.	Dumas *fils*: *La Dame aux Camélias*
1849	No longer able to teach or concertize, he returns to Paris in January. The Stirling sisters help him financially. He moves to suburb, then to Place Vendôme. Sister Louise comes to nurse him. Dies night of October 17.	Continued troubles in Paris. June 13 Communist uprising suppressed.	Meyerbeer: *Le Prophète*

BIBLIOGRAPHY

Anonymous. *Conducteur de l'étranger à Paris.* Paris, 1832.
———. *Le Récit d'un vieux Gentilhomme Polonais;* L. Mickiewicz, editor. Paris, c. 1865
Askenazy, Szymon. *Napoleon a Polska* [Napoleon and Poland]. 3 vols. Warsaw, 1919.
Balzac, Honoré de. *Lettres à Madame Hanska.* Paris, 1967.
Barea, Ilsa. *Vienna.* London, 1966.
Barry, Joseph. *Infamous Woman—The Life of George Sand.* Garden City, N.Y., 1977.
Barzun, Jacques. *Berlioz and the Romantic Century.* 2 vols. Boston, 1950.
———. *Romanticism and the Modern Ego.* Boston, 1943.
Beckett, W. *Liszt.* London, 1956.
Belotti, Gastone. *F. Chopin l'uomo.* 3 vols. Milan, 1974.
Berlioz, Hector. *Evenings with the Orchestra.* New York, 1956.
———. *Memoirs.* Edited by David Cairns. New York, 1969.
Beylin, Karolina. *Tajemnice Warszawy* [The Secrets of Warsaw]. Warsaw, 1956.
Binental et Chowaniec. *Frédéric Chopin, George Sand et leurs amis.* Paris, 1937.
Bone, A. E. *Jane Wilhelmina Stirling.* London, 1960.
Book of the Congress 1963, The. First International Musicological Congress Devoted to the Works of Frederic Chopin (Warsaw, 16–22 February, 1960). Warsaw, 1963.
Börne, Ludwig. *Gesammelte Schriften.* 5 vols. Vienna, 1968.
Boucourechlieu, André. *Chopin, a Pictorial Biography.* London, 1963.
Bourniquel, Camille. *Chopin.* Paris, 1956.
Bronarski, Ludwig. *Chopin et l'Italie.* Lausanne, 1944.
———. *Etudes sur Chopin.* Lausanne, 1944.
———. *Szkice Chopinowskie* [Chopin Sketches]. Warsaw, 1961.
Broszkiewicz, J., ed. *Guide Chopin Illustré.* Warsaw, 1960.

Brzowski, Jósef. *Z dziennika* [From Diary]. Quoted after "Preludia o Chopinie" [Preludes on Chopin], by F. Hoesick. *Echo Muzyczne,* no. 8 (1900). Warsaw.

Cate, Curtis. *George Sand.* New York, 1975.

Chainaye, Suzanne. *De quoi vivait Chopin?* Paris, 1951.

Chainaye, Suzanne, and Chainaye, Denise. *Majorque, Chopin et George Sand.* "Bulletin de la Classe des Beaux-Arts." Brussels, 1961.

Chopin, F. *Collected Letters.* Edited by H. Opienski. London, 1932.

———. *Gesammelte Briefe.* Edited by B. Scharlitt. Leipzig, 1911.

———. *Selected Correspondence.* Translated and edited by Arthur Hedley. New York, 1963.

Clarke, Cyril. *The Composer in Love.* New York, 1951.

Comettant, Oscar. *Histoire de cent mille pianos et d'une salle de concert.* Paris, 1890.

Cortot, Alfred. *Aspects de Chopin.* Paris, 1949.

———. *Notizen über Chopin.* Frankfurt, 1962.

Courthion, Pierre. *Romanticisme.* Lausanne, 1961.

Craik, G. L. *Paris and Its Historical Scenes.* 2 vols. London, 1831.

Czartkowski, Adam, and Jeżewska, Zofia. *Chopin Żywy w Swoich Listach i w Oczach Współczesnych* [Chopin Alive in His Letters and the View of His Contemporaries]. Warsaw, 1967.

Delabonde, Arthur, Mrs. *Representative Painters of the XIXth Century.* London, 1899.

Delaborde, Henri. *Delaroche.* Berlin, n.d.

Delacroix, Eugène. *Correspondance Générale.* Edited by André Joubin. 5 vols. Paris, 1935.

———. *Journal.* Edited by Hubert Wellington. London, 1951.

Davison, J. W. *From Mendelssohn to Wagner.* Edited by Henry Davison. London, 1912.

Dulęba, Władysław. *Chopin.* Cracow, 1975.

Eigeldinger, Jean-Jacques. *Chopin vu par ses élèves.* Neufchâtel, 1970.

Einstein, Alfred. *Music in the Romantic Era.* New York, 1947.

Erhardt, Ludwik. *"Listy Chopina do Delfiny Znów Aktualne"* [Chopin's Letters to Delfina Again in the Spotlight]. *Sztandar Mlodych,* no. 249 (October 18, 1961). Warsaw.

———. *Music in Poland.* Warsaw, 1975.

———. *Ponizej Muzyki* [Below Music]. Warsaw, 1972.

Escholier, E. *Delacroix et les femmes.* Paris, 1963.

Escudier, Léon. *Mes souvenirs: Les virtuoses.* Paris, 1868.

Fellinger, I. *Verzeichnis der Musikzeitschriften des 19. Jahrhunderts.* Regensburg, 1968.

Fitzlyon, April. *The Price of Genius—A Life of Pauline Viardot.* London, 1964.

Forster, M. Charles. *Pologne.* Paris, 1840.

Ganche, Édouard. *Dans le souvenir de Frédéric Chopin.* Paris, 1925.

———. *Frédéric Chopin, sa vie et ses oeuvres.* Paris, 1913.

———. *Souffrances de Frédéric Chopin.* Paris, 1935.

Gavoty, Bernard. *Frédéric Chopin.* Paris, 1974.

German, Franciszek. *Chopin i Literaci Warszawscy* [Chopin and the Writers of Warsaw]. Warsaw, 1960.
Gide, André. *Notes on Chopin.* New York, 1949.
Glinski, Matteo. *Chopin the Unknown.* Windsor, Canada, 1963.
_____, ed. *Chopin's Letters to Delfina.* Windsor, Canada, 1961.
Gribble, Francis. *George Sand and Her Lovers.* New York, 1907.
_____. *The Passions of the French Romantics.* New York, 1910.
Hadden, J. Cuthbert. *Chopin.* London, 1934.
Halecki, O. *A History of Poland.* New York, 1942.
Hamerow, T. S. *Restoration, Revolution, Reaction.* Princeton, 1966.
Handelsman, A. *Adam Czartoryski.* 4 vols. Warsaw, 1948.
Harasowski, Adam. *The Skein of Legends Around Chopin.* Glasgow, 1967.
Haynie, Henry. *Paris, Past and Present.* New York, 1902.
Hedley, Arthur. *Chopin.* London, 1964.
Heine, Heinrich. *Sämtliche Werke.* 7 vols. Leipzig, 1910.
Heller, C. S. *On the Edge of Destruction—Jews of Poland Between the Two World Wars.* New York, 1977.
Hipkins, E. J. *How Chopin Played.* London, 1937.
Hoesick, Ferdinand. *Chopin, His Life and Works.* 4 vols. 3rd ed. Cracow, 1962–68.
Holcman, Jan. *The Legacy of Chopin.* New York, 1954.
Iwaszkiewicz, Jarosław. *Chopin.* Paris, 1966.
_____. "Chopin—the Man." *Polish Perspectives,* no. 2, pp. 83–87. Warsaw, 1958.
Jachimecki, Zdzisław, ed. *Warszawa Miasto Chopina* [Warsaw, Chopin's City]. Warsaw, 1950.
Janta, Aleksander. *Przyjemnie Zapoznać* [Nice to Meet You]. Polish Cultural Foundation. London, 1972.
Jones, Howard Mumford. *Revolution and Romanticism.* Cambridge, Mass., 1974.
Jordan, Ruth. *George Sand.* New York, 1976.
Karasowski, Maurice. *Life and Letters of Chopin.* London, 1879.
Kelly, Linda. *The Young Romantics.* London, 1976.
Kieniewicz, Stefan, and Kula, Witold. *Historia Polski* [A History of Poland]. 3 vols. Warsaw, 1958.
Kobylańska, Krystyna. *Chopin in His Native Land. Documents and Souvenirs.* Cracow, 1956.
_____. *Korespondencja Fryderyka Chopina z Rodziną* [Chopin's Correspondence with His Family]. Warsaw, 1972.
_____. *Rękopisy Utworów Chopina Katalog* [Catalogue of Manuscripts of Chopin's Works]. 2 vols. Warsaw, 1977.
_____. "Spowiedz Ludwicki" [Louise's "Confession"]. *Ruch Muzyczny,* nos. 20 and 21, Warsaw, 1968.
Korngold, Luise. *Lieber Meister Chopin.* Vienna, 1960.
Kott, Jan, and Lorentz, Stanisław. *Warszawa Wieku Oświecenia* [Warsaw During the Age of Enlightenment]. Warsaw, 1954.

Kott, Jan, ed. *Zygmunt Krasiński: Sto Listów Do Delfiny* [Zygmunt Krasiński: A Hundred Letters to Delfina]. Warsaw, 1966.

Kridl, Manfred. *A Survey of Polish Literature and Culture.* New York, 1956.

Kukiel, Marian. *Dzieje Polski Porozbiorowe 1795–1921* [A History of Poland After the Partitions]. London, 1963.

Lang, Paul Henry. *Music in Western Civilization.* New York, 1941.

Lansdale, Maria Hormor. *Paris.* Philadelphia, 1898.

Leclercq, P. *Chopin et son époque.* Liège, 1947.

Legouvé, E. *Soixante ans de souvenirs.* Paris, 1886.

Liszt, Franz. *Frédéric Chopin.* Paris, 1852.

Loesser, Arthur. *Men, Women and Pianos.* New York, 1954.

Long, Dr. Edward. *A History of the Therapy of Tuberculosis and the Case of Frederic Chopin.* Lawrence, Kansas, 1956.

Longford, Elizabeth. *The Life of Byron.* Boston, 1976.

Lubin, Georges. *Nohant.* Paris, 1976.

———. "Autour de la mort de Chopin." *La Revue des Deux Mondes,* Paris, April 1, 1962.

L. W. M. *Chopin.* Cambridge, Mass., 1894.

Maine, Basil. *Chopin.* New York, 1933.

Mallet, Francine. *George Sand.* Paris, 1976.

Marchand, Leslie A. *Byron: A Portrait.* London, 1971.

Marek, G. R. *Gentle Genius—The Story of Felix Mendelssohn.* New York, 1972.

Margetson, Stella. *Leisure and Pleasure in the 19th Century.* New York, 1969.

Marix-Spire, Thérèse. *Les Romantiques et la Musique. Le Cas George Sand.* Paris, 1955.

Maurois, André. *Frédéric Chopin.* Montreal, 1942.

———. *Lélia.* New York, 1953.

———. *Olympio* [Life of Victor Hugo]. New York, 1956.

———. *Prometheus* [Balzac]. New York, 1965.

———. *The Titans* [Dumas]. New York, 1957.

Michałowski, Kornel. *Bibliografia Chopinowska.* Cracow, 1970.

Mickiewicz, Adam. *Pan Tadeusz.* New York, 1962.

———. *Poems.* Edited by G. R. Noyes. New York, 1944.

Milosz, Czesław. *The History of Polish Literature.* New York, 1969.

Mirska, Maria, and Hordyński, Władysław. *Chopin na obczyźnie. Dokumenty i pamiątki* [Chopin Abroad. Documents and Souvenirs]. Cracow, 1965.

Miżwa, Stephen P., ed. *Frederic Chopin.* New York, 1949.

Moriolles, Alexandre, Nicolas de. *Mémoires sur l'émigration, la Pologne et la Cour du Grand Duc Constantin.* Paris, 1902.

Mowat, R. B. *The Romantic Age.* London, 1937.

Murdoch, William. *Chopin, His Life.* New York, 1935.

Murgia, Adelaide. *Delacroix.* London, 1968.

———. *The Life and Times of Chopin.* Philadelphia, 1967.

Musielak, Henri. "Dokumenty dotyczace spadku po F. Chopinie" [Documents Concerning F. Chopin's Legacy]. *Ruch Muzyczny,* nos. 13, 14, and 15, Warsaw, 1978.

Musset, Alfred de. *Correspondance, 1827–1857.* Edited by Léon Séché. Paris, 1907.

Newman, Ernest. *The Man Liszt.* New York, 1935.

Niecks, F. *Frederick Chopin as Man and Musician.* London, 1888.

Norwid, Cyprian. *Dziela Zebrane* [Collected Works]. 2 vols. Warsaw, 1966.

Okey, Thomas. *The Story of Paris.* London, 1906.

Opieński, Henryk, ed. *Chopin's Letters.* New York, 1953.

Orga, Ates. *Chopin: His Life and Times.* London, 1976.

Perényi, Eleanor. *Liszt—The Artist as Romantic Hero.* Boston, 1974.

Pierrot, M. Roger, ed. *George Sand, Visages du Romantisme.* Paris, 1977.

Pleasants, Henry. *The Great Singers.* New York, 1966.

Pourtalès, Guy de. *Chopin ou le Poète.* Paris, 1927.

Pritchett, V. S. *Balzac.* New York, 1973.

———. *The Gentle Barbarian* [Turgenev]. New York, 1977.

Prochazka, J. *Chopin und Böhmen.* Prague, 1968.

Raikes, Thomas. *A Portion of the Journal.* 2 vols. London, 1858.

Sand, George. *Correspondance* [1837–50]. Edited by Georges Lubin. 4 vols. Paris, 1968–1972.

———. *Oeuvres autobiographiques.* Edited by Georges Lubin. 2 vols. Paris, 1970–1971.

———. Various works, especially: *Lettres d'un voyageur,* Paris, 1836. *Consuelo,* Paris, 1843. *Lucrezia Floriani,* Paris, 1846.

Schenk, H. G. *The Mind of the European Romantics.* New York, 1967.

Scholes, Percy A. *The Oxford Companion to Music.* London, 1938.

Schonberg, Harold. *The Great Pianists.* New York, 1963.

Shelley, Henry C. *Old Paris.* Boston, 1912.

Sigmann, J. *1848.* New York, 1973.

Sitwell, Sacheverell. *Liszt.* Boston, 1934.

Sliwiński, Artur. *Maurycy Mochnacki.* Lwów, 1910.

Smoter, Jerzy Maria. *Spór o "Listy" Chopina do Delfiny Potockiej* [Controversy over Chopin's "Letters" to Delfina Potocka]. 1st ed. 1967; 2d ed. (supplemented) 1976. Warsaw.

———. *L'Album de Chopin.* Cracow, 1975.

Straszewicz, J. *I Polacchi della Rivoluzione del 29 Novembre 1830.* 2 vols. Capolago, 1833.

Stromenger, Karol. *Fryderyk Chopin. W Stulecie śmierci* [F.C. On the Hundredth Anniversary of His Death]. Łódz, 1949.

Stromenger, Karol, and Sydow, Bronisław Edward. *Almanach Chopinowski.* Warsaw, 1949.

Sutherland, Donald. *On, Romanticism.* New York, 1971.

Swiderek, Janina. "Ostatnie słowa Chopina—Mikołaja" [The Last Words of Chopin—Nicolas]. *Ruch Muzyczny,* no. 4, Warsaw, 1976.

Sydow, Bronisław Edward. *Bibliografia F. F. Chopina.* Warsaw, 1954.

———, ed. *Korespondencja Fryderyka Chopina* [Chopin's Correspondence]. 2 vols. Warsaw, 1955.

Talmon, J. L. *Romanticism and Revolt.* London, 1967.

Kott, Jan, ed. *Zygmunt Krasiński: Sto Listów Do Delfiny* [Zygmunt Krasiński: A Hundred Letters to Delfina]. Warsaw, 1966.

Kridl, Manfred. *A Survey of Polish Literature and Culture.* New York, 1956.

Kukiel, Marian. *Dzieje Polski Porozbiorowe 1795–1921* [A History of Poland After the Partitions]. London, 1963.

Lang, Paul Henry. *Music in Western Civilization.* New York, 1941.

Lansdale, Maria Hormor. *Paris.* Philadelphia, 1898.

Leclercq, P. *Chopin et son époque.* Liège, 1947.

Legouvé, E. *Soixante ans de souvenirs.* Paris, 1886.

Liszt, Franz. *Frédéric Chopin.* Paris, 1852.

Loesser, Arthur. *Men, Women and Pianos.* New York, 1954.

Long, Dr. Edward. *A History of the Therapy of Tuberculosis and the Case of Frederic Chopin.* Lawrence, Kansas, 1956.

Longford, Elizabeth. *The Life of Byron.* Boston, 1976.

Lubin, Georges. *Nohant.* Paris, 1976.

———. "Autour de la mort de Chopin." *La Revue des Deux Mondes,* Paris, April 1, 1962.

L. W. M. *Chopin.* Cambridge, Mass., 1894.

Maine, Basil. *Chopin.* New York, 1933.

Mallet, Francine. *George Sand.* Paris, 1976.

Marchand, Leslie A. *Byron: A Portrait.* London, 1971.

Marek, G. R. *Gentle Genius—The Story of Felix Mendelssohn.* New York, 1972.

Margetson, Stella. *Leisure and Pleasure in the 19th Century.* New York, 1969.

Marix-Spire, Thérèse. *Les Romantiques et la Musique. Le Cas George Sand.* Paris, 1955.

Maurois, André. *Frédéric Chopin.* Montreal, 1942.

———. *Lélia.* New York, 1953.

———. *Olympio* [Life of Victor Hugo]. New York, 1956.

———. *Prometheus* [Balzac]. New York, 1965.

———. *The Titans* [Dumas]. New York, 1957.

Michałowski, Kornel. *Bibliografia Chopinowska.* Cracow, 1970.

Mickiewicz, Adam. *Pan Tadeusz.* New York, 1962.

———. *Poems.* Edited by G. R. Noyes. New York, 1944.

Milosz, Czesław. *The History of Polish Literature.* New York, 1969.

Mirska, Maria, and Hordyński, Władysław. *Chopin na obczyźnie. Dokumenty i pamiątki* [Chopin Abroad. Documents and Souvenirs]. Cracow, 1965.

Miżwa, Stephen P., ed. *Frederic Chopin.* New York, 1949.

Moriolles, Alexandre, Nicolas de. *Mémoires sur l'émigration, la Pologne et la Cour du Grand Duc Constantin.* Paris, 1902.

Mowat, R. B. *The Romantic Age.* London, 1937.

Murdoch, William. *Chopin, His Life.* New York, 1935.

Murgia, Adelaide. *Delacroix.* London, 1968.

———. *The Life and Times of Chopin.* Philadelphia, 1967.

Musielak, Henri. "Dokumenty dotyczące spadku po F. Chopinie" [Documents Concerning F. Chopin's Legacy]. *Ruch Muzyczny,* nos. 14, 15, and 16, Warsaw, 1978.

INDEX